SOUTHERN LAW JOURNAL

I0036864

EDITOR-IN-CHIEF

Diana M. Brown
Sam Houston State University

ASSOCIATE EDITOR

Laura L. Sullivan
Sam Houston State University

REVIEWERS

Susan R. Dana
Black Hills State University

Michelle Evans
Texas State University – San Marcos

Paul W. Fulbright
University of Houston-Downton

Jennifer Barger Johnson
University of Central Oklahoma

Susan Park
Boise State University

Patricia Pattison
Texas State University – San Marcos

Marcia Staff
University of North Texas

Lee Usnick
University of Houston – Downtown

Tricia A. Wald
Southwestern Oklahoma State
University

ONLINE JOURNAL EDITOR AND WEB MASTER

Ray Teske
University of Texas – San Antonio

The *Southern Law Journal* is an official publication of the
Southern Academy of Legal Studies in Business
ISSN: 1056-2184
ISBN: 978-1-63498-892-6
Listed in *Ulrich's International Periodical Directory* and *Cabell's Directory*
Available at www.southernlawjournal.com and through
EBSCO, an electronic university database

From the Editor's Desk . . .

The *SLJ* **Style Sheet** may be found at our website: www.southernlawjounal.com. If you plan to submit, please follow the *SLJ* Style Sheet closely. Contributors should visit our website for recently revised *SLJ* **Submission Policies.** Although it is expected that most *SLJ* articles will be presented at the SALSB Annual Conference, conference presentation is not a prerequisite for publication.

Hard copies of back issues of the SLJ can be found in over two hundred regional libraries. Current issues can be obtained by contacting the editor at SLJSubmission@comcast.net. In addition, the full text of all *SLJ* articles may be accessed through EBSCO's "Academic Research Complete" database, accessible through over 90% of the world's Electronic University holdings.

Thank you in advance for helping the *SLJ* team continue to advance the quality, exposure, and prominence of the *SLJ* for many decades to come.

Questions and submissions should be directed to: SLJSubmission@comcast.net.

Kind regards,
Diana Brown,
Editor-in-Chief
Southern Law Journal

REPOSITORY LIBRARIES FOR THE SOUTHERN LAW JOURNAL
(BACK ISSUES)

Abilene Christian University .... Brown Library
Amberton University .... Library Resources Center
Angelo State University .... Porter Henderson Library
Arkansas State University of Jonesboro .... Dean B. Ellis Library
Arkansas Tech University .... Pendergraft Library and Technology Center
Arlington Baptist College .... Earl K. Oldham Library
Austin College .... George T. and Gladys H. Abell Library Center
Baylor Law School .... Baylor Law Library
Baylor University .... Baylor Collections of Political Materials
Baylor University .... University Libraries
Cameron University .... Cameron University Library
Concordia University Austin .... Founders Library
Dallas Baptist University .... Vance Memorial Library
East Central University .... Linscheid Library
East Texas Baptist University .... Jarrett Library
Grambling State University .... A.C. Lewis Memorial Library
Harding University .... Brackett Library
Hardin-Simmons University .... Hardin-Simmons University Library
Henderson State University, Arkadelphia .... Huie Library
Hendrix College .... Olin C. Bailey Library
Howard Payne University .... Walker Memorial Library
Lamar University Beaumont .... Mary and John Gray Library
Langston University .... G. Lamar Harrison Library
Louisiana College .... Richard W. Norton Memorial Library
Louisiana State University in Shreveport .... Noel Memorial Library
Louisiana State University Law School .... Prescott Memorial Library
Louisiana Tech University .... Paul M. Herbert Law Center
Loyola University New Orleans Law Library .... The Law Library
Loyola University New Orleans .... J. Edgar and Louise S. Monroe Library
Lyon College .... Mabee-Simpson Library
McMurry University .... Jay-Rollins Library
McNeese State University Library .... Frazar Memorial Library
Midwestern State University .... Moffett Library
Nicholls State University .... Ellender Memorial Library
North Central Texas .... North Central Texas College Library
Northeastern Oklahoma State University .... John Vaughan Library
Northwestern State University .... Watson Memorial Library
Northwood University .... Hach Library
Ohio Northern University College of Law .... Taggart Law Library
Oklahoma City University .... Gold Star Library
Oklahoma Panhandle State University .... Marvin E. McKee Library
Oklahoma State University–Stillwater .... Edmond Low Library
Ouachita Baptist University, Arkadelphia .... Riley-Hickingbotham Library
Rice University .... Fondren Library
Rogers State University .... Stratton Taylor Library
Sam Houston State University .... Newton Gresham Library
Schreiner University .... William Logan Library
South Texas College of Law .... The Fred Parks Law Library
Southeastern Louisiana University .... Linus A. Sims Memorial Library
Southeastern Oklahoma State University .... Henry G. Bennett Memorial Library
Southern Arkansas University, Magnolia .... Magale Library
Southern Methodist University .... Bridwell Library
Southern Methodist University .... Underwood Law Library
Southern University Law Center .... Southern University Law Center Library
Southwestern Christian College .... Doris Johnson Library
Southwestern Oklahoma State University .... Al Harris Library

4

SALSB EXECUTIVE COMMITTEE
(2020)

APPROPRIATION OF LIKENESS AND INFORMED CONSENT IN THE AGE OF SURVEILLANCE CAPITALISM

ROGER W. REINSCH[*]
SONIA GOLTZ[**]
MARAT BAKPAYEV[***]

I. INTRODUCTION

More than half of the world's population now performs a wide range of daily activities in a computer-mediated fashion.[1] For instance, people use digital platforms to communicate, shop, or study. With the birth of social media, people increasingly go online for various social or professional activities, be it chatting with friends or family, finding a date, participating in discussions about politics, or getting the news. More than 70 percent of adult Americans are using at least one social media site; that number goes up to more than 90 percent for those who are 18-29 years old. The use of technology increased further after the COVID-19 pandemic hit, with many people working and socializing from home using software such as Zoom and Facebook Livestream. According to Nielsen Reports, screen time during COVID-19—including television, computers, tablets, and smartphones—has increased to over 13 hours a day. Being in a digital environment is the new normal. This means that the use of information technology has gone well beyond the traditional boundaries of the workplace, becoming ubiquitous. It also means that the bulk of big data is generated through what has been called its everydayness.

The term big data refers to the extremely large data sets generated that could be analyzed to reveal patterns, trends, and associations in terms of human behavior and interactions. The data trail a person leaves with each use of the Internet can be stitched together to create a "digital image." When a person likes friends' posts on Facebook, searches for information on Google, or shares their location in a new restaurant using a check-in—

---

[*] Ph.D., professor, Labovitz School of Business and Economics, University of Minnesota-Duluth.

[**] Ph.D., professor, Mickus Endowed Faculty Fellow in Business Impact, College of Business, Michigan Technological University.

[***] Ph.D., assistant professor, Labovitz School of Business and Economics, University of Minnesota-Duluth.

[1] Internet World Stats: Usage and Population Statistics, World Total Population - 7,796,949,710; number of internet users - 4,648,228,067; percentage of Internet users in the world - 59.6 %

all that is a part of the trail the person leaves. Social networking sites (hereinafter "SNS") and other platforms then use all this information based on data mining. Data mining refers to the processes companies use to search through raw data and turn it into sellable information, for instance, by creating algorithms to find patterns. As a result, an extremely personal image is created for each individual. Companies actively employ that image for monetization because the data can be used to drive people's behavior in a specific direction (sometimes referred to as a hypernudge or choice architecture). Big data mining is used to profile users and market products or influence voters. This raises questions of the possibility of an invasion of privacy through misappropriation of one's name or likeness; therefore, we suggest the need to expand the legal concept of taking one's image to include taking one's digital image without permission for personal (or organizational) gain without proper informed consent.

II. OVERVIEW

Various digital platforms create an individual's digital image. Examples of such platforms include social networking websites, such as Facebook, Instagram, Snapchat, and WhatsApp. People literally extend themselves online digitally, creating avatars, sharing their stories online, or developing certain self-narratives.[2] However, the digital images created are much broader than each of us think because of the various relationships with online platforms. Every day, people create not only a self that is mostly consciously projected into the media but also a different type of digital image, one that consists of digital traces across multiple platforms. Awareness of this second type of image is, at best, a very general one: most consumers "view the relationship between a consumer and a social networking service as a simple exchange: The consumer provides personal information to the SNS, and the SNS provides a valuable service to the consumer."[3]

This online exchange usually begins with a request by the provider to provide some personal data or accept a consent agreement by checking a box. Although many individuals provide the data or check the box to be able to proceed to the SNS, in most cases—even after having access to the agreement—what is being done with an individual's digital image is either not contemplated by that individual, or that individual has some vague idea

---

[2] Russell W. Belk, *Extended Self in a Digital World*, 40 Journal of Consumer Research 477, *see* discussion on page 481, (2013).
[3] Jan Whittington & Chris Jay Hoofnagle, *Unpacking Privacy's Price*, 90 N.C. L. REV. 1327, 1328 (2012).

about what is being done.[4] Moreover, it is common for consumers to click to indicate their consent to the agreement without even a cursory reading of the document itself.[5] Overall, the social exchange view of the interaction that individuals often take is missing a complete understanding of the high value of the trade over time for the social networking service, as described by Whittington.

> Personal information forms the currency of the exchange, making these services free in the sense that consumers need not reach for their wallets when using SNSs such as Facebook, LinkedIn... For instance, to enroll in Facebook, a user provides her name, email address, date of birth, and sex. She is then encouraged to link her account with friends and interact with them socially. The data provided, the social graph, and the varied interactions among the friends become the basis for targeted advertising .... These and other third-party applications support the Facebook network, which is then marketed as free to users.[6]

The industry that takes digital data, processes it, and uses it to generate profits has been called "surveillance capitalism."[7] Surveillance capitalists take this comprehensive image created from an individual's data without asking for the right to that image or for the right to use it as they wish for their own benefit. In the agreements found on websites, companies claim they are not selling personal data, which is true because there is no direct sale of individual-level data, but companies are very obtuse about the fact that they are monetizing that data in other ways once it is aggregated. Google's privacy terms state: "We may combine the information we collect among our services and across your devices for the purposes described above. For example, if you watch videos of guitar players on YouTube, you might see an ad for guitar lessons on a site that uses our ad products. Depending on your account settings, your activity

---

[4] Masooda Bashir, Carol Hayes, April Lambert, and Jay Kesan, *Online Privacy and Informed Consent: The Dilemma of Information Asymmetry*, 52 PROC. OF THE ASS'N FOR INFO. TECH. 1, 5 (2015).

[5] *See generally* Yannis Bakos, Florencia Marotta-Wurgler and David R. Trossen, *Does Anyone Read the Fine Print? Consumer Attention to Standard Form Contracts*, 43 J. OF LEGAL STUD. 1, (2014).

[6] Whittington, et al, *supra* note 13, at 1328, we are labeling "social graph" as "digital image."

[7] Shoshana Zuboff, *Big Other: Surveillance Capitalism and the Prospects of an Information Civilization*, 30 J. OF INFO. TECH. 75, 76 (2015).

on other sites and apps may be associated with your personal information in order to improve Google's services and the ads delivered by Google." The policy goes on to say, "We do not share your personal information with companies, organizations, or individuals outside of Google except in the following cases," with the stated exceptions listed under the following headings: "without your consent," "with domain administrators," "for external processing," and "for legal reasons." However, this policy never expressly states that Google is selling access to aggregate information about the user.[8]

Surveillance capitalism has proliferated with few limits placed on it, primarily due to the dependency that has been created.[9] "Dependency on free services by consumers has become close to addiction, fed by anxieties of loss of inclusion."[10] Also, in some cases, there is a real need to use the services, and there is no viable alternative because the company has a monopolistic control over the market. Arguably, because of this level of dependency, there may be circumstances where consent is not freely given, even when users know what is being done with the data. The dependency also makes unclear the degree to which that consent is really "informed."

It is not uncommon for individuals to often sign up for services provided by SNSs and without considering that, although there is an exchange of free access to the SNS for the user's information, this exchange is not a one-time occurrence—it is ongoing. Surveillance capitalism refers to the use of *accumulating information* to "predict and modify human behavior as a means to produce revenue and market control."[11] In other words, the image is continuously evolving, and the revenue possibilities build as the consumer uses these websites more frequently and for more purposes. Every time the user uses the SNS, they provide more information for their digital image. Additionally, social media sites often rely on in-depth interactions within friendship communities,[12] in which individuals may divulge information they would not normally divulge to others. For these reasons, the exchange is actually "a continuous transaction with atypical attributes. These exchanges make

---

[8] Google Privacy Policy, https://policies.google.com/privacy?hl=en-US (effective July 1, 2020).

[9] *See generally* Zuboff, *supra* note 17.

[10] Graham Greenleaf, *Elements of Zuboff's Surveillance Capitalism*, 160 PRIVACY LAWS & BUS. INT'L REP. 29, 30 (2019).

[11] *Id.* at 75.

[12] Brian D. Wassom, *Uncertainty Squared: The Right of Publicity and Social Media*, 63 SYRACUSE L. REV. 227, 228 (2013).

it very difficult for consumers to determine the value of what they are trading."[13]

Therefore, most consumers do not understand the entire picture of what happens when they use what is advertised as a free SNS. Consumers fail to understand precisely to what they are agreeing and what the value of that information is to the SNSs. Also, even if the consumer has some understanding of what is being done with their image, multiple barriers exist that dissuade attempts at controlling the flow of personal information. As Whittington noted, "ease of transfer, difficulty of monitoring transfer, and persistence of digital data allow SNSs to present formidable barriers to anyone attempting to control the flow of value from the personal information that they provide to SNSs. Information-intensive companies exacerbate these problems by relying upon consumer ignorance of the rules, or using masking practices,[14] once they have collected personal information from consumers."[15]

III. AN INDIVIDUAL'S LIKENESS: MOVING TOWARDS THE DIGITALLY GENERATED DOUBLE

The concept of a person's image is defined within privacy law, evolving with case law over the last several decades. A key aspect of privacy law is the prohibition of the use of a person's name or likeness for monetary gain. Likeness is often viewed as being something that makes the person identifiable. Prosser, for example, stated that one's identity is not being appropriated, "unless the context or the circumstances, or the addition of some other element, indicates that the name is that of the plaintiff."[16] Typically, this means using a person's name, nickname, or visual image; sometimes it has included using an attribute that evokes that person's identity, such as presenting a picture of a racing driver's car or creating a figure that mimics a celebrity's well-known poses in an ad.[17] The law has typically chosen not to list the various ways in which use of a name or likeness can occur in order to provide for a broad definition that

---

[13] Whittington, *supra* note 13, at 1328.
[14] "Data masking is also referred to as data obfuscation, data anonymization, or pseudonymization. It is the process of replacing confidential data by using functional fictitious data such as characters or other data. Main purpose of data masking is to protect sensitive, private information in situations where the enterprise shares data with third parties." Cem Dilmegani, Top 8 Data Masking Techniques, AI MULTIPLE (May 24, 2022), https://research.aimultiple.com/data-masking/.
[15] *Id.* at 1329.
[16] William L. Prosser, *Privacy*, 48 CALIF. 383, 403-404 (1960)
[17] Motschenbacher v. R.J. Reynolds Tobacco Co., 498 F.2d 821 (9th Cir. 1974); White v. Samsung Elec. Am., Inc., 917 F.2d 1395 (9th Cir. 1992).

can be applied under different circumstances.[18] For example, Prosser, writing in 1960, long before the invention of the Internet, acknowledged that a person's identity and/or likeness can be very broad.[19]

This broad definition is particularly needed in today's world because image appropriation is occurring in many new and surprising ways previously not imagined. Thus, although past cases brought under privacy law may have focused on certain types of characteristics, such as revealing a specific combination of race, gender, and age that made it more likely a person was identifiable, currently because of technology, the previous conception of what described an individual's likeness seems quite narrow and rigid:

> Just by browsing the internet, you're unwittingly creating a profile with online tracking companies that can estimate your age, gender, income level, interests, political beliefs, job title, and so on, down to the tiniest things such as allergies. Some online tracking companies are so good at creating profiles based on your browsing habits that they can link completely different devices as being both from the same person.[20]

Often, when discussing the data created by an individual from behaviors, such as clicks and likes on a social media site or search histories, the phrase "behavioral footprint" is used.[21] It refers to the fact that an image is not made up of just physical characteristics—it also includes behavioral ones. The actual outcome is much more than either a physical image of the person or the behavioral footprint—it is a combination of all of those aspects. However, even these two descriptors fall far short of capturing what is presently occurring. These social networking services know not just physical characteristics, such as one's gender, age, race, and body size, but also aspects such as political philosophy, religion (or lack thereof), sexual orientation, hobbies, likes

---

[18] *See infra* Appropriation as Defined in Tort Law (II.B.)

[19] Prosser, *supra* note 25, at 389 (when he stated, "Without any attempt to exact definition....").

[20] *How Data Mining Uses Your Personal Information*, PEOPLEFINDERS (May 21, 2020), https://blog.peoplefinders.com/how-data-mining-uses-your-personal-information.

[21] *See, e.g.* Syed Sardar Muhammad, Bidit Lal Dey & Vishanth Weerakkody, *Analysis of Factors that Influence Customers' Willingness to Leave Big Data Digital Footprints on Social Media: A Systematic Review of Literature*, 20 INFO. SYST. FRONT 559 (2018), ("Big data digital footprints are digital DNA that customers generate and leave on digital platforms when they interact with and use various media channels, including social media," at 559) (citations omitted).

and dislikes, economic standing, and location. In other words, organizations capturing big data can create an amazingly developed picture of each individual and may even have more information than do some of that person's friends and relatives. For example, Google has information "that includes everything from search activity to emails its users send and receive."[22] "This is user-generated data harvested from the haphazard ephemera of everyday life, especially the tiniest details of our online engagements—captured, datafied abstracted, aggregated, packaged, sold, and analyzed. This includes everything from Facebook likes and Google searches to tweets, emails, texts, photos, songs, and videos, location and movement, purchases, every click, misspelled word, every page view, and more."[23]

For a simple example of the information that is available, the reader could conduct a quick Google search of their name. Most likely, what comes up will be surprising; however, this is just the tip of the iceberg, unfortunately. For instance, one of the authors downloaded their Facebook information. The information, almost a half a gigabyte, included every message sent, every advertisement seen, every comment made, every "like," and so forth. This information provided a very personal and detailed image. With all this information being available in such detail—down to specific allergies—it is easy to conclude that a digital image creates a person's likeness relying on an "aspect of identity." In fact, it is often even more of an image of the person than is a photograph, their name, or anything else that would have been considered an image prior to the Internet. The image that data mining allows the SNS to create includes some extremely personal information that a simple photograph would never disclose.

In other words, based on many individual data points such as visual images, likes, personal data input by the user, clicks, and so forth, the SNSs and similar platforms can put together a complex three-dimensional rich picture of each person that exists in a type of virtual reality. In some sense, a good analogy for what this image is would be a hologram or a doppelganger. However, neither is entirely correct because a hologram is a 3-D image, but not necessarily a double, whereas a doppelganger is literally a double, but not necessarily a 3-D image. A hologram is often visually indistinguishable from its physical

---

[22] Aimee Picchi, *Facebook: Your Personal Info for Sale*, CBS NEWS: MONEYWATCH (March 21, 2018), https://www.cbsnews.com/news/facebook-your-personal-info-for-sale.
[23] Shoshana Zuboff, *A Digital Declaration*, FRANKFURTER ALLGEMEINE (Sept. 9, 2014), https://www.faz.net/aktuell /feuilleton/debatten/the-digital-debate/shoshan-zuboff-on-big-data-as-surveillance-capitalism-13152525.html

counterpart.[24] Some have called this a "data double."[25] As Jones states, "Each of us has a 'data double,' a digital duplicate of our lives captured in data and spread across assemblages of information systems."[26] In an article about self-tracking, Bode and Kristensen labeled what the self-trackers created a "digital doppelganger."[27] This description, however, misses the mark because the person's image that is generated by big data is dynamic and multidimensional. Also, the digital double is not simply created by a person—it is generated by others as well. Therefore, to differentiate the digital double from other descriptions, it will be referred to as a "Digitally Generated Double" (DGD). DGD is a multidimensional, dynamically evolving, digitally generated image of the person that goes well beyond the traditional simple digital image and is more in line with the ideas of both a hologram (3-D) *and* a Doppelgänger. This digitally generated double is, in essence, sold to the highest bidder, who then often uses it for marketing of political purposes.

The image that is being created through data mining is very comprehensive and does identify the individual who created that data trail. Data mining doubtlessly creates a person's image, but is that image appropriated in a legal sense?

IV. APPROPRIATION AS DEFINED IN TORT LAW

Modern tort law relating to the invasion of privacy refers to different types of violations, as classified initially by Prosser, with the appropriation of one's image being one of these: "The law of privacy comprises four distinct kinds of invasion of four different interests of the plaintiff, which are tied together by a common name, but otherwise have almost nothing in common except that each represents an interference with the right of the plaintiff, in the phrase coined by Judge Cooley, 'to be let

---

[24] Amelia Carrozzi, Mathew Chylinski, Jonas Heller, Tim Hilken, Debbie Keeling, & Ko de Ruyter,
What's Mine is a Hologram? How Shared Augmented Reality Augments Psychological Ownership, 48 J. OF INTERACTIVE MARKETING 71, 72 (2019).
[25] *See*, Kevin D. Haggerty & Richard V. Ericson, *The Surveillant Assemblage*, 51 BRIT. J. OF SOC., 605, 613 (2000) (citations omitted)
https://onlinelibrary.wiley.com/doi/abs/10.1080/00071310020015280).
[26] Kyle M. L. Jones, *What is a Data Double?*, DATA DOUBLES (May 1, 2018),
https://datadoubles.org/2018/05/01/ what-is-a-data-double.
[27] Matthias Bode & Dorthe Brogård Kristensen, (2016). *The Digital Doppelgänger Within: A Study on Self-Tracking and the Quantified Self Movement*, ASSEMBLING CONSUMPTION 119,119 (Domen Bajde & Robin Canniford ed., (2016),
https://www.researchgate.net/publication/303738926_The_digital_doppelganger_within_ A_study_on_self-tracking_and_the_quantified_self-movement.

alone.'"[28] Briefly, the four areas include: intrusion upon the plaintiff's seclusion or solitude, publicity, which places the plaintiff in a false light, public disclosure of a private embarrassing fact, and appropriation, for the defendant's advantage, of the plaintiff's likeness.

As Prosser stated, with regard to the dimension of appropriation of likeness, "first of all (what must be established is) whether there has been appropriation of an aspect of the plaintiff's identity."[29] As discussed, this aspect must somehow evoke the name of the plaintiff. The next question is "whether the defendant has appropriated the name or likeness for his own advantage."[30] Similarly, a more recent article states that a tortious appropriation must meet three criteria. First, the defendant must have used an aspect of identity protected by law, such as name or likeness; second, this must have been done for purposes of commercial gain or other exploitative reasons; and third, the individual whose likeness was used must not have given consent for the offending use.[31]

The underlying reasons behind the appropriation tort, historically, have been twofold.[32] The first is to protect an individuals' dignity. For example, the way one's image was used might have been offensive and humiliating and may cause mental distress as a result of the loss of control of the use of one's image. A second reason, invoked later, arises from the protection of property rights.[33] In this view, an individual has an ownership interest, akin to a natural copyright, in terms of determining the commercial use of one's identity. This has been called the "right of publicity."[34] The right of publicity has generally been treated as a type of intellectual property, particularly in the case of social media.[35]

The use of a personal attribute without permission for commercial or personal gain has been found in a variety of cases that, together, serve to illustrate the number of ways appropriation can occur. Ford used a voice impersonator to sing a famous song sung initially by Bette Midler without her permission.[36] Johnny's Portable Toilets used the slogan "Here's Johnny" as a brand name for portable toilets because it sufficiently evoked

---

[28] Prosser, *supra* note 25, at 389, *see* Cooley, Torts 29 (2d ed. 1888).

[29] *Id.* at 403 (emphasis added).

[30] *Id.* at 405.

[31] *Using the Name or Likeness of Another*, DIGITAL MEDIA LAW PROJECT (August 5, 2020), http://www.dmlp.org/legal-guide/using-name-or-likeness-another.

[32] *See* Robert C. Post, *Rereading Warren and Brandeis: Privacy, Property, and Appropriation*, 41 CASE WESTERN RES. L. REV. 647 (1991).

[33] *e.g., see* Canessa v. Kislak, Inc., 97 N.J. Super 327, 235 A.2d 62 (1967).

[34] *e.g.,* Post, *supra* note 39, at 675; *also see*, Brian D. Wassom, *supra* note 22.

[35] Wassom, *supra* note 22, at 227.

[36] Midler v. Ford Motor Co., 849 F.2d 460 (9th Cir. 1988).

Johnny Carson's identity.[37]   In a more recent case, the defendants used a video of the plaintiff playing at the Montreux Jazz Festival in 1974. The plaintiff was a well-known guitar player, and the defendants produced a two-part DVD of his performance and comments without his permission. In this case, the court emphasized the existence of appropriation for purposes of advantage. Regarding the plaintiff's claims, the court said,

> Unlike the other privacy torts, "appropriation does not require falsity." Also, unlike the other privacy torts, the right protected by the appropriation tort is not "plaintiff's right 'to be let alone.'" Instead, the right protected "'is in the nature of a property right,' which the tort recognizes as being violated whenever 'the defendant makes use of the plaintiff's name or likeness for his own purposes and benefit.'" Any unauthorized use of a plaintiff's name or likeness, however inoffensive in itself, is actionable if that use results in a benefit to another.[38]

As Brian D. Wassom pointed out, "Many of the courts and legislatures that have articulated the right, however, recognize that any attempt to exhaustively list the forms that publicity right infringements can take is simply an invitation to creative infringement to devise some other means of appropriating someone's identity. Much like the concept of 'identity' itself, therefore, the idea of 'appropriating' that identity must necessarily remain fluid."[39]   This is, in part, because the technology of social media itself is incredibly fluid, with individual forums and applications appearing and disappearing rapidly.[40]   Another factor in determining the need for fluidity is that the algorithms organizations use for data mining are constantly shifting and evolving. For example, to handle large data sets, artificial intelligence, especially machine learning, is now being applied to dynamically analyze and generate algorithms.[41]

Therefore, both the concept of what invokes an image and the concept of the appropriation of that image, meaning for one's benefit and without permission, should remain fluid. This is particularly important

[37] Carson v. Here's Johnny Portable Toilets, Inc., 698 F.2d 831 (6th Cir. 1983).
[38] Armstrong v. Eagle Rock Entertainment, Inc., 655 F.Supp.2d 779, 785 (2009) (citations omitted).
[39] Wassom, *supra* note 22, at 231.
[40] *Id.* at 227.
[41] *e.g.,* Fuchun Sun, Guang-Bin Huang, Q. M. Jonathan Wu, Siji Song & Donald C. Wunsch II, *Efficient and Rapid Machine Learning Algorithms for Big Data and Dynamic Varying Systems*, 47 IEEE TRANSACTIONS ON SYSTEMS, MAN, AND CYBERNETICS: SYSTEMS, 2625 (Oct. 1, 2017) https://ieeexplore.ieee.org/document.

given the enormous changes technology has generated in terms of both how a personal image can be captured and appropriated.

V. APPROPRIATION IN THE ERA OF SURVEILLANCE CAPITALISM

The monetization of data mining has been labeled surveillance capitalism, which has been described as follows:

> ...a market-driven process where the commodity for sale is your personal data, and the capture and production of this data relies on mass surveillance of the internet. This activity is often carried out by companies that provide us with free online services, such as search engines (Google) and social media platforms (Facebook). These companies collect and scrutinize our online behaviors (likes, dislikes, searches, social networks, purchases) to produce data that can be further used for commercial purposes. And it's often done without us understanding the full extent of the surveillance.[42]

Surveillance capitalism began with the discovery of behavioral surplus,[43] which was turned into surveillance assets through commodification.[44] As with industrial capitalism, in which raw materials are transformed into goods and services, personal data from users and about users can be commodified. This commodification has been enabled by the language that has been used to label this data. "These data flows have been labeled by technologists as 'data exhaust.' Presumably, once the data are redefined as waste material, their extraction and eventual monetization are less likely to be contested."[45] This is a use of language that stimulates most people to think of the norm, backed up by a Supreme

---

[42] *Explainer: What is Surveillance Capitalism and How Does it Shape Our Economy?*, THE CONVERSATION (June 24, 2019) https://theconversation.com/explainer-what-is-surveillance-capitalism-and-how-does-it-shape-our-economy-119158.

[43] Zuboff defines behavioral surplus as, "There's data and information collected about people that is used specifically to inform the particular products that are served back to them, but there's this other data, what you've termed behavioral surplus, that's information that doesn't have an immediate use but is itself a kind of control and power that these organizations possess that gives them an advantage over other companies." Noah Kulwin, *Shoshana Zuboff on Surveillance Capitalism's Threat to Democracy The Harvard Business School Professor Discusses Her New Book*, INTELLIGENCER (Feb. 24, 2019), https://nymag.com/intelligencer/2019/02/shoshana-zuboff-q-and-a-the-age-of-surveillance-capital.html?regwall-newsletter-signup=true#_=_

[44] Surveillance assets coined by Zuboff, *supra* note 17, at 81.

[45] *Id.* at 79.

Court decision, that once people place their trash on the curb for collection, it is no longer considered private and can be searched by others because it has been essentially abandoned.[46] However, the difference is that the trash at the curb is placed there with the purpose of abandoning it, and with full knowledge that it will remain at the curb, visible to others.

Here, the first element of appropriation includes not just the physical characteristics of a person but "certain other personal attributes as well." Since it is apparent that SNSs have a considerable amount of information about the "personal attributes" of individuals, the concept of "appropriation" should now include DGDs, in other words, data about an individual obtained through information technology sources. Just as is the case with physical images, digital images should not be appropriated without consent.

The second element of appropriation requires that the image be used for exploitative purposes. This requires the image to have some commercial value.[47] When the common law rule for appropriation was first created, there was no value in most ordinary people's personal images—this applied mostly to celebrities. The internet has changed this: information about ordinary people has now become valuable. In fact, "The personal data that social media ... users generate enrich the world's largest tech companies."[48] Additionally, this revenue is growing exponentially. For example, in 2017, Facebook's advertising revenue was $40 billion,[49] and in 2018, Facebook generated $55 billion in advertising revenue.[50] In 2019, about 98.5% of Facebook's global revenue was generated from advertising, whereas only around 2% was generated by payments and other fee revenue. Facebook advertising revenue stood at close to $69.7 billion USD in 2019, a new record for the company and a significant increase in comparison to the previous years.[51] Questions of appropriation of one's image raise issues similar to those raised over a century ago by the court in the *Pavesich v. New England Life* case, which held: "as long

---

[46] *See* California v. Greenwood, 486 U.S. 35 (1988).

[47] *See* Wassom, *supra* note 22, at 232.

[48] Jennifer Zhu Scott, *You Should be Paid for Your Facebook Data*, QUARTZ (April 11, 2018), https://qz.com/ 1247388/you-should-be-paid-for-your-data.

[49] Kurt Wagner, *This is How Facebook Uses Your Data for Ad Targeting*, VOX (Apr. 11, 2018), https://www.vox.com/2018/4/11/17177842/facebook-advertising-ads-explained-mark-zuckerberg.

[50] Hanna Kozlowska, *How much is your data worth?*, QUARTZ (July 8, 2019), https://qz.com/1655610/how-can-you-measure-the-worth-of-your-data.

[51] J. Clement, *Facebook: Advertising Revenue Worldwide 2009-2021*, STATISTA (Feb 28, 2020), https://www.statista.com/statistics/271258/facebooks-advertising-revenue-worldwide/#:~:text=In%202019%2C %20Facebook%20generated%20close,U.S.%20dollars%20in%20ad%20revenues.

as the advertiser uses him for these purposes, he cannot be otherwise than conscious of the fact that he is for the time being under the control of another, that he is no longer free, and that he is, in reality, a slave, without hope of freedom."[52] The simple fact is that Facebook uses personal data to make money by selling access for targeted advertising. This leads to the conclusion that "social media may be the most direct means imaginable to support the argument that anyone and everyone's identity has some level of commercial value."[53] "This new form of information capitalism aims to predict and modify human behavior as a means to produce revenue and market control."[54]

Traditional marketing is built around the concepts of segmentation, targeting, and positioning (STP).[55] The STP framework assumes that during the process of segmentation, potential consumers are subdivided into various homogenous groups based on identified criteria. Most attractive segments are then targeted with marketing tactics, such as, for instance, advertising activities aimed at developing specific positioning of the products or services. For example, Coca-Cola identifies a growing segment of health-conscious consumers and targets them with a new product, positioning it as healthy.

With the availability of data, the technical capacities of marketers to segment and target consumers are significantly improved. Marketers now can look at browsing behavior[56] or purchase history.[57] Various data mining techniques are now actively used by businesses to segment consumers in order to acquire them as customers, develop relationships with them, and retain them as customers.[58] Marketers can now segment

---

[52] Pavesich v. New England Life Ins. Co., 122 Ga. 190, 220 (Ga. 1905).
[53] Wassom, *supra* note 22, at 235.
[54] Zuboff, *supra* note 17, at 75.
[55] *See generally*, Wendell R. Smith, *Product Differentiation and Market Segmentation as Alternative Marketing Strategies*, 21 J. OF MKT. 3 (1956); Philip Kotler, *Marketing Management: Analysis, Planning, Implementation And Control*, 9th ed. Upper Saddle River, NJ: Prentice Hall (1997).
[56] *See generally* Nikhil Agarwal, Susan Athey, & David Yang, *Skewed Bidding in Pay-Per-Action Auctions for Online Advertising*, 99 AM. ECON. REV. 441 (2009); Ye Chen, Dmitry Pavlov, & John F. Canny, *Large-Scale Behavioral Targeting*, Proceedings of the 15th ACM SIGKDD International Conference on Knowledge Discovery and Data Mining (2009), https://dl.acm.org/doi/pdf/10.1145/1557019.1557048.
[57] *See generally*, Edward C. Malthouse, & Ralf Elsner, *Customisation with Crossed-Basis Sub-Segmentation*, 14 J. OF DATABASE MKT & CUSTOMER STRATEGY MGMT 40 (2006).
[58] *See generally*, Konstantinos Tsiptsis, & Antonios Chorianopoulos, *Data Mining Techniques in CRM: Inside Customer Segmentation*, John Wiley & Sons Ltd. (2011).

consumers on a micro-level, personalizing their communication with each individual consumer.[59]

One of the widely used and known technologies to target specific consumers is referred to as behavioral re-targeting. Re-targeting works as follows. Marketers place a code on their website. When consumers visit the website to see the offerings, a small pixel tag (1 x 1 image) is downloaded unnoticeably. When a consumer leaves the website and browses the Internet later, cookie technology[60] allows marketers to re-target those consumers whose information was tracked. Generally, cookies are referred to as "first-party" and "third-party." While first-party cookies come directly from websites (a publisher) users are visiting, third-party cookies are set by other domains tracking the users across multiple websites, including SNSs. Advertising is based on the recognition of the consumers—allowing the deploying of specific, rather than generic advertisements. For example, consumers who shop for sports shoes and then browse other websites will be likely to encounter advertisements that are specific to the previously seen sports.[61]

As can be seen from the preceding explanation, Facebook, Google, and others do not actually sell an individual's data in the usual sense of the term. Instead, "Facebook has become an advertising behemoth because it can slice and dice its users into targeted groups that companies want to reach. Its 'core audience' targeting provides advertisers with four types of information about users: demographics, location, interests, and behaviors, according to its ad-targeting site for advertisers."[62] One of the reasons Facebook doesn't directly sell personal data is "[i]t's valuable, and by not allowing other entities to it, Facebook can monetize that same data repeatedly. If it sold the data to an advertiser, that data would lose its value."[63] Facebook's leaders acknowledge this strategy. Following is a portion of the conversation between Zuckerman and a congressman during a Congressional hearing on data privacy:

[59] See generally, Joe Ciuffo, Artificial Intelligence in Marketing, Chapter 6, ARTIFICIAL INTELLIGENCE AND MACHINE LEARNING FOR BUSINESS FOR NON-ENGINEERS, Edited by Frank M. Groom & Steven S. Jones, CRC Press, Taylor & Francis Group (2019).

[60] A cookie is a piece of data from a website that is stored within a web browser that the website can retrieve at a later time. Cookies are used to tell the server that users have returned to a particular website. TREND MICRO, https://www.trendmicro.com/vinfo/us/security/definition/cookies#:~:text=A%20cookie% 20is%20a%20piece,returned%20to%20a%20particular%20website.

[61] See generally, Anja Lambrecht, & Catherine Tucker, When Does Retargeting Work? Information Specificity in Online Advertising, 50 J. OF MKT. RES. 561 (2013).

[62] Picchi, supra note 30.

[63] Kaleigh Rogers, Let's Talk About Mark Zuckerberg's Claim that Facebook 'Doesn't Sell Data', MOTHERBOARD (April 11, 2018), https://www.vice.com/en_us/article/8xkdz4/does-facebook-sell-data.

"There's a very common misperception about Facebook—that we sell data to advertisers. And we do not sell data to advertisers. We don't sell data to anyone," Zuckerberg testified on Tuesday.

"What we allow is for advertisers to tell us who they want to reach, and then we do the placement. "But as Representative Greg Walden, the chair of the House Committee on Energy and Commerce, pointed out on Wednesday, user data is how Facebook makes money even if it's not selling the data outright.

"I understand that Facebook does not sell user data, *per se*, in the traditional sense," Walden said. "But it's also just as true that Facebook's user data is probably the most valuable thing about Facebook—in fact it may be the only truly valuable thing about Facebook."[64]

Because Google is visited most often, it is the largest big data company. Google's management did not want to create a fee-for-service model:

They opted instead for an advertising model. The new approach depended upon the acquisition of user data as the raw material for proprietary analyses and algorithm production that could sell and target advertising through a unique auction model with even more precision and success. As Google's revenues rapidly grew, they motivated ever more comprehensive data collection. The new science of big data analytics exploded, driven largely by Google's spectacular success.[65]

In addition to Facebook and other social media sites and platforms like Google, which collect and sell data, there are also the Internet-of-Things (IoT) devices.[66] These consumer devices that are connected to the Internet include such things as smart speakers, smart TVs,[67] smart

---

[64] *Id.*

[65] Zuboff, *supra* note 17, at 79 (citation omitted).

[66] *See supra* note 54.

[67] Ananda Mitra, *Television as a Surveillance Tool*, INTECHOPEN (March 13th 2019), (For example, "In February 2018, an analysis by the reputed magazine Consumer Reports announced that their testing revealed that the increasingly ubiquitous 'smart TV' was

appliances, smart thermostats, smart security, and many other devices that connect to the Internet from the user's home or business. "All those interconnected devices produce an amount of data that is almost literally unimaginable. IoT data is measured in zettabytes, a unit equal to one trillion gigabytes. Cisco estimates that by the end of 2019, the IoT will generate more than 500 zettabytes per year in data—and in the years beyond, that number is expected to grow exponentially, not linearly."[68]

The fact is that this data is also being shared with third parties:

> What the researchers found was astounding – 72 of the 81 IoT devices shared data with third parties completely unrelated to the original manufacturer. And the data they shared went far beyond just basic information about the physical device being used—it also included IP addresses, device specifications and configurations, usage habits, and location data. Some of these third parties were names you might expect—such as Google, Amazon and Akamai—because it is these companies that are providing the Wi-Fi, Internet networking or cloud storage functionality needed to run these IoT products. But there were plenty of other devices making third-party contact with companies located around the world (and not just in the U.S. or UK).[69]

Just as with data from social media sites, the value of IoT data is expected to be significant, rising exponentially. Projections are that by 2030, the market value of data being transacted in IoT marketplaces could rise to 3.6 trillion because more than 1 million organizations would be monetizing their IoT data. The data being transacted every day at that point is hard to imagine since it is 12 exabytes, or 27,000 times the entire contents of the U.S. Library of Congress.[70]

---

capable of 'watching' the viewer and keeping a detailed record of the viewer's TV watching patterns and related behavior.") https://www.intechopen.com/books/the-future-of-television-convergence-of-content-and-technology/television-as-a-surveillance-tool.
[68] Melissa Liton, *How Much Data Comes from the IoT?*, SUMO LOGIC (February 7, 2018), https://www.sumologic.com/blog/iot-data-volume.
[69] Nicole Lindsey, *Smart Devices Leaking Data To Tech Giants Raises New IoT Privacy Issues*, CPO MAGAZINE (October 1, 2019), https://www.cpomagazine.com/data-privacy/smart-devices-leaking-data-to-tech-giants-raises-new-iot-privacy-issues.
[70] *Value of Data: The Dawn of the Data Marketplace*, ACCENTURE: HIGH TECH (Sept. 7, 2018), https://www.accenture.com/us-en/insights/ high-tech/dawn-of-data-marketplace#:~:text=the%20data%20 marketplace-,The%20dawn%20of %20 the%20data%20marketplace,trillion%20in%20value%20by%202030.

There is no doubt that personal data is being gathered by numerous tech companies and devices; it is then being sold to others, and the market for that private data is vast. The fact that this DGD is being monetized shows that the second element of appropriation is met.

Some would argue that these surveillance assets are stolen: "Critics of surveillance capitalism might characterize such assets as 'stolen goods' or 'contraband' as they were taken, not given."[71] This gets at the third aspect of appropriation—whether or not permission was given to use the assets for financial gain. Therefore, the next question we consider concerns whether consent has been obtained. These companies would most likely claim it has. However, the form of consent that has been obtained by most of them is likely insufficient, and everyone should have detailed information about everything that is happening with their DGD and what may and may not be done with that information. These individuals should also have input regarding their entitlement to damages when that information is being appropriated for the economic benefit of the SNSs.

VI. Informed Consent in the Era of the Internet

The last element required for wrongful appropriation of one's image is that the person did not previously provide informed consent for its use. Generally, to comprehend something, one must have full information of what they are agreeing to, which is the common dictionary definition of informed, "you have all the information or knowledge that you need."[72] This clearly means that, without having all the information and/or knowledge that a user needs to make a decision, such as exactly how information will be used, the consent cannot be informed; rather, it is just consent. It has been suggested that the current use of consent is "often not meaningful."[73] Often, the focus has been on whether or not consent has been provided. In most cases, when people trade their personal information for use of a social media site, some form of consent occurs in that they see an agreement from the provider pop up on the screen and must check a box indicating that they accept the agreement. However,

---

[71] Zuboff, *supra* note 17, at 81.

[72] Vocabulary.com, https://www.vocabulary.com/dictionary/informed.

[73] Daniel J. Solove, *Privacy Self-Management and the Consent Dilemma*, 126 HARV. L. REV. 1880, 1881 (2013)

informed consent is a "process (that) involves multiple elements, including disclosure, comprehension, voluntary choice, and authorization."[74]

There are two aspects of informed consent that have not received adequate attention: comprehension and voluntariness. What does comprehension entail? As Bashir stated:

> Comprehension here refers to an individual's accurate interpretation of the significance of disclosures. A user cannot give informed consent when the length, terminology, or organization of a privacy policy interferes with his comprehension of the contents of the policy. To be fully informed, individuals should be able to restate a disclosure agreement using different words and apply its contents to a different, but similar situation.[75]

Therefore, part of the problem with informed consent currently is that information technology has extensively changed the subject matter of the consent—compared to the past when things were simpler, namely, the extent of the information collected and how it can be used to create a personal image. For example, a 2015 survey showed that, while:

> ... respondents knew some of the uses of cloud computing, many failed to understand the breadth of services reliant on cloud computing, betraying a lack of knowledge about the fundamental nature of the technology. This is problematic because if users do not understand the basics of the technology design, how can they be expected to give informed consent? Without this basic aspect of comprehension, the consent process has significantly less meaning.[76]

---

[74] Christine Grady, *Enduring and Emerging Challenges of Informed Consent*, 372 N. ENGL. J. MED. 855 (2015); *see also*, Thea van der Geest, Willem Pieterson, & Peter de Vries, *Informed Consent to Address Trust, Control, and Privacy Concerns in User Profiling*, ("the process by which a fully informed user participates in decisions about his or her personal data.") at 9 (2004), (citation omitted) https://www.researchgate.net/publication/242073709_ Informed_Consent_to_Address_Trust_Control_and_Privacy_Concerns_in_User_Profiling.
[75] Masooda Bashir, Carol Hayes, April D. Lambert & Jay P. Kesan, *Online Privacy and Informed Consent: The Dilemma of Information Asymmetry*, 52 PROC. OF THE ASS'N FOR INFO. SCI. AND TECH. 1, 2 (2016), https://asistdl.onlinelibrary.wiley.com/doi/full/10.1002/pra2.2015.145052010043.
[76] *Id.* at 4-5.

If something as relatively simple as the technology is not understood, then understanding what is done with the gathered information is even more challenging to understand. "Modern data analytics … can deduce extensive information about a person from these clues. In other words, little bits of innocuous data can say a lot in combination. Solove referred to this as the 'aggregation effect.'"[77] For example, "Cambridge University and Microsoft Research show how the patterns of Facebook likes can very accurately predict your sexual orientation, satisfaction with life, intelligence, emotional stability, religion, alcohol use and drug use, relationship status, age, gender, race, and political view—among many others."[78] As a result, obtaining informed consent becomes more complicated, relying on people to be able to make "rational choices about the costs and benefits of consenting to the collection, use and disclosure of their personal data."[79] This includes understanding that over time there are various entities collecting and aggregating individual data for a variety of uses that benefit these entities rather than the consumer who provided the data. Given that most individuals, even the most rational and knowledgeable ones, have a difficult time understanding the complex and long-term implications of this ongoing collection and use of their data, the traditional concept of individuals being able to provide informed consent is no longer useful.

A recent survey showed the following results regarding comprehension:

> Comprehension is deficient in the online consent process because people are often unaware of how websites and cloud service providers handle their personal information. Our knowledge data clearly shows that many people lack sufficient comprehension about several important issues related to cloud computing, online security, and the data trade for personal information online. For example, 25% of respondents were unable to correctly answer a basic multiple-choice question about the fundamental nature of cloud computing, 23% were unaware that free webmail services store customer information in the cloud, and 44% did not know that free websites could make money by

---

[77] Solove, *supra* note 79, at 1889-1890) (citations omitted).
[78] Avantika Monnappa, *How Facebook is Using Big Data – The Good, the Bad, and the Ugly*, SIMPLILEARN (Nov. 22, 2019, updated June 8, 2020), https://www.simplilearn.com/how-facebook-is-using-big-data-article.
[79] *Id.*

selling user information directly to marketing companies. Furthermore, because the knowledge-based questions were either true/false or multiple-choice, respondents were likely able to guess their way to higher knowledge scores by eliminating improbable answer options.[80]

Beyond the few individuals who have pointed out the meaninglessness of informed consent in the era of the Internet, the law has not sufficiently grappled with the issue of informed consent and the use of personal data collected through the Internet. As an initial matter, the law has primarily treated informed consent as a binary dimension. As Solove states, "The law's current view of consent is incoherent, and the law treats consent as a simple binary (that is, it either exists or it does not). Consent is far more nuanced, and privacy law needs a new approach that accounts for the nuances without getting too complex to be workable."[81] A simple "I agree" is not enough for informed consent here. Second, and related to the first point, the law has not reflected the more sophisticated understanding of the limits of human decision-making. These two issues together raise several concerns about the adequacy of the law to deal with current conditions: What does consent to something really mean? What should the law recognize as valid consent? Also, many transactions occur with some kind of inequality in knowledge and power—when are these asymmetries so substantial as to be coercive?

The issue of whether the consent that is given when visiting a website is actually informed is an important one. The view, as Solove points out, seems to be that the law is binary and a simple "I agree" is enough for informed consent.

In order to illustrate why comprehension is difficult, we will look at what Facebook's and Google's consent (terms of use) policy is. As Wagner says, "It's also clear that many people don't know the details of how Facebook's advertising business works."[82] We would add that most people do not know or understand how Google's and many others' advertising business works. Therefore, we will look at what Facebook's and Google's consent (term of use) policies state.

Facebook's policy is detailed, especially about what it does not do,[83] but it leaves out one significant bit of information—the fact that it monetizes the information and sell access to it even though it does not sell it *per se*. Here is what Facebook notes:

---

[80] Bashir, etal, *supra* note 81, at 8.
[81] Solove, *supra* note 79, at 1901.
[82] *Id.*
[83] Facebook Terms of Service, https://www.facebook.com/terms.php.

We don't charge you to use Facebook or the other products and services covered by these Terms. Instead, businesses and organizations pay us to show you ads for their products and services. By using our Products, you agree that we can show you ads that we think will be relevant to you and your interests. We use your personal data to help determine which ads to show you.

We don't sell your personal data to advertisers, and we don't share information that directly identifies you (such as your name, email address or other contact information) with advertisers unless you give us specific permission. Instead, advertisers can tell us things like the kind of audience they want to see their ads, and we show those ads to people who may be interested. We provide advertisers with reports about the performance of their ads that help them understand how people are interacting with their content. See Section 2 below to learn more.[84]

Section 2 goes into more detail about how this information is collected and used and emphasizes that the identity of users is protected and that they have some control. Still, it omits some critical aspects, such as that Facebook is benefitting directly monetarily:

2. How our services are funded

Instead of paying to use Facebook and the other products and services we offer, by using the Facebook Products covered by these Terms, you agree that we can show you ads that businesses and organizations pay us to promote on and off the Facebook Company Products. We use your personal data, such as information about your activity and interests, to show you ads that are more relevant to you.

Protecting people's privacy is central to how we've designed our ad system. This means that we can show you relevant and useful ads without telling advertisers who you are. We don't sell your personal data. We allow advertisers to tell us things like their business

---

[84] *Id.*

goal, and the kind of audience they want to see their ads (for example, people between the age of 18-35 who like cycling). We then show their ad to people who might be interested.

We also provide advertisers with reports about the performance of their ads to help them understand how people are interacting with their content on and off Facebook. For example, we provide general demographic and interest information to advertisers (for example, that an ad was seen by a woman between the ages of 25 and 34 who lives in Madrid and likes software engineering) to help them better understand their audience. We don't share information that directly identifies you (information such as your name or email address that by itself can be used to contact you or identifies who you are) unless you give us specific permission. Learn more about how Facebook ads work here.

We collect and use your personal data in order to provide the services described above to you. You can learn about how we collect and use your data in our Data Policy. You have controls over the types of ads and advertisers you see, and the types of information we use to determine which ads we show you. Learn more.[85]

Google's privacy terms are even more complicated than Facebook's because it collects a lot more information about each individual such as all the search terms and so on.[86] These terms were updated and were in effect beginning July 1, 2020 and were created to meet the California law that went into effect on January 1, 2020.[87] Concerning the California Consumer Privacy Act (CCPA), Google states that they do not sell personal information, however, the information is shared.[88] The policy also describes the categories of the information collected.[89] Google does state, however, that it uses the information to customize service for the user.[90]

---

[85] *Id.*
[86] The terms can be found at https://policies.google.com/privacy.
[87] *See generally,* Google Privacy Policy (July 1, 2020)
https://policies.google.com/privacy/archive/20200331-20200701?gl=US&hl=en
[88] *Id.*
[89] *Id.*
[90] *Id.*

Provide personalized services, including content and ads

> We use the information we collect to customize our services for you, including providing recommendations, personalized content, and customized search results. For example, Security Checkup provides security tips adapted to how you use Google products. And Google Play uses information like apps you've already installed and videos you've watched on YouTube to suggest new apps you might like.
>
> Depending on your settings, we may also show you personalized ads based on your interests. For example, if you search for "mountain bikes," you may see an ad for sports equipment when you're browsing a site that shows ads served by Google. You can control what information we use to show you ads by visiting your ad settings.[91]

However, what Google does not indicate is that it sells access to the aggregated information, which includes user information, to those advertisers. In addition to the above U.S. policy, there is an E.U. privacy policy.[92] The reason that Google has two sets of terms is because the European Union has a privacy directive that is much more comprehensive than that of the U.S.[93] However, neither set of rules discloses that these companies are monetizing the personal data.

Both Facebook's and Google's disclosures, do not meet some of the requirements of informed consent. As discussed previously, there are four requirements, and two of those do not appear to be met, namely disclosure and comprehension. It would seem that with all of the information that both of the companies provide, the disclosure requirement would be met, however, there is no disclosure about the fact that they use user information to directly profit (i.e., rather than profiting by meeting the customer's needs only). The fact that Facebook and Google make money off the individual's data seems to be a critical fact that a person should know before they can fully consent, and that aspect is totally missing. The other part, comprehension, seems to be problematic as well.

---

[91] *Id.*

[92] Google EU User Consent Policy and the GDPR, (May 18, 2020) https://www.termsfeed.com/blog/gdpr-google-eu-user-consent-policy.

[93] General Data Protection Regulation (GDPR), Regulation (EU) 2016/679, https://gdpr-info.eu.

The fact that there is so much information on these sites is part of the problem; the average person would not comprehend the subject matter of the consent.

There was a 2011 class action case against Facebook that involved the issue of informed consent.[94] That lawsuit concerned Facebook's "Sponsored Stories."[95] When a user clicked a "like" button, Facebook would use that interaction to create an advertisement that was then sent to that user's friends on Facebook. It turned those users into spokespersons for Facebook advertisers. The suit claimed that it was not legal to use people's names and people's photos for advertising without permission. Facebook argued that consent was given "by registering for and using Facebook website under its Terms of Use, which informs members that '(y)ou can use your privacy setting to limit how your name and profile picture may be associated with commercial, sponsored, or related content served or enhanced by us." In response, the *Fraley* court said:

> Facebook made a similar argument in *Cohen* I, but the court there was not persuaded, concluding that "[n]othing in the provisions of the Terms documents to which Facebook has pointed constitutes a clear consent by members to have their name or profile picture shared in a manner that discloses what services on Facebook they have utilized, or to endorse those services." Plaintiffs here contend that they never consented in any form to the use of their names or likenesses in Sponsored Stories, noting that Sponsored Stories were not even a feature of Facebook at the time they became registered members, and alleging that Plaintiffs were never asked to review or renew their Terms of Use subsequent to Facebook's introduction of the Sponsored Stories feature, which operates on an opt-out basis. The gravamen of Plaintiffs' consent argument is that even if the Statement of Rights and Responsibilities can be broadly construed to encompass Sponsored Stories, such "consent" was fraudulently obtained and, thus, not knowing and willful. As was the case in *Cohen* I, the Court determines that whether Facebook's Statement of Rights and Responsibilities, Privacy Policy, or Help Center pages unambiguously give Defendant the right to

---

[94] Fraley v. Facebook, Inc., 830 F. Supp. 2d 785 (2011).
[95] *Id.*

use Plaintiffs' names, images, and likenesses in the form of Sponsored Story advertisements for Facebook's commercial gain remains a disputed question of fact and is not proper grounds for dismissal at this time.[96]

This ruling supports the conclusion that the consent obtained by Facebook and other corporations with similar consent agreements does not meet the requirement that it is informed consent. The ruling focused on the introduction of the program following the consent agreement with no attempt to ask users to review the new features and renew consent. The nature of technology and big data is ever-changing and, therefore, obtaining valid consent can be difficult at best, particularly if consent agreements are not updated.

However, there are other difficulties in obtaining truly informed consent. As Solove said, "Even if most people were to read privacy policies routinely, people often lack enough expertise to adequately assess the consequences of agreeing to certain present uses or disclosure of their data."[97] Solove noted that the cognitive problems present numerous hurdles, such as:

> (1) people do not read privacy policies; (2) if people read them, they do not understand them; (3) if people read and understand them, they often lack enough background knowledge to make an informed choice: and (4) if people read them, understand them, and can make an informed choice, their choice might be skewed by various decision-making difficulties.[98]

Solove's fourth and final point refers to findings in social science of many departures from what is thought to be rational, such as people's propensity to be influenced by how decisions are framed. This research then influenced law, including trial procedures, contract law, tort law, criminal law, tax law, corporate law, family law, and policy formation.[99] For example, tort law, which has a strong state of mind focus, became

---

[96] Fraley, at 805-806 (citations omitted) (note: this case was later settled for a relatively small amount for each plaintiff), https://www.thrillist.com/news/nation/fraley-vs-facebook-class-action-lawsuit-15-dollar-check-settlement.
[97] Solove, *supra* note 79, at 1886.
[98] *Id.* at 1888.
[99] Donald C. Langevoort, *Behavioral Theories of Judgment and Decision Making in Legal Scholarship: A Literature Review*, 51 VANDERBILT L. REV. 1499, 1511-1512 (1998) .

concerned about biases in risk perception, such as in consumer choice.[100] Still, the law has been criticized for hanging onto the idea that people are rational decision-makers in many cases.[101] This has been the case for informed consent agreements concerning digitally collected data. In particular, the law has mostly ignored the fact that making a truly informed decision agreeing to consent is a near impossibility given the overwhelming number of ways the data could be used as well as the risks this use could incur. In fact, this has been noted by others as well: "As technical capability advances, what can be achieved with data mining and initiatives outpaces statutory regulation, as well as the social norms that frame individual human understandings."[102] Online users are motivated to press the button to access the service and are unlikely to read the agreement or understand it if they do.[103] Data uses are conceptually abstract and challenging to convey, particularly in terms of the potential harm to the user; furthermore, legalistically framed online consent agreements are complex, obscure, and lengthy that agreement to them is not truly informed.[104]

Another problem with making informed consent is what Solove calls "the problem of aggregation."[105] A person might share a single piece of data, such as being a female, which by itself may be relatively innocuous. Later that person is on the Internet looking for pregnancy test kits or researching breast cancer. With big data, those relatively separate pieces of information are aggregated, and that can now provide information to a business that this person is either trying to get pregnant or is already pregnant. The breast cancer search provides information that the person may think they have breast cancer. Before surveillance capitalism, marketers would not have all the information that is available now; many times segmentation would be approached with a probability that a specific person could be targeted with an advertisement. For example, if the advertisement is placed on a billboard, marketers would not know who is seeing the ad precisely at a given moment. This started to change with the availability of data. Zuboff noted the further

---

[100] *Id.* at 1512-1513.
[101] Russell B. Korobkin, & Thomas S. Ulen, *Law and Behavioral Science: Removing the Rationality Assumption from Law and Economics*, 88 CAL. L. REV. 1051, *see* discussion at 1126-1127 (2000).
[102] Vivien M. Rooney & Simon N Foley, *An Online Consent Maturity Model: Moving from Acceptable Use Towards Ethical Practice*, 18 NSPW: Proceedings of the New Security Paradigms Workshop 64, 64 (August 2018), https://dl.acm.org/doi/abs/10.1145/3285002.3285003.
[103] *Id.* at 64.
[104] *Id.* at 65.
[105] Solove, *supra* note 79, at 1889.

development of personalization and predictive capacities when "user profile information," or "UPI" could be derived based on users' actions.[106] One example is Target's use of predictive analytics to determine who is pregnant and in the second trimester so they could send coupons for baby clothes to the pregnant woman, which resulted in an angry father, who didn't know his teenage daughter was pregnant, complaining to the store.[107] As shown, tracking has become hyper-targeted, meaning targeting a specific individual at a key point in time. This kind of information is quite valuable to businesses that are interested in getting access to potential customers.[108]

The point is that, with big data being able to analyze existing information and combine that data with new information, it is "virtually impossible for a person to make meaningful judgments about the cost and benefits of revealing certain personal data. To enable a person to make a rational decision about sharing data, that person would need to have an understanding of the range of possible harms and benefits so as to do a cost-benefit analysis."[109] One of the key findings of the Bashir survey was that the respondents lacked sufficient comprehension to provide informed consent.[110]

Even if one could understand the complex picture of what is being gathered and how it is being used, there is an additional problem of voluntariness. Consent not only requires full knowledge, but it also requires that the person voluntarily agrees. There has to be "actual willingness that an act...shall occur"[111] As Bashir stated:

> Voluntariness is also a troubling issue online today because people are often presented with a forced choice dilemma: accept a cloud service provider's terms and conditions or do not use the service. While such a forced choice may not meet the level of coercion that would invalidate a contract under the law, it cannot be seen as meaningfully voluntary. Our survey results illustrate

---

[106] Shoshana Zuboff, *The Age of Surveillance Capitalism*, Published by PublicAffairs, an imprint of Perseus Books, LLC, a subsidiary of Hachette Book Group, Inc., (1st Edition January 2017), *see generally* discussion beginning on page 57.

[107] Kashmir Hill, *How Target Figured Out A Teen Girl Was Pregnant Before Her Father Did*, (Feb 16, 2012), https://www.forbes.com/sites/kashmirhill/2012/02/16/how-target-figured-out-a-teen-girl-was-pregnant-before-her-father-did/#3ba969866686.

[108] *See*, Solove, supra note 79, at 1889-1890 for a more detailed discussion.

[109] *Id*. at 1890.

[110] *See*, Bashir *et al*, *supra* note 81, at 8.

[111] West's Encyclopedia of American Law, edition 2, https://legal-dictionary.thefreedictionary.com/consent.

this perception of coercion, as the vast majority of respondents (81%) indicated that in at least one incident, they had submitted information online when they wished they were not required to do so.[112]

The dilemma exists because we rely on many websites for our daily activities. The use of computers is ubiquitous, and much of that involves gathering information. We need sites such as Google for activities, so our choice is to either not use the sites at all or agree to their terms. Granted, we do not need to use most social media sites, but the use of many sites, such as LinkedIn, are almost a necessity for important tasks, like job hunting. "Recruiters: social media is used by 93% of all recruiters to search and verify candidate's information, with LinkedIn being the most popular site to use. If you aren't on social media, recruiters can't find you for open jobs or verify your employment information."[113]   Therefore, regarding the sites we must use in today's world, the agreement to the terms on those sites is not genuinely voluntary.

Finally, there is another issue concerning how the aggregated information about an individual is being used: persuasive technology.[114] This means that it is used not only to track information about users but also to persuade them, "designed to change people's attitudes and behaviors."[115] For instance, specific behaviors are conditioned with incentives, such as sharing an ad with others or spending even more time with the technology platform. An example is found in Facebook, which uses buttons such as "like" so that others positively reinforce the act of posting. These types of conditioning techniques make it more likely users are genuinely unable to rationally process the true cost structure of sharing information on a platform.

Based on all of the above, it is clear that a person's DGD is being created by many companies and devices and that image is being monetized in various ways for those who mine the information. Since these websites never fully disclose what information they are using, how they are using it, and that they make most of their revenue from this information, we believe that the consent given to SNSs is not informed because the consent does not meet the legal standard of informed consent.

---

[112] Bashir, *et al, supra* note 81 at 9.

[113] Jessica Howington, *Why Your Online Job Search Is So Important*, Flexjobs (March 13, 2015) https://www.flexjobs.com/blog/post/online-job-search-important.

[114] *See generally*, Fogg, *supra* note 10.

[115] Maurits Kaptein & Aart van Halteren, *Adaptive Persuasive Messaging to Increase Service Retention: Using Persuasion Profiles to Increase the Effectiveness of Email Reminders*, 17 Pers Ubiquit Comput 1173, 1173 (2013) https://doi.org/10.1007/s00779-012-0585-3.

VII. RECENT PRIVACY LEGISLATION

At the international level, the EU General Data Protection Regulation (EU2016/679) (hereinafter, GDPR) took effect in 2018. On the local level, the California Consumer Privacy Act of 2018 took effect on January 1, 2020 (hereinafter, CCPA).[116] At the time of this writing, in the U.S., only California had passed legislation to regulate consumer privacy. Massachusetts,[117] New York,[118] and Maryland[119] all have legislation at various stages, but none have yet been signed into law.[120] Also, none of the proposed legislation in those states does more than the California legislation, and some do less.[121] Both the GDPR and the CCPA are strict about permissible uses of the collected data. A consumer may opt-out of the collection of the information and the sale of personal data under both laws. However, neither of these laws prevents the sites from aggregating data and selling access to that information to others. This data is also known as anonymous, deidentified, pseudonymous, or aggregated data.[122] "The CCPA does not restrict a business's ability to collect, use, retain, sell, or disclose a consumer information that is deidentified or aggregated."[123] Pseudonymous data is not considered personal data under the GDPR.[124] As long as the aggregated data is anonymous, the GDPR does not restrict what the data collector may do with it.

Thus, websites such as Facebook, Google, are not greatly affected by either of these pieces of legislation.[125] The laws primarily constrain smaller actors in the online advertising world.[126] Even though the legislation will not affect the way Google makes most of its revenue,

---

[116] CAL. CIV. CODE § 1798.100-1798.199.
[117] https://malegislature.gov/Bills/192/HD3847.
[118] https://www.nysenate.gov/legislation/bills/2021/s6701.
[119] https://mgaleg.maryland.gov/mgawebsite/Legislation/Details/sb0011?ys=2022RS.
[120] For complete and up to date coverage of U.S. privacy laws, *see* https://www.varonis.com/blog/us-privacy-laws/
[121] https://www.varonis.com/blog/us-privacy-laws.
[122] Laura Jehl & Alan Friel, *CCPA and GDPR Comparison Chart*, PRACTICAL LAW, https://www.bakerlaw.com/webfiles/Privacy/2018/Articles/CCPA-GDPR-Chart.pdf.
[123] *Id.*
[124] *Id.*
[125] *See, e.g.*, Antonio Garcoa Martinez, *Why California's Privacy Law Won't Hurt Facebook or Google*, WIRED, (August 31, 2018), https://www.wired.com/story/why-californias-privacy-law-wont-hurt-facebook-or-google.
[126] *Id.*

Google is lobbying to weaken the legislation.[127] The websites have to provide more information and have an opt-out option for collecting and selling personal data, but they do not have to do anything about the aggregated data they sell access to, meaning their bottom line will not be affected much by these laws.

However, there may be some additional threats to Google, Facebook and others with regard to their revenue.[128] As discussed, the GDPR and the CCPA attempted to protect consumer privacy. However, "[d]iscussions now focus on what comes next. Every week, members of the World Wide Web Consortium, or W3C, an international standards organization founded by a creator of the web, Tim Berners-Lee, dial into a video call to work out the options."[129] "The participants are all trying desperately to nudge the tiller in a direction that satisfies their needs. But the captain steering the ship is undoubtedly Google, whose $162 billion in 2019 revenue makes it the gatekeeper for almost half of all global digital ad spending."[130] Therefore, although an industry standards organization is discussing the self-regulation of data usage, it is unlikely that these discussions will have much effect on how Google and Facebook make their revenue.

VIII. RECOMMENDATIONS

Website users leave a very comprehensive trail, a digital image that is very detailed and continuously evolving as they use the Internet. The digitally generated double is essentially an image on steroids. The law is clear that a person owns their image and that it cannot be used for another person's benefit without permission. However, SNSs and other platforms are using this image for their own gain, constituting an appropriation of that image that it is being monetized without informed consent. Informed consent requires comprehension and voluntariness, neither of which exists under the current consent agreements utilized by SNSs.

With regard to comprehension, since these websites do not fully disclose the uses and monetization of the collected data, more clarity is

---

[127] Kartikay Mehrotra, Laura Mahoney & Daniel Stoller, *Google and Other Tech Firms Seek to Weaken Landmark California Data-Privacy Law*, LOS ANGELES TIMES, (Sept. 4, 2019) https://www.latimes.com/business/story/2019-09-04/google-and-other-tech-companies-attempt-to-water-down-privacy-law.

[128] Alex Webb, *Google's Cookie Fight Will Shape Future of Digital Advertising*, BUSINESSWEEK (July 20,2020), https://www.bloomberg.com/news/articles/2020-07-16/google-s-cookie-overhaul-could-reshape-the-digital-ad-industry

[129] *Id.*

[130] *Id.*

required. Websites must make it clear that the individual's data is aggregated with other consumer information, and access to that pooled information is sold. Therefore, a statement is needed that says something such as: Even though we do not directly sell your personal data, we do aggregate your data with the data of others who have similar interests based your Internet use. For example, if you visit and/or search for information on classic cars, your data may be pooled with others who have a similar interest. That aggregated data is sold to advertisers who want may try to sell you items based on your interests, which means that you may be shown advertisements from businesses that want to sell your car parts and related items. If you wish, you may opt-out of allowing the pooling of your information. However, we do want you to know that this site is free because of the revenue received from the marketers who pay for access to the pooled data. This means that without your consent to our selling such information, we may no longer be able provide a service to you at no cost.

Such disclosure may cause some consumers to opt-out, but with a reasonable explanation as to why the sale of such information is important, many consumers would probably not opt-out. Obviously, the risk of such disclosure is that if too many consumers opt-out, the platform's revenue may drop to a non-sustainable point. A viable alternative in the circumstance that an individual opts out would be the loss of free access to the SNS; instead, the site could charge a user fee on an annual basis. Therefore, the tradeoff is that the site is free with the understanding that an individual's aggregated data can be sold, or it is not free if the individual decides not to allow the site to sell their pooled information.

There is a third alternative. Some sites benefit the individual in some manner. For example, Google benefits the user by providing information that the user wants and/or needs. In that case, Google and sites like it could still disclose what they are doing with a user's information. But the fact that the user is benefitting from using the site could be considered a *quid pro quo*, allowing Google to sell the pooled information. On the other hand, sites like Facebook generally do not benefit users beyond maintaining connections between family and friends. The users do not really need much of what is on Facebook; therefore, those sites would use the option of a user agreement to allow them to sell the information or to charge a fee for site access.

Full disclosure also means that it is imperative for companies to seek renewed consent agreements with users as they add features that collect additional data. This might be difficult given that typically new features are rolled out continuously; however, companies could be asked to group or chunk features and then obtain consent from each consumer prior to mining the data, just as they are sure to obtain payment before any premium content can be used.

Another aspect of the comprehensibility of informed consent agreements involves clear, understandable language. Purposely creating obtuse consent agreements that are difficult to understand is not obtaining true consent. An individual should not have to consult a lawyer to understand the agreement they are signing. Furthermore, consent documents should not be constructed in such a way as to take advantage of the less-than-rational decision tendencies of individuals, such as through how they are framed. Legalistic and business utility approaches to obtaining consent often invite game-playing on the part of corporations that encourages incomprehensibility or framing as ways to overwhelm the individual's rational decision processes.

Of course, even if both comprehensibility and full disclosure are achieved, to genuinely provide consent, an individual should have some other viable options for obtaining the needed service. Most moral philosophers agree that using one's power to get someone to do something when they have few alternatives is a restriction of freedom and, therefore, a form of coercion.[131] Additionally, in law, informed consent must be voluntarily given, not coerced.[132] Coerced in this context means that the service that is provided is one that is generally needed by users. Google is a good example of such a service. Google is undoubtedly one of the largest and most apparent monopolies in the world. In fact, the company monopolizes several different markets, including search and advertising. Bing, Google's closest search competitor, has just 2% of the market— hardly a significant threat to Google's 90%. Google also controls about 60% of the global advertising revenue on the Internet.[133] Therefore, companies that have a monopoly on a service cannot obtain true voluntary consent because of the asymmetric imbalance of power they have over consumers when the service they provide is needed. For that reason, a business that is a monopoly and that provides something most consumers need in today's world should work to create and support alternatives to the provided services that do not require consent where personal data is needed to obtain the services. That alternative could be a fee-for-service model outlined above.

---

[131] *See generally,* Sonia Goltz, *On Power and Freedom: Extending the Definition of Coercion,* 43 PERSPECTIVES ON BEHAVIOR SCIENCE 137 (2020) http://link.springer.com/article/10.1007/s40614-019-00240-z
[132] Christine Grady, *Enduring and Emerging Challenges of Informed Consent,* 372 N. ENGL. J. MED. 855 (2015).
[133] Joseph Mercola, *Google - One of the Largest Monopolies in the World,* MERCOLA (June 16, 2018), https://articles.mercola.com/sites/articles/archive/2018/06/16/google-one-of-the-largest-monopolies.aspx.

The focus here is on obtaining full informed and voluntary consent, rather than the suggestion that revenue generated from each consumer's information be shared with the consumer. The incremental revenue derived from an individual consumer is most likely *de minimus* and being forced to share that revenue may create an expense that would detrimentally affect the bottom line. For example, "Facebook profits off of its 1.4 billion daily users in a big way: According to its most recent filings with the Securities and Exchange Commission, the average revenue per user in 2017 was $20.21 ($6.18 in the fourth quarter alone). Users in the U.S. and Canada were worth even more because of how big the markets are."[134] Therefore, requiring Facebook to share a portion of $20 with each consumer would cost the company a significant amount of money, not just due to sharing the revenue but also in terms of record keeping and making the payments to millions of users.

To make SNSs and others comply with these recommendations, it would likely be necessary for states to pass legislation detailing the content of the consent agreements. The current legislation in California, other states, and the E.U. does not force the SNSs to clearly disclose what they are doing with one's information and how they are making money off that information. The current laws only prevent the sale of personal data but not the sale of access to the aggregated data that includes one's information. The various governments need to create and pass legislation that forces a clear explanation of what is done with the information and then allow users to make the choice, including the option to pay for services when the user wants to completely opt-out of providing any of the personal information being used in any way. Doing this would ensure that there is informed consent and that, with the options, the consent is voluntary.

IX. CONCLUSION

The current situation is characterized by: 1) people increasingly spending their time online, leaving so much data about themselves that a digitally generated double can be created; 2) companies creating many incentives to entice people to leave more data about themselves; 3) companies appropriating data to create a digitally generated double and benefitting from it because it forms the basis for a new type of marketing;

---

[134] Julia Glum, *This Is Exactly How Much Your Personal Information Is Worth to Facebook*, MONEY (March 21, 2018), https://money.com/how-much-facebook-makes-off-you.

and 4) people not benefitting from their data being collected and sold, not fully understanding it, and not having much choice about it. People should be fully informed in a way that allows them to comprehend the full picture and voluntarily make decisions about the use of their data. If the users choose not to allow the sale of their data, they could still benefit from company services through the payment of fees. The bottom line is that the legal framework should reflect the complexities that come with the digital age; much work remains to be done to ensure the consent agreements fully disclose the terms under which the information will be used and the options available to users who would like to opt out.

THE BATTLE OVER FIDUCIARY RESPONSIBILITY OF PENSION FUND MANAGERS: THE TRUMP ADMINISTRATION TAKES ON THE ESG MOVEMENT

FRANK J. CAVALIERE[1*]
RICARDO COLON[**]
TONI MULVANEY[***]
MARLEEN SWERDLOW[****]

ABSTRACT

The ESG Movement is one of the most potent forces affecting the investment world today. ESG stands for "environmental/ social/governance" and it is the latest iteration of the long-established Corporate Social Responsibility (CSR) movement. ESG has been embraced by managers of some of the world's largest pension plan administration companies, such as BlackRock. The goal of the Movement is to pressure boards of directors and top management of companies where pension plan managers own significant shares of stock into doing what these pension plan managers consider to be "the right thing", even if the actions they promote result in less profitability for those companies, at least in the short run. Stockholders are not generally considered to owe fiduciary duties to the companies in which they own stock. Pension plan managers, however, are fiduciaries of the beneficiaries of their respective pension plans. How does being a fiduciary harmonize to being a promoter of ESG when following the tenets of that Movement can result in less profitability for the plans they manage? The Trump Administration has expressed doubt over the legality of ESG-motivated actions as they relate to federally-regulated qualified pension plans subject to the Employee Retirement Income Security Act of 1974 (ERISA). According to an Administration Executive Order, the fiduciary duty of a pension plan manager subject to ERISA is to "maximize" profits for the plan beneficiaries. This paper will discuss the origins and precepts of the ESG

---

[*] J.D., University Professor of Business Law, Lamar University, Beaumont, Texas.
[**] LL.M., J.D., Associate Professor of Accounting, Lamar University, Beaumont, Texas.
[***] J.D., Associate Dean for Undergraduate Studies and Administration, Professor of Business Law, Lamar University, Beaumont, Texas.
[****] J.D., Professor of Business Law, Lamar University, Beaumont, Texas.

Movement, the fiduciary responsibilities of pension plan trustees, the concerns of ESG proponents that making profits at the expense of the planet and the health of the global population is counter-productive, and arguments about whether ERISA mandates fiduciaries to maximize profits.

I. INTRODUCTION

The Environmental, Social and Governance (ESG) movement is one of the most important forces impacting investment strategies today. Some of the largest U.S. mutual fund administrators and pension plan managers are proponents of the Movement. In 2019, ESG funds attracted over $20 billion in funding from investors.[2] The rise of the ESG Movement may have implications for pension plan managers who have fiduciary duties to participants and beneficiaries of the pension plans they administer. Is the responsibility of these pension managers to maximize the benefits of their participants and beneficiaries or should they consider ESG factors when making investment decisions? Recently, the administration of Donald J. Trump issued guidance expressing concerns about the use of ESG factors for making investment decisions, particularly with respect to pension plans regulated by the Employee Retirement Income Security Act (ERISA) of 1974.[3]

This paper analyzes the origins and precepts of the ESG Movement as it evolved from the concept of enlightened self-interest and corporate social responsibility. It discusses the tenets of the ESG Movement and analyzes the fiduciary responsibilities of pension plan managers. In light of a recent Executive Order and Field Advisory Bulletin from the Department of Labor, this paper analyzes arguments for and against consideration of ESG considerations in investment decisions made by pension plan managers. Finally, the paper concludes that fiduciary responsibilities of plan managers allow them to consider ESG considerations in determining an investment strategy that maximizes the risk-adjusted return to plan participants and beneficiaries. However, the consideration of ESG issues, in isolation, does not seem to be supported

---

[2] Greg Iacurci, *Money Moving into Environmental Funds Shatters Previous Record*, CNBC, Jan. 14, 2020, https://www.cnbc.com/2020/01/14/esg-funds-see-record-inflows-in-2019.html

[3] Exec. Order No. 13868, 84 Fed. Reg. 15495 (Apr. 15, 2019); Field Assistance Bulletin No. 2018-01 (Apr. 23, 2018).

by the Modern Prudent Investor Rule, the "prudent man" standard of care, or the most recent administrative guidance issued on ERISA plans by the Department of Labor.

II. ENLIGHTENED SELF-INTEREST

The concept of self-interest is essential to understanding the capitalist economic system. According to the father of capitalism, Adam Smith, "[i]t is not from the benevolence of the butcher, the brewer, or the baker that we expect our dinner, but from their regard to their own interest."[4] Less well-known is his earlier work, *The Theory of Moral Sentiments*, wherein he expressed a more philosophical approach, premised on the need of people to live in sympathy with one another:

> Without this sacred regard for general rules, no-one's conduct can be much depended on. It is what constitutes the most essential difference between a man of principle and honour and a worthless fellow. The man of principle keeps steadily and resolutely to his maxims on all occasions, preserving through the whole of his life one even tenor of conduct. The worthless fellow acts variously and accidentally, depending on whether mood, inclination, or self-interest happens to be uppermost. Indeed, men are subject to such variations of mood that without this respect for general rules a man who in all his cool hours was delicately sensitive to the propriety of conduct might often be led to act absurdly on the most trivial occasions, ones in which it was hardly possible to think of any serious motive he could have for behaving in this manner.[5]

Implicit in Smith's contention, and an article of faith among many critics of business is that it is more important to take the "long-run" view of business success, rather than a "short-run" perspective. According to

---

[4] Smith, Adam, "An Inquiry into the Nature and Causes of the Wealth of Nations" (The Wealth of Nations) (1776) Book 1, Chapter 2, "Of the Principle which gives occasion to the Division of Labour", http://geolib.com/smith.adam/won1-02.html

[5] ADAM SMITH, THE THEORY OF MORAL SENTIMENTS 85 (1759), http://www.earlymoderntexts.com/assets/pdfs/smith1759.pdf

Archie Carroll, one of the leading advocates for businesses acting in socially responsible ways, "[t]he long-range self-interest view, sometimes referred to as 'enlightened self-interest' holds that if business is to have a healthy climate in which to operate in the future, it must take actions now to ensure its long-term viability."[6]

III. THE SOCIAL RESPONSIBILITY OF BUSINESS

Social responsibility is often studied in the context of principles sometimes referred to as the "managerial ideology of business." Managerial ideology is defined as "a stream of discourse that promulgates, however unwittingly, a set of assumptions about the nature of … corporations, employees, managers, and the means by which the latter can direct the other two."[7] One of the key elements of managerial ideology has long been the idea known as "corporate social responsibility" (CSR) and the debate that it presents between optimum profits and maximum profits, which can be summarized as follows:

> Executives who accept the idea of enlightened self-interest today must be willing to accept optimum profits rather than maximum profits. In most annual reports, a CEO tells the company's stockholders that every measure is being taken to ensure maximum profits. In the planning session with managers, however, the same CEO may accept optimum profits, which is a satisfactory level of profits considering external pressures, such as government regulation. Executives who make social responsibility decisions based on long-run goals are trading maximum short-run profits (the most that could be made this quarter) for optimum profits (what they are willing to make this quarter in light of other developments).[8]

---

[6] ARCHIE B. CARROLL, BUSINESS & SOCIETY 40 (2015).

[7] Stephen R. Barley & Gideon Kunda, *Design and Devotion: Surges of Rational and Normative Ideologies of Control in Managerial Discourse*, 37 ADMIN. SCI. QUARTERLY 363, 363 (1992).

[8] JOHN H. JACKSON, ROGER L. MILLER & SHAWN G. MILLER, BUSINESS AND SOCIETY TODAY 159 (1997).

Today, the concept of corporate social responsibility is intimately associated with the stakeholder concept. The stakeholder concept involves the idea that a business manager must respect the legitimate expectations of a large and ever-expanding array of people, organizations, entities,[9] and even the natural environment itself.[10] According to professors Edward Freeman and Heather Elms, businesses that want to be successful in the twenty-first century cannot follow a pure profit maximization motive, which is blamed for contributing to the collapse of many companies and corporate scandals –Enron, Wells Fargo, Lehman Brothers, General Motors – all of which have cost U.S. citizens and taxpayers trillions of dollars.[11] Instead, Freeman and Elms argue that "the social responsibility of business is to create value for its stakeholders."[12] They summarize their theory as follows:

> The stakeholder approach sets forth a new conceptualization of business, in which business is understood as a set of relationships and management's job is to help shape these relationships. Business is about how customers, suppliers, employees, financiers, communities, and managers interact to create value, and there is no single formula for balancing or prioritizing stakeholders. Creating that balance is part of what management is all about, and it will be different for different companies at different times.[13]

---

[9] ARCHIE B. CARROLL, BUSINESS & SOCIETY 66 (2015) ("In short, a stakeholder may be thought of as 'any individual or group who can affect or is affected by the actions, decisions, policies, practices, or goals of the organization'").

[10] ARCHIE B. CARROLL, BUSINESS & SOCIETY 67 (2015). "When the concept of sustainability first became popular, however, the natural environment was given priority, but the natural environment has often been neglected. In keeping with sustainability, the natural environment, nonhuman species, and future generations would be considered among business's important stakeholders." Id.

[11] Edward Freeman & Heather Elms, *The Social Responsibility of Business is to Create Value for Stakeholders*, MIT SLOAN (Jan. 4, 2018), https://sloanreview.mit.edu/article/the-social-responsibility-of-business-is-to-create-value-for-stakeholders/ *Contra* Milton Friedman, *The Social Responsibility of Business is to Increase its Profits*, N.Y. TIMES, Sept. 13, 1960, http://umich.edu/~thecore/doc/Friedman.pdf

[12] *Id.*

[13] *Id.*

Adopting social responsibility principles, Larry Fink, the Chief Executive Officer of BlackRock, the world's largest pension plan management company, has stated that "[c]ompanies must benefit all of their stakeholders, including shareholders, employees, customers and the communities in which they operate."[14] Similarly, the Business Roundtable, an association of chief executive officers of America's leading corporations, has released a new Statement on the Purpose of the Corporation. In the new Statement, the executives acknowledge a fundamental commitment to all stakeholders and agree to undertake the following actions:

> **[Deliver] value to our customers**. We will further the tradition of American companies leading the way in meeting or exceeding customer expectations.
> **[Invest] in our employees**. This starts with compensating them fairly and providing important benefits. It also includes supporting them through training and education that help develop new skills for a rapidly changing world. We foster diversity and inclusion, dignity and respect.
> **[Deal] fairly and ethically with our suppliers.** We are dedicated to serving as good partners to the other companies, large and small, that help us meet our missions.
> **[Support] the communities in which we work**. We respect the people in our communities and protect the environment by embracing sustainable practices across our businesses.
> **Generat[e] long-term value for shareholders**, who provide the capital that allows companies to invest, grow and innovate. We are committed to transparency and effective engagement with shareholders.

---

[14] Liz Moyer, *BlackRock Says it's Time to Take Action on Guns, May Use Voting Power to Influence*, CNBC, Mar. 2, 2018, https://www.cnbc.com/2018/03/02/blackrock-says-its-time-to-take-action-on-guns-may-use-voting-power-to-influence.html

Each of our stakeholders is essential. We commit to **deliver value to all of them**, for the future success of our companies, our communities and our country.[15]

The 2019 Statement supersedes previous statements by Business Roundtable which were based on shareholder primacy—"that corporations exist principally to serve shareholders"—creating a new framework that better reflects the way corporations can and should operate in the twenty-first century.[16]

IV. THE ESG MOVEMENT

By harnessing the economic power of mutual fund and pension plan administrators, the ESG movement seeks to get corporations to act more responsibly. ESG stands for environmental, social, and governance, and it has been called an offshoot of the CSR, or corporate social responsibility movement, which was directed at the officers and boards of directors of corporations to encourage them to act more in the interests of society.[17] Like CSR, ESG is a fluid concept or theory, and the "issues" with which it is concerned change over time.

ESG is based on the adage "money talks."[18] It represents an organized, investment-centric, top-down approach to measure firm performance in three very different endeavors, namely: environmental sustainability, social equity, and corporate governance.[19] Environmental criteria may include a company's energy use, waste, pollution, natural resource conservation, treatment of animals, and risk management.[20]

---

[15] Press Release, Business Roundtable, Business Roundtable Redefines the Purpose of a Corporation to Promote 'An Economy that Serves All Americans' (Aug. 19, 2019) (emphasis added), https://www.businessroundtable.org/business-roundtable-redefines-the-purpose-of-a-corporation-to-promote-an-economy-that-serves-all-americans

[16] *Id.*

[17] Frank Cavaliere, *The UN Global Compact and Principles for Responsible Investing,* [152] THE PRACTICAL LAWYER, no. 4, 2019, at 8.

[18] Frank Cavaliere, Frank Badua & Ricardo Colon, *Should Accounting for Sustainability be Mandatory?*, Today's CPA, May-June 2020, at 35 [hereinafter *Accounting for Sustainability*].

[19] *Id.*

[20] COLUMBIA PACIFIC WEALTH MANAGEMENT, *WHAT YOU SHOULD KNOW ABOUT ESG INVESTING,* https://www.columbiapacificwm.com/blog/insights/general/what-you-should-know-about-esg-investing/

Social criteria look at the company's business relationships.[21] Governance criteria can refer to transparent accounting, stockholder voting opportunities, use of political contributions, avoiding conflicts of interest, and not engaging in illegal practices.[22] The metrics used to document and report a company's performance in these three areas differ significantly from one another, and from traditional accounting measures that focus on financial performance.[23]

The SEC has not adopted specific disclosure requirements with respect to ESG. Today, ESG reporting relies on the concept of materiality. Issues about sustainability that are material to a company's financial condition or results of operations must be disclosed.[24] Additionally, ESG disclosures are required whenever they are necessary to prevent other financial statement disclosures from being materially incomplete or misleading and to inform investors' proxy decisions.[25] Management is responsible for identifying which ESG issues are material to a company.[26]

The landscape for ESG reporting has become more difficult to navigate as numerous companies have adopted sustainability disclosure frameworks developed by different non-governmental organizations including the Global Reporting Initiative (GRI), International Integrated Reporting Committee (IIRC), Task Force on Climate-Related Financial Disclosures (TCFD), Carbon Disclosure Project (CDP), and the Sustainability Accounting Standards Board (SASB).[27] Currently, SASB is widely accepted as a reporting framework that is aligned with the requirements of the U.S. securities laws in terms of ESG disclosures.[28] At

---

[21] *Id.*

[22] *Id.*

[23] *Accounting for Sustainability, supra* note 17.

[24] Mary J. White, Chair, Securities and Exchange Commission, Keynote Address at the International Corporate Governance Network Annual Conference: Focusing the Lens of Disclosure to Set the Path Forward on Board Diversity, Non-GAAP, and Sustainability (June 27, 2016), http://www.sec.gov/news/speech/chair-white-icgn-speech.html

[25] *Id.*

[26] Congress first introduced the concept of materiality in Section 17(a)(2) of the Securities Act of 1933. Afterwards, Congress also included the concept of materiality in Section 18(a) of the Securities Act of 1934. For public company disclosures, SEC Rule 405 defines the term "material". SEC Staff Accounting Bulletin No. 99 – Materiality, sets forth standards for assessing materiality for preparers of financial statements as well as auditors.

[27] *Accounting for Sustainability, supra* note 17, at 38.

[28] *Id.*

least 308 companies use SASB for sustainability reporting.[29] SASB is comprised of seventy-seven industry-specific sets of sustainability accounting standards covering a range of industry-specific sustainability areas of interest to investors such as water management for beverage companies, data security for technology firms, and supply chain management for consumer goods manufacturers and retailers.[30]

V. BACKGROUND ON THE CONCEPT OF FIDUCIARY RESPONSIBILITY

The term "fiduciary" is often bandied about, but can differ in meaning depending on the context, and specifically whether it is premised on the historical common law or whether it has been modified by statutes. The typical situations involving this relationship include trusts, agency relationships, partnerships, and corporations. Historically, the fiduciary concept arose from the law of trusts, where the trustee has title, but not beneficial ownership, of the property delivered from one person, for the benefit of another, under the terms of a written agreement.[31] The common law standards of faithfulness imposed on trustees were rigid.[32] The trustee is required to manage the trust corpus first and foremost with the needs of beneficiaries in mind and self-dealing is strictly prohibited.[33]

Virtually all qualified pension plan assets are held in the form of trusts.[34] The trustee has a duty to manage the trust assets in the manner of

---

[29] The complete list of companies using SASB can be found at https://www.sasb.org/company-use/sasb-reporters/

[30] Janine Guillot, Director of Capital Markets Policy and Outreach, Sustainability Accounting Standards Board, Discussion Regarding Disclosures on Sustainability and Environmental, Social and Governance Topics (December 13, 2018), http://www.sec.gov/video/webcast-archive-player.shtml?document_id=iac121318

[31] Joseph T. Walsh, *The Fiduciary Foundation of Corporate Law,* 27 JOURNAL OF CORPORATION LAW, no. 3, 2002, at 333, https://papers.ssrn.com/sol3/papers.cfm?abstract_id=338541 ("The fiduciary concept, as we know, had its origin in the law of trusts, where its literal meaning 'faithfulness' correctly described the duty or responsibility owed by one who held title, but not ownership, to property of another, who lacked legal title but could, in equity, claim the benefits of ownership. This latter individual is referred to as the beneficiary, or in earlier cases, the cestui que trust, *i.e.*, he for whom the trust was created.")

[32] *Id.*

[33] *Id.*

[34] U.S. DEPARTMENT OF LABOR EMPLOYEE BENEFITS SECURITY ADMINISTRATION, FAQS ABOUT RETIREMENT PLANS AND ERISA, https://www.dol.gov/sites/dolgov/files/ebsa/about-ebsa/our-activities/resource-center/faqs/retirement-plans-and-erisa-for-workers.pdf, at 13: "The funds must be held in trust or invested in an insurance contract. The employers' creditors cannot make a claim on retirement plan funds."

a reasonable prudent person, in other words, not to take inordinate risks. The prudent person legal standard was established in *Harvard College v. Amory*, where the court stated "[a]ll that can be required of a trustee to invest is, that he shall conduct himself faithfully and exercise a sound discretion. He is to observe how men of prudence, discretion and intelligence manage their own affairs, not in regard to speculation, but in regard to the permanent disposition of their funds, considering the probable income, as well as the probable safety of the capital to be invested."[35]

Private pension plans are regulated by the Employee Retirement Income Security Act of 1974 (ERISA), 29 U.S.C. § 1001, et seq. Although the ERISA statute only applies to private pension funds, many public funds also follow its provisions, particularly with respect to the standards of care expected of fiduciaries.[36] ERISA adopts the prudent man standard of care and provides, in pertinent part:

[A] fiduciary shall discharge his duties with respect to a plan solely in the interest of participants and beneficiaries and—

(A) for the exclusive purpose of:
(i) providing benefits to participants and their beneficiaries; and
(ii) defraying reasonable expenses of administering the plan;
(B) with the care, skill, prudence, and diligence under the circumstances then prevailing that a prudent man acting in a like capacity and familiar with such matters would use in the conduct of an enterprise of a like character and with like aims;
(C) by diversifying the investments of the plan as to minimize the risk of large losses, unless under the circumstances it is clearly prudent not to do so; and
(D) in accordance with the documents and instruments governing the plan insofar as such documents and instruments are consistent with the provisions of this

---

[35] 9 Pick. 446, 461 (Sup. Jud. Ct. Mass. 1830).
[36] PRINCIPLES FOR RESPONSIBLE INVESTMENT & UN ENVIRONMENT PROGRAMME, FIDUCIARY DUTY IN THE 21ST CENTURY 75 (2015) [hereinafter *Fiduciary Duty*].

subchapter and subchapter III of this chapter.[37]

State law governs public pension plans.[38] Most states follow the Uniform Prudent Investor Act of 2002 (UPIA).[39] In turn, UPIA adopts the Modern Prudent Investor Rule set forth in the Restatement (Third) of Trusts.[40] The Modern Prudent Investor Rule sets forth the duties of fiduciaries as follows:

> The trustee has a duty to the beneficiaries to invest and manage the funds of the trust as a prudent investor would, in light of the purposes, terms, distribution requirements, and other circumstances of the trust.
> (a) This standard requires the exercise of reasonable care, skill, and caution, and is to be applied to investments not in isolation but in the context of the trust portfolio and as a part of an overall investment strategy, which should incorporate risk and return objectives reasonably suitable to the trust.
> (b) In making and implementing investment decisions, the trustee has a duty to diversify the investments of the trust unless, under the circumstances, it is prudent not to do so.
> (c) In addition, the trustee must: (1) conform to fundamental fiduciary duties of loyalty and impartiality; (2) act with prudence in deciding whether and how to delegate authority and in the selection and supervision of agents; and
> (3) incur only costs that are reasonable in amount and appropriate to the investment responsibilities of the trusteeship.
> (d) The trustee's duties under this Section are subject to the rule of § 91, dealing primarily with contrary investment provisions of a trust or statute.[41]

---

[37] 29 U.S.C. § 1104(a) (2020).
[38] *Fiduciary Duty, supra* note 35, at 73
[39] *Id.*
[40] *Id.*
[41] RESTATEMENT (THIRD) OF TRUSTS § 90 (AM. LAW INST. 2006).

The Modern Prudent Investor Rule is more flexible than the rules set forth under ERISA because it gives fiduciaries a range of diversification strategies, requiring only that investment choices be made with appropriate skill, care and prudence, and for the benefit of plan participants and beneficiaries.[42]

VI. THE U.S. GOVERNMENT ENTERS THE DEBATE

On April 23, 2018 the Department of Labor issued a Field Assistance Bulletin to its agents dealing with the ESG Movement's inroads into corporate decision-making:

> Fiduciaries must not too readily treat ESG factors as economically relevant to the particular investment choices at issue when making a decision. It does not ineluctably follow from the fact that an investment promotes ESG factors, or that it arguably promotes positive general market trends or industry growth, that the investment is a prudent choice for retirement or other investors. Rather, ERISA fiduciaries must always put first the economic interests of the plan in providing retirement benefits. A fiduciary's evaluation of the economics of an investment should be focused on financial factors that have a material effect on the return and risk of an investment based on appropriate investment horizons consistent with the plan's articulated funding and investment objectives.[43]

More recently, in 2019, President Trump issued Executive Order 13868, titled "Promoting Energy Infrastructure and Economic Growth." This Executive Order extols the virtue and importance of the energy industry, particularly petrochemical companies, which are a huge target for environmental activists. The Purpose section of the Executive Order signals a clear departure from the Obama-era environmental approach and

---

[42] *Fiduciary Duty, supra* note 35, at 74.
[43] Field Assistance Bulletin No. 2018-01 (Apr. 23, 2018), https://www.dol.gov/sites/default/files/ebsa/employers-and-advisers/guidance/field-assistance-bulletins/2018-01.pdf

a shift to policies that may be more amenable to the energy sector. The ESG-related language is found in Section 5(b) of the Executive Order:

> To advance the principles of objective materiality and fiduciary duty . . . the Secretary of Labor shall, within 180 days of the date of this order, complete a review of available data filed with the Department of Labor by retirement plans subject to the Employee Retirement Income Security Act of 1974 (ERISA) in order to identify whether there are discernible trends with respect to such plans' investments in the energy sector. Within 180 days of the date of this order, the Secretary shall provide an update to the Assistant to the President for Economic Policy on any discernable trends in energy investments by such plans. The Secretary of Labor shall also, within 180 days of the date of this order, complete a review of existing Department of Labor guidance on the fiduciary responsibilities for proxy voting to determine whether any such guidance should be rescinded, replaced, or modified to ensure consistency with current law and policies that promote long-term growth and maximize return on ERISA plan assets.[44]

The Executive Order is silent on how the data gathered by the Department of Labor will be used. It seems reasonable to assume that the data may be used to enforce the guidance issued in 2018 on ESG plans which provides that plan fiduciaries cannot focus solely on ESG factors when making investment decisions.[45]

---

[44] Exec. Order No. 13868, 84 Fed. Reg. 15495 (Apr. 15, 2019), https://www.federalregister.gov/documents/2019/04/15/2019-07656/promoting-energy-infrastructure-and-economic-growth.

[45] Betty Moy Huber, *Recent Executive Order on Energy Infrastructure and Economic Growth – ESG Disclosure and Proxy Voting Implications*, BRIEFING: GOVERNANCE, Apr. 2019, https://www.briefinggovernance.com/2019/04/recent-executive-order-on-energy-infrastructure-and-economic-growth-esg-disclosure-and-proxy-voting-implications/

VII. ARGUMENTS FOR ESG'S FIDELITY TO FIDUCIARY DUTY UNDER ERISA

The primary reason to apply ESG principles to pension plans is to save the planet, because the E in ESG appears the primary motivator for the movement. Likewise, Larry Fink, the CEO of BlackRock, has stated that the "key to long-term success for companies is 'understanding the societal impact of your business' and how it will 'affect your potential for growth.'"[46] Most recently, in its 2020 letter to chief executive officers, Fink stated that "sustainability and climate-integrated portfolios can provide better risk-adjusted returns to investors."[47] Similarly, Larry Beeferman, Director of the Pensions and Capital Stewardship Project at Harvard Law School, stated "[t]he literature on [Socially Responsible Investing] is robust enough to say that there is a serious question around whether or not ESG issues are important to investment performance" and "at a minimum, due diligence processes must include assessment of the need to take account of [ESG] issues in investment decision-making."[48] A 2018 survey by the Callan Institute, which reports trends on ESG adoption by U.S. institutional funds, found that incorporation of ESG factors into the investment decision-making process of portfolio managers almost doubled to 43% in 2018 compared to 23% in 2013, and that the most frequently stated reason for incorporating ESG concerns is to achieve an improved risk and return profile.[49]

Other arguments that favor fiduciary investing based on ESG factors are similar to the arguments used against shareholder primacy. First, ignoring ESG factors forces trustees to "focus myopically on short-term earnings reports at the expense of long-term performance."[50] Second, failure to consider ESG factors "discourages investment and innovation, harms employees, customers and communities; and causes companies to indulge in reckless, sociopathic, and socially irresponsible behavior".[51]

---

[46] Liz Moyer, BlackRock says it's time to take action on guns, may use voting power to influence, https://www.cnbc.com/2018/03/02/blackrock-says-its-time-to-take-action-on-guns-may-use-voting-power-to-influence.html.

[47] BLACKROCK, A FUNDAMENTAL RESHAPING OF FINANCE (2020), https://www.blackrock.com/corporate/investor-relations/larry-fink-ceo-letter

[48] *Fiduciary Duty, supra* note35, at 74.

[49] CALLAN INSTITUTE, 2018 ESG SURVEY 2 (2018), https://src.bna.com/JfS

[50] LYNN STOUT, THE SHAREHOLDER VALUE MYTH: HOW PUTTING SHAREHOLDERS FIRST HARMS INVESTORS, CORPORATIONS, AND THE PUBLIC, *Preface* (2012).

[51] *Id.*

Ultimately, disregarding ESG factors "threatens the welfare of consumers, employees, communities, and investors alike."[52]

VIII. Arguments Against ESG Fidelity to Fiduciary Duty under ERISA

Recently, Max Schanzenbach of Northwestern University, and Robert Sitkoff of Harvard University, have challenged the assertion that investment management by pension trustees is required to consider ESG implications under fiduciary law principles. Both -authors reject the premise that a trustee must consider ESG factors.[53] First, as a matter of law, the Modern Prudent Investor Rule does not contain categorical rules of permissible or impermissible investments, because a trustee may invest in any type of investment so long as it is "part of an overall investment strategy having risk and return objectives reasonably suitable to the trust."[54] Second, mandating ESG investing is inappropriate because ESG factors are too fluid and their application too subjective.[55] Third, a prudent trustee could conclude that ESG factors do not give rise to a profitable trading opportunity and cannot be exploited cost-effectively for profit.[56] Fourth, an ESG investment mandate could prohibit many forms of passive investments because it would not allow trustees to invest in a broad market index funds that lack ESG investment options.[57] Passive investing is widely used, and in certain cases, represents a superior investing strategy, particularly when there is "little hope of outperforming the market."[58] Fifth, ESG factors, like any investment factor, may be over-valued in the market, and a trustee may engage an anti-ESG strategy upon concluding that firms with high ESG scores are overvalued.[59] Sixth, mandating ESG investing relies on the assumption that all trusts have a long-term time

---

[52] *Id.*
[53] Schanzenbach, Max Matthew and Sitkoff, Robert H., *Reconciling Fiduciary Duty and Social Conscience: The Law and Economics of ESG Investing by a Trustee*, 72 STANFORD L. REV. 381 (2020); Northwestern Law & Econ Research Paper No. 18-22; Harvard Public Law Working Paper No. 19-50, https://ssrn.com/abstract=3244665 or http://dx.doi.org/10.2139/ssrn.3244665
[54] *Id.* at 50. (Citing Unif. Prudent Inv'r Act § 2(b), (e) (Unif. Law Comm'n 1994).
[55] *Id.*
[56] *Id.* at 51.
[57] *Id.* at 52.
[58] *Id.* (Citing Fifth Third Bancorp v. Dudenhoeffer, 134 S. Ct. 2459, 2471 (U.S. 2014)).
[59] *Id.* at 52.

horizon. In point of fact, some trusts have a short time horizon, which means that a fiduciary should favor firms with low ESG scores since investments with high ESG scores will take too long to achieve the desired return on investment.[60] Schanzenbach and Sitkoff conclude that "mandating a long-term ESG perspective for trustees or other investment fiduciaries is manifestly contrary to both law and economics."[61]

It is also troubling that influential individuals like Larry Fink, Chief Executive Officer of Blackrock, have become arbiters of which investments ought to be preferred by fiduciaries. Ultimately, trustees have a responsibility to maximize return on investment, not to "optimize profits" based on subjective standards of what is "best" for society.

IX. CONCLUSION

The growth of the ESG Movement raises important questions in terms of the fiduciary duties of pension plan trustees. The key question discussed in this paper is whether ESG factors should be a mandatory consideration for trustees of pension plans. Fiduciary responsibilities for pension fund managers have developed piecemeal through the common law, trust law, and federal and state statutory law. Fiduciary responsibilities of pension plan trustees have thus evolved to allow the consideration of ESG concerns.[62]

Against this backdrop, the administration of President Donald J. Trump has issued guidance emphasizing that ERISA fiduciaries must always put the economic interests of their pension plans first and that ESG issues should not be presumed to be economically relevant to investment choices. Ultimately, the debate seems to boil down to different interpretations of fiduciary duties and responsibilities. While one interpretation sanctions considering ESG factors to determine risk and return in the context of the overall investment strategy for a portfolio, the other interpretation requires fiduciaries to maximize profits by making investment decisions considering only economic factors.

The pressure on pension fund managers to consider ESG factors and to balance those factors with the potentially conflicting fiduciary responsibilities inherent in the management of pension funds will continue given growing market awareness of the relevance of ESG issues,

---

[60] Id. at 53.
[61] Id.
[62] *Fiduciary Duty, supra* note 35, at 78-80.

increasing disclosures by public companies on ESG performance, and wider societal interest in issues related to climate change and human rights.[63]

---

[63] *Id.* at 78.

PRACTICAL STRATEGIES TO PROTECT CORPORATE TRADE SECRETS AND AVOID MISAPPROPRIATION CLAIMS

WADE DAVIS[*]
JEFFREY POST[**]

I. INTRODUCTION

As one of the four principle categories of intellectual property rights, along with patents, copyrights, and trademarks, knowledge of trade-secret law is essential to conducting business and thriving in today's economy. The U.S. Chamber of Commerce estimates that trade secrets protect U.S. assets worth an estimated 5 trillion and 5.5 trillion dollars.[1] Many businesses view trade secret protection as more critical than any other form of intellectual property - including patents.[2]

Knowledge of trade secrets might be the difference between protecting critical business assets or them ending up in a competitor's hands. It may also mean the difference between facing a large jury verdict and reaching a quick, favorable resolution to a claim. By focusing on the Federal Defend Trade Secrets Act and Minnesota's application of the Uniform Trade Secret Act, this article provides a practical guide to understand how these statutes operate in a real business environment. As always, businesses should seek legal advice regarding the details of the Act's implementation in their particular jurisdiction. This article is does not provide legal advice; rather, it is designed to help companies and legal practitioners spot red flags in their operations and strategically protect their trade secrets and intellectual property.

This article provides a practical overview to trade secret law for businesses seeking to protect their trade secrets and avoid trade secret claims. Section I identifies the types of information that are protectable as a trade secret and common categories that are often not protectable. Section II discusses ways that trade secrets can be misappropriated and common defenses to misappropriation. Section III examines the damages

---

[*] J.D., Associate Professor of Business Law, Minnesota State University, Mankato.
[**] Shareholder at Fredrikson and Byron, P.A.; J.D, University of Minnesota.
[1] Brian T. Yeh, *Protection of Trade Secrets: Overview of Current Law and Legislation,* Congressional Research Service, at 13, Apr. 22, 2016; U.S. Chamber of Commerce, *The Case for Enhanced Protection of Trade Secrets in the Trans-Pacific Partnership Agreement,* at 10, available at https://www.uschamber.com/sites/default/files/legacy/international/files/Final%20TPP%20Trade%20Secrets%208_0.pdf
[2] *Id.*

and remedies that are available. Section IV describes proactive steps companies can take to head-off trade secrets claims asserted by others. Section V offers recommendations to protect a company's trade secrets from misappropriation by others. Finally, Section VII identifies common companion claims brought in trade secret litigation.

II. DEFINING TRADE SECRETS

A wide variety of information potentially qualifies as a trade secret, including "all forms and types of financial, business, scientific, technical, economic, or engineering information, including patterns, plans, compilations, program devices, formulas, designs, prototypes, methods, techniques, processes, procedures, programs, or codes."[3] Trade secrets are protected under common law, state statutes, and the Federal Defend Trade Secrets Act.[4] As explained in this section, information must meet an additional three-factor test before it can be considered a trade secret.[5]

With the exception of New York, every state in has adopted the Uniform Trade Secrets Act in one form or another.[6] New York relies on common law, including Section 757 of the Restatement of torts, and criminal law to govern trade secrets protection and claims [7] Although the federal statute does not preempt or displace any other trade secrets claims or remedies, the state uniform trade secrets statutes often "displace conflicting tort, restitutionary, and other law of this state providing civil

---

[3] 18 U.S.C. § 1839(3); MINN. STAT. § 325C.01; Berkley Risk Adm'rs Co., LLC v. Accident Fund Holdings, Inc., Civ. No. 16-2671, 2016 U.S. Dist. LEXIS 113421, (D. Minn. Aug. 24, 2016) ("The definition of 'trade secret' in the federal statute and MUTSA are substantially similar.").

[4] See cf, 18 U.S.C. §1831 et seq. (federal "Defend Trade Secrets Act"), MINN. STAT. Ch. 325C (Minnesota "Uniform Trade Secrets Act). Parties can use the Defend Trade Secrets Act to establish jurisdiction in federal court. CH Bus Sales, Inc. v. Geiger, No. 18-cv-2444; 2019 WL 23374492019 U.S. Dist. LEXIS 92067, *4 (D. Minn. Jun. 3, 2019) (remanding lawsuit back to state court where dismissed federal trade secret claim was the only basis for federal jurisdiction).

[5] 18 U.S.C. § 1839(3); MINN. STAT. § 325C.01; Electro-Craft Corp. v. Controlled Motion, Inc., 332 N.W.2d 890, 899-902 (Minn. 1983).

[6] See Peter Steinmeyer, *Massachusetts Becomes 49th State to Adopt Uniform Trade Secrets* Act, EPSTEIN BECKER GREEN (Aug. 21, 2018) (noting that more recently Massachusetts became the 49th state to adopt the UTSA). The Uniform Trade Secrets Act, published by the Uniform Law Commission in 1979 and amended in 1985, is a uniform law proposed for adoption by individual states.

[7] See, e.g., Paz Sys., Inc. v. Dakota Grp. Corp., 514 F. Supp. 2d 402, 407 (E.D.N.Y. 2007); E.J. Brooks Co. v. Cambridge Sec. Seals, 105 N.E.3d 301, 316 (N.Y. 2018).

remedies for misappropriation of trade secrets[8]" but does not affect contract and civil remedies not based on trade secrets, or criminal remedies.

A. Information - Trade Secret Requirements

First, the information must not be generally known or readily ascertainable to be protected.[9] If the information is "available in trade journals, reference books, or published materials," the information is generally known.[10] Where only a small group of people have the ability to design the trade secret and it cannot readily be reverse engineered, the trade secret is not readily ascertainable.[11] The "requirement for a trade secret that information sought to be protected must not be generally known or readily ascertainable is satisfied if the information is not quickly available through proper means."[12] The fact that some of the information that constitutes the trade secret is in the public realm is not dispositive of whether information constitutes a trade secret.[13] For instance, a compilation of publicly available information may constitute a trade secret if significant effort was necessary to compile the information, the information is not readily ascertainable, and it affords a competitive advantage.[14]

Second, the information must gain independent economic value from not being generally known.[15] "Generally, if substantial time and money would be required of a competitor to develop the same information,

---

[8] MINN. STAT. §325C.07.

[9] *Id.*; *Electro-Craft Corp.*, 332 N.W.2d at 897 ("Without a proven trade secret there can be no action for misappropriation, even if defendants' actions were wrongful.").

[10] Surgidev Corp. v. Eye Tech., Inc., 648 F. Supp. 661, 688 (D. Minn. 1986).

[11] Scott Equip. Co. v. Stedman Mach. Co., Civ. No. 06-906, 2003 WL 21804868, *2 (D. Minn. July 31, 2003).

[12] *Surgidev*, 648 F. Supp. at 688 (citing *Electro-Craft*, 332 N.W.2d 890).

[13] AvidAir Helicopter Supply, Inc. v. Rolls-Royce Corp., 663 F.3d 966, 974 (8th Cir. 2011); CHS Inc. v. Petronet, LLC, Civ. No. 10-94, 2011 WL 1885465, *8 (D. Minn. May 18, 2011).

[14] *AvidAir*, 663 F.3d at 972; *but see* Strategic Directions Group v. Bristol-Myers Squibb Co., 293 F.3d 1062, 1065 (8th Cir. 2002) (compilation of known information is insufficient to establish trade secret); *Berkley Risk Adm'rs Co.*, 2016 U.S. Dist. LEXIS 113421 at *5-6.

[15] 18 U.S.C. § 1839(3)(B); *Electro-Craft*, 332 N.W.2d at 900.

that information has economic value."[16] If introducing the information into the marketplace allows another business to produce a competing product, and if the competition results in lower profit margins, the information derives independent economic value from its secrecy.[17]

Third, a plaintiff must show that it made reasonable efforts to maintain the secrecy of the trade secret.[18] Trade secret law "does not require the maintenance of absolute secrecy; only partial secrecy or qualified secrecy has been required under the common law."[19] For instance, a party "acted reasonably to maintain secrecy by requiring a confidentiality agreement from [the defendant] and marking its documents and files as confidential."[20] The law is also clear that the mere existence of a confidentiality agreement is insufficient to establish that the covered information constitutes a trade secret.[21]

> *PRACTICE POINTER:* Evaluating whether information
> constitutes a trade secret is difficult and experienced
> counsel is a necessity. Often, the more technical the
> information a company is seeking to protect, the more
> likely a jury, judge, or arbitrator is to consider the
> information is a trade secret. Thus, the process for coating
> a medical device will more likely be treated as a trade

---

[16] *Surgidev*, 648 F. Supp. at 692; *see also AvidAir,* 663 F.3d at 973 (holding that the key question is not whether duplication is possible, but "whether the duplication of the information would require a substantial investment of time, effort, and energy.").

[17] Wyeth v. Natural Biologics, Inc., Civ. No. 98-2469, 2003 WL 22282371, *19 (D. Minn. Oct. 2, 2003); I-Sys., Inc. v. Softwares, Inc., Civ. No. 02-1951, 2004 WL 742082, *14 (D. Minn. Mar. 29, 2004).

[18] 18 U.S.C. § 1839(3)(A); *Electro-Craft*, 332 N.W.2d at 901.

[19] *Surgidev*, 648 F. Supp. at 692-93.

[20] K-Sun Corp. v. Heller Invs., Inc., Nos. C4-97-2052, C6-97-2053, 1998 WL 422182, *3 (Minn. Ct. App. July 28, 1998); Macy's Retail Holdings, Inc. v. Cty. of Hennepin, 27-CV-13-6683, 2018 Minn. Tax LEXIS 16, *11-12 (Minn. Tax. Ct. Mar. 12, 2018) (maintaining confidentiality agreements with lenders, accountants, auditors, and prospective buyers" constitutes reasonable efforts to maintain secrecy).

[21] *Electro-Craft*, 332 N.W.2d at 901-02; Bison Advisors LLC v. Kessler, Civ. No. 14-3121, 2016 U.S. Dist. LEXIS 107244, 2016 WL 4361517, *11 (D. Minn. Aug. 12, 2016) (granting summary judgment to dismiss trade secrets claim where defendants signed confidentiality agreement because they did not otherwise treat information as confidential); Coyne's & Co. v. Enesco, LLC, No. 07-4095, 2010 U.S. Dist. LEXIS 83630, 2010 WL 3269977, *16 (D. Minn. Aug. 16, 2010); RING Comput. Sys., Inc. v. ParaData Comput. Networks, Inc., No. C4-90-889, 1990 Minn. App. LEXIS 922, 1990 WL 132615, *2 (Minn. Ct. App. Sept. 10, 1990) (holding that "signing of a confidentiality agreement, without more, is not enough").

secret than the business plan for a franchise concept. Moreover, the more specific the information that is sought to be protected, as opposed to more general categories of information, the more likely it will be protected. Finally, a trade secret must be describable in a fashion that a judge or jury can understand. When evaluating a client's trade-secret claim, we often utilize the one-sentence test. Parties who can explain their trade secret in one sentence generally have a stronger claim than those who cannot.

B. Information Excluded

Numerous categories of information have been found not to constitute trade secrets as a matter of law. Generally, less technical information is less likely to be considered a trade secret. Furthermore, the plaintiff must identify its trade secrets with specificity.[22] The following categories of information have been held not to be trade secrets: "Reasonable measures" to protect secrecy of the information are required,

---

[22] Therapeutics LLC v. Beatty, 354 F. Supp. 3d 957, 967 (D. Minn. 2018); Cambria Co. LLC v. Schumann, No. 19-CV-3145, 2020 U.S. Dist. LEXIS 11373, *10 (D. Minn. Jan. 23, 2020) (denying preliminary injunction where trade secrets were not clearly defined and the plaintiff did not allege that the defendant physically took information from its former employer); *CH Bus Sales*, 2019 U.S. Dist. LEXIS 46093, *22-23 (D. Minn. Mar. 20, 2019) (stating that, post-*Twombly* and *Iqbal*, a plaintiff must describe trade secrets with more than conclusory statements and with sufficient information to infer more than a possibility of misconduct.); *see also* Cambria Co. LLC v. Schumann, No. 19-CV-3145 (NEB/TNL) 2020 U.S. Dist. LEXIS 11373, *10 (D. Minn. Jan. 23, 2020) (denying preliminary injunction where trade secrets are not clearly defined and the plaintiff does not allege that the defendant took any physical information from his employer); Wilson v. Corning, Inc., 171 F. Supp. 3d 869, 882-83 (D. Minn. 2016); WEG Elec. Corp. v. Pethers, Civ. No. 16-47, 2016 U.S. Dist. LEXIS 49208, 6 (D. Minn. 2016) (lack of specificity weakens claim); Loftness Specialized Farm Equip. Inc. v. Twiestmeyer, Civ. No. 11-1506 (DWF/TNL), 2012 WL 1247232, *7 (D. Minn. Apr. 13, 2012); Hot Stuff Foods, LLC v. Dornbach, 726 F. Supp. 2d 1038, 1044 (D. Minn. 2010); Luigino's Inc. v. Peterson, 317 F.3d 909, 912 (8th Cir. 2003); *but see* TE Connectivity Networks, Inc. v. All Sys. Broadband, Inc., Civ. No. 13-1356 ADM/FLN, 2013 WL 6827348, *3 (D. Minn. Dec. 26, 2013) (holding that while a plaintiff may not rely on conclusory statements to establish its trade secrets, a plaintiff is not required to reveal exact parameters of a trade secret); Superior Edge, Inc. v. Monsanto Co., 964 F. Supp. 2d 1017, 1042 (D. Minn. 2013); Hypred S.A. & A & L Labs., Inc. v. Pochard, Civ. No. 04-2773, 2004 U.S. Dist. LEXIS 11293, *12 (D. Minn. Jun. 18, 2004) (dissolving temporary restraining order where plaintiff failed to specify trade secrets beyond stating that they were "dealer information," "product formulation and manufacturing secrets").

but the statutes generally do not specifically define what efforts are "reasonable." The mere "intention to keep material confidential is not enough to confer trade secret protection," a party must take concrete and tangible measures to ensure that the information remain secret.[23]

1. Customer Lists and Related Information

Although it comes as a surprise to many business people, a company's customer list usually is not a trade secret.[24] The primary reason for denying trade secret status to customer lists is that the identity of customers is readily ascertainable and often lose their value over a short period of time.[25] Courts are also reticent to deem information provided by customers regarding the customer's needs and orders.[26] An underlying rationale is that courts do not want to create backdoor non-competes through the trade secret statute.[27] Additionally, there is a strong public interest in preserving competition.[28]

In limited circumstances, a customer list might be protected. A customer list that contains more than bare customer names and includes a

---

[23] Nw. Airlines v. Am. Airlines, 853 F. Supp. 1110, 1115 (D. Minn. 1994); Denson Int'l Ltd. v. Liberty Diversified Int'l, Inc., Civ. No. 12-3109, 2015 U.S. Dist. LEXIS 116092, *15 (D. Minn. Sept. 1, 2015) (denying injunction where plaintiff argued that "the importance of confidentiality was widely assumed" in the business community without taking specific steps to designate the information as confidential).

[24] Katch, LLC v. Sweetser, 143 F. Supp. 3d 854, 868-69 (D. Minn. 2016) (identity of key customers and pricing that can be determined by asking customers is not a trade secret); see also Newleaf Designs, LLC v. Bestbins Corp., 168 F. Supp. 2d 1039, 1044 (D. Minn. 2001) (citing Lasermaster Corp. v. Sentinel Imaging, 931 F. Supp. 628, 637-38 (D. Minn. 1996)); Harley Auto. Group, Inc. v. AP Supply, Inc., Civ. No. 12-1110, 2013 WL 6801221, *7 (D. Minn. Dec. 23, 2013); Equus Computer Sys. v. N. Computer Sys., Inc., Civ. No. 01-657, 2002 WL 1634334, *4 (D. Minn. July 22, 2002); Universal Hosp. Servs., Inc. v. Henderson, Civ. No. 02-951, 2002 WL 1023147, *4 (D. Minn. May 20, 2002); Oberfoell v. Kyte, No. A17-0575, 2018 Minn. App. Unpub. LEXIS 74, *21-22 (Minn. Ct. App. Jan. 22, 2018); Wells Fargo Ins. Servs. USA v. King, No. 15-CV-4378, 2016 U.S. Dist. LEXIS 8279, *22-23 (D. Minn. Jan. 25, 2016).

[25] Wells Fargo Ins. Servs. USA, 2016 U.S. Dist. LEXIS 8279 at *23; Equus, 2002 WL 1634334, *3-4; Associated Med. Ins. Agents, L.L.C. v. G.E. Med. Protective Co., No. A03-1373, 2004 WL 615002, *4 (Minn. Ct. App. Mar. 30, 2004).

[26] Tension Envelope Corp. v. JBM Envelope Co., 876 F.3d 1112, 1122 (8th Cir. 2017) (applying Missouri trade circuit law).

[27] Equus, 2002 WL 1634334, *5 (citing Int'l. Bus. Mach. Corp. v. Seagate Tech., Inc., 941 F. Supp. 98, 101 (D. Minn. 1992)); WEG Elec. Corp., 2016 U.S. Dist. LEXIS 49208 at *7.

[28] Lasermaster, 931 F. Supp. at 637.

customer's buying, pricing and payment history may be considered a trade secret.[29] Moreover, if the customer list segregates customers into high-volume or high-margin categories, the list might be protected as a trade secret.[30] Even if the customer list constitutes a trade secret, a party can waive trade secret status by providing a reference list that contains current customers to potential customers.[31] An effective way for a business to protect customer information, however, is to enter into a valid non-competition or non-disclosure agreement.

2. General Knowledge in the Industry

Information that is not known to the general public, but widely known within an industry, is not a trade secret.[32] For instance, an executive's knowledge of contact people within a given industry is not a trade secret.[33]

3. Personal Expertise and General Business Information

General marketing intelligence, pricing structures, business expertise, or business plans do not constitute trade secrets.[34] Generally, courts will not protect broad categories of business information.

---

[29] *Equus*, 2002 WL 1634334, *4; Dexon Computer, Inc. v. Modern Enter. Solutions, No. A16-0010, 2016 Minn. App. Unpub. LEXIS 741, *11-12 (Minn. Ct. App. Aug. 1, 2016) (affirming temporary restraining order where the information contained information on more than 10,000 potential customers along with networking, research and sales information about specific customers).

[30] *Equus*, 2002 WL 1634334, *4.

[31] *Id.*; *Associated Med.*, 2004 WL 615002, *4.

[32] Fox Sports Net N., LLC v. Minn. Twins P'ship, 319 F.3d 329, 336 (8th Cir. 2003).

[33] *Id.*

[34] *Electro-Craft*, 332 N.W.2d at 900 ("The law of trade secrets will not protect talent or expertise, only secret information."); *Newleaf Designs*, 168 F. Supp. 2d at 1044; *Seagate Tech.*, 941 F. Supp. at 100; Luigino's, Inc. v. Peterson, 317 F.3d 909, 912 (8th Cir. 2003); Integrated Process Sols., Inc. v. Lanix LLC, No. 19-CV-567, 2019 U.S. Dist. LEXIS 43808, *12 (D. Minn. Mar. 18, 2019) (holding that statement that trade secrets include financial records; bidding information; and standards, blocks, and software is insufficiently precise to identify trade secret); Goodbye Vanilla, LLC v. Aimia Proprietary Loyalty United States, Inc., 304 F. Supp. 3d 815 (D. Minn. 2018) (granting summary judgment where plaintiff e-mail "containing quotations and recommendations" rises to the level of trade secrets); *WEG Elec. Corp.*, 2016 U.S. Dist. LEXIS 49208 at *5 ("[C]ustomer, inventory, and pricing lists, as well as documents containing other institutional knowledge and operation strategies - generally do not constitute trade

4. Variations on a Widely Used Process

Variations on a widely used process do not constitute trade secrets.[35] Thus, one court refused to grant trade secret protection to a computer system that merely combined well-known subsystems.[36]

5. Obsolete Information

It should come as no surprise that obsolete information is not considered a trade secret because it has no economic value.[37] The trick, however, is determining when information becomes considered obsolete. In one case, an executive's knowledge of telecast agreements that had been superseded by other agreements was not considered a trade secret, because his knowledge was obsolete.[38] In another case, information regarding business strategies that was six months old was considered obsolete and therefore no longer a trade secret.[39]

---

secrets"); *Denson Int'l Ltd.*, 2015 U.S. Dist. LEXIS 116092 (granting summary judgement where alleged trade secrets included information "about our employment, our staff levels, our staff levels, our salaries, our overhead, our expenses, . . . [and] our profit margins" because the information was general and trade secrets were not specifically identified); Excel Mfg. v. Wondrow, No. A15-1325, 2016 Minn. App. Unpub. LEXIS 385, *11-12 (Minn. Ct. App. Apr. 18, 2016) (holding that "laundry list" of items such as "design prints, product specifications, pricing information, marketing plans and potential customers" are "general categories of information that do not qualify as trade secrets."). Keep in mind that business information such as "detailed customer pricing data" and "sales analysis and strategies" might constitute trade secret if a company takes "significant time, effort, and expense" to maintain its confidentiality, it is not knowable through proper means, and value is derived from its privacy. *See, e.g.,* Deluxe Fin. Servs., LLC v. Shaw, Civ. No. 16-3065, 2017 U.S. Dist. LEXIS 122795, 7-8 (D. Minn. Aug. 3, 2017) (denying motion to dismiss where trade secrets were sufficiently alleged in complaint). Furthermore, courts will often give plaintiffs more leeway at the motion to dismiss stage at the outset of the litigation. Management Registry v. A.W. Cos., No. 0:17-cv-05009, 2019 WL 7838280, 2019 U.S. Dist. LEXIS 226063, *28-29 (D. Minn. Sept. 12, 2019); TE Connectivity Networks, Inc., 2013 U.S. Dist. LEXIS 180392 at *8-10 (denying motion to dismiss where "somewhat vague" allegations were sufficient to state a trade secrets claim "when the allegations are viewed as a whole").

[35] *Electro-Craft*, 332 N.W.2d at 899.

[36] *Id.* (citing Jostens, Inc. v. Nat'l Computer Sys., 318 N.W.2d 691, 700-01 (Minn. 1982)).

[37] *Fox Sports Net*, 319 F.3d at 336; *WEG Elec. Corp.*, 2016 U.S. Dist. LEXIS 49208 at *7; *Katch*, LLC, 143 F. Supp. 3d 854.

[38] *Id.*

[39] Lexis-Nexis v. Beer, 41 F. Supp. 2d 950, 959 (D. Minn. 1999).

6. Easily Reverse-Engineered Information

If an item is available in the marketplace and easily reverse-engineered, then the item does not constitute a trade secret.[40]

7. Publicly Filed Information

Once information is disclosed in a patent application, it loses its trade secret status.[41] Likewise, other information that is submitted to a public entity, such as in a public government bid, may lose trade secret protection. Thus, it is important to determine whether information submitted to a public entity falls within an exception to state or federal open-records laws and, if so, to follow the procedures to confidentially submit the information.

> *PRACTICE POINTER:* One of the dilemmas a plaintiff seeks in any litigation and particularly a trade secret litigation is that the litigation itself might result in disclosure of the trade secret, particularly as federal courts are requiring parties to plead and identify the elements with a greater degree of specificity.[42] It is therefore critical for parties to establish procedures, such as protective orders, confidentiality designations, and filing documents under seal to prevent such disclosures. The federal statute instructs courts to "enter such orders and take such other action as may be necessary and appropriate to preserve the confidentiality of the trade secrets" consistent with the state and federal rules of procedure and evidence, and other related laws.[43]

---

[40] *Electro-Craft*, 332 N.W.2d at 899.

[41] Coenco, Inc. v. Coenco Sales, Inc., 940 F.2d 1176, 1179 n.3 (8th Cir. 1991); Wilson v. Corning, Inc., 171 F. Supp. 3d 869, 882 (D. Minn. 2016) (a claim for a trade secret cannot be made for misappropriation after the trade secret is published in a patent application); Accent Packaging, Inc. v. Leggett & Platt, Inc., 707 F.3d 1318, 1329 (Fed. Cir. 2013) ("As a matter of law, any specifications and tolerances disclosed in or ascertainable from the asserted patents became publicly available . . . when the . . . patent application was published and, as such, could not constitute a trade secret [a few months later] when [the defendant] is alleged to have engaged in misappropriation.")

[42] *See infra* note 22.

[43] 18 U.S.C. § 1835.

III. MISAPPROPRIATION DEFINED

The trade secret statutes defining misappropriation three ways: acquisition through improper means, disclosure, or use.[44] A party asserting a claim for misappropriation has the burden to prove both that the information at issue is a trade secret and that the defendant misappropriated it.[45]

A. Improper Acquisition

The trade secret statutes prohibit the acquisition of a trade secret by improper means such as "theft, bribery, misrepresentation, breach or inducement of a breach of a duty to maintain secrecy, or espionage through electronic or other means."[46] Improper means also likely includes lawful conduct which is improper under the circumstances; for example, an airplane overflight used as aerial reconnaissance to determine the competitor's plant layout during construction of the plant.[47] A party that later acquires a trade secret is also liable if it knows or has reason to know that the trade secret was initially acquired by improper means.[48]

Importantly, it is not improper to learn a trade secret through reverse engineering, independent development, or other lawful means.[49] Reverse engineering is starting with the known product and working backward to determine the method by which it was developed.[50] Independent derivation occurs with another party develops the product or process from its own independent efforts. Finally, a party may acquire a trade secret through legitimate means such as through permission and voluntary sharing.

---

[44] 18 U.S.C. § 1839(5); *Electro-Craft*, 332 N.W.2d at 897; *Goodbye Vanilla, LLC*, 304 F. Supp. 3d at 820. The statute of limitations for misappropriation of trade secrets under federal and Minnesota law is three years. 18 U.S.C. § 1836(d); MINN. STAT. § 325C.06.

[45] CPI Card Grp., Inc. v. Dwyer, 294 F. Supp. 3d 791, 807 (D. Minn. 2018); Widmark v. Northrup King Co., 530 N.W.2d 588, 592 (Minn. Ct. App. 1995).

[46] 18 U.S.C. § 1839(6)(A).

[47] Unif. Trade Secrets Act § 1, com.

[48] 18 U.S.C. § 1839(5)(A).

[49] 18 U.S.C. § 1839(6).

[50] Kewanee v. Bicron, 416 U.S. 470, 476 (1974); David S. Almeling, *et al. A Statistical Analysis of Trade Secret Litigation in Federal Courts*, 45 GONZ. L. REV. 291, 324 (2009/10).

B. Disclosure

Misappropriation also happens when a non-owner discloses another's trade secrets without authorization.[51] In limited circumstances, a trade secret owner can successfully assert that a departing employee will inevitably disclose trade secrets if they move to a similar position in another company.[52] In jurisdictions where the inevitable disclosure theory is available, the plaintiff must meet a high bar to show that there is a high degree of probability that the other party will disclose the trade secret information.[53]

C. Use

While the statutes focus on improper acquisition or disclosure of trade secrets, courts will also examine whether a party actually uses or intends to use the trade secret information. For instance, evidence that a departing employee intended to take his former employer's protected information may be insufficient to show misappropriation if there is no additional evidence that the employee actually took or used the information.[54]

IV. POTENTIAL EXPOSURE

Trade secret cases are distinguished from normal commercial disputes by the availability of a wider range of damages (including punitive damages), the possibility that the defendant will be responsible for the plaintiff's attorney fees, and the availability of injunctive relief.

---

[51] 18 U.S.C. 1832(a)(2); MINN. STAT. §325C.01, subd. 3(ii).

[52] To establish inevitable misappropriation, the party seeking the injunction has the heavy burden of establishing a "high degree of probability" that the party possessing the trade secret will inevitably disclose it. Honeywell Int'l Inc. v. Stacey, No. 13-CV-3056, 2013 WL 9851104, *6 (D. Minn. Dec. 11, 2013); *see also* Prime Thereapeutics LLC v. Beatty, 354 F.Supp.3d 957, 968-72 (D. Minn. 2018) (denying injunctive relief where plaintiff failed to sufficient evidence to meet the very high bar to show inevitable disclosure); United Prods. Corp. of Am. v. Cederstrom, No. A05-1688, 2006 Minn. App. Unpub. LEXIS 594, *14 (D. Minn. Jun. 6, 2006) (same); *Katch, LLC*, 143 F. Supp. 3d at 872-73 (same); Mid-Am. Bus. Sys. v. Sanderson, Civ. No. 17-3876, 2017 U.S. Dist. LEXIS 166463, *20-21 (D. Minn. Oct. 6, 2017) (same).

[53] *See id. Prime Therapeutics LLC*, 354 F.Supp.3d at 968-72.

[54] *Integrated Process Sols.*, 2019 U.S. Dist. LEXIS 43808 at *13 (denying injunction).

A. Money Damages

A plaintiff can recover both its lost profits and for any unjust enrichment the defendant received from the theft.[55] In lieu of damages measured by other means, a court may impose a reasonable royalty for the defendant's use of the trade secret.[56]

A trade secret defendant faces greater liability than the defendant in a normal commercial dispute. In a normal dispute, a defendant's maximum liability would be for the plaintiff's losses. A trade secret defendant is not only liable for the plaintiff's losses stemming from the misappropriation, but also for any unjust enrichment the defendant received from the misappropriation.[57] The only limitation is that the unjust enrichment damages cannot have been taken into account in determining the plaintiff's losses.[37]

For example, a hypothetical plaintiff in the business of manufacturing software has its development work stolen. As a result of the theft, the defendant is able to put competing software on the market. Consequently, the plaintiff lost $10 million in sales, the defendant gained $10 million in sales, and the defendant saved $2 million in software development costs. In this scenario, the plaintiff could recover $12 million. It would be impermissible for the plaintiff to recover both its lost sales and the defendant's increased sales, because the defendant's increased sales have already been taken into account in calculating plaintiff's lost sales.

B. Injunction

A defendant does not just face the possibility of a large damages award. The plaintiff is also entitled to enjoin the defendant from using the trade secret where the plaintiff can prove likelihood of success on the merits and irreparable harm.[58] In our hypothetical scenario, the plaintiff would be entitled to an injunction preventing the defendant from selling the software.

---

[55] 18 U.S.C. § 1836(b)(3)(B)(i)(II); Children's Broad. Corp. v. The Walt Disney Co., 357 F.3d 860, 865 (8th Cir. 2004) (citing MINN. STAT. § 325C.03(a)).

[56] 18 U.S.C. § 1836(b)(3)(B)(ii); MINN. STAT. § 325C.03(a).

[57] MINN. STAT. § 325C.03.

[58] 18 U.S.C. § 1836(b)(3)(A); MINN. STAT. § 325C.02. Note, that while irreparable harm was often associated with trade secret misappropriation, recent courts have found that against a presumption of irreparable harm. See MPAY Inc. v. Erie Custom Computer Applications, 970 F.3d 1010, 1019-21 (8th Cir. 2020).

An injunction may not be issued where, even if there is evidence that a former employee possessed or possesses trade secrets, there is no evidence that the employee will disclose or use that information, particularly where employees commit to not using or disclosing the information.[59]

In situations where a former employee takes significant proprietary information, computers and data, Minnesota courts may issue injunctive relief ordering the former employee to return all information, prohibiting further disclosure or communication regarding the trade secrets, using or copying trade secrets, making all computers and electronic devices available for computer forensic duplication and examination, and submitting an affidavit regarding all destroyed information.[60]

The length of the injunction is determined by the period of time that would be required for independent development of the trade secret.[61] The time period of the injunction can be extended to eliminate any commercial advantage that a defendant derived from the misappropriation.[62]

The risk that a company faces is aptly illustrated by the Eighth Circuit's decision in the *Wyeth* case. The defendant was a pharmaceutical company that misappropriated another company's process for producing estrogen.[63] The Eighth Circuit upheld the district court's decision to permanently enjoin the defendant from producing estrogen.[64] The Eighth Circuit adopted the district court's reasoning that a permanent injunction was appropriate for two reasons: (1) no competitor had ever replicated the process during the decades the process had existed; and (2) the defendant had engaged in conduct, namely destroying evidence and giving false testimony, that demonstrated that the defendant could not be trusted to

---

[59] Midwest Sign & Screen Printing Supply Co. v. Robert Dalpe & Laird Plastics, Inc., 386 F. Supp. 3d 1037, 1053-54 (D. Minn. 2019) (denying injunction where employee forwarded confidential information to their home email because there was no evidence that the employee would subsequently use or disclose the information); *CPI Card Grp.*, 294 F. Supp. 3d at 804; *Mid-Am. Bus. Sys.*, 2017 U.S. Dist. LEXIS 166463 (denying trade secrets injunction where the plaintiff merely speculates that the defendant will use information).

[60] Advanced Control Tech., Inc. v. Iversen, Civ. No. 19-1608, 2019 WL 3037089, 2019 U.S. Dist. LEXIS 117355, *2-5 (D. Minn. Jul. 3, 2019).

[61] *Wyeth*, 2003 WL 22282371, *27 (citing *Surgidev*, 648 F. Supp. at 696).

[62] 18 U.S.C. § 1836(b)(3)(B)(i)(II); MINN. STAT. § 325C.02(a).

[63] *Wyeth*, 395 F.3d at 899.

[64] *Id.* at 903.

undertake future research into developing an alternative process without relying on the misappropriated trade secrets.[65] The injunction put the defendant out of business.

> *PRACTICE POINTER*: It may not always be in a company's best interest to immediately pursue an injunction if it only suspects theft. Rushing to seek injunctive relief without strong evidence of both a trade secret and misappropriation or inevitable misappropriation of the trade secret risks an early adverse determination from a court that the company is unlikely to succeed on the merits. Once a court makes that determination, it will be difficult to reverse its initial impression and, at best, likely dooms a company to protracted litigation.

C. Willful and Malicious Risks Double Damages

In addition to lost profits, unjust enrichment, and reasonable royalties, a defendant whose misappropriation was willful and malicious will be liable for the plaintiff's attorneys' fees as well as exemplary damages up to twice the value of actual damages.[66] A trio of trade secret cases have identified the following conduct as willful and malicious:[67]

- Defendant's management is aware that it might be utilizing trade secrets, but proceeds with the project without investigating;
- Without informing the plaintiff of the defendant's decision to reject a business opportunity, defendant's management continues to solicit trade secrets under the pretext of negotiations and then transfers that information in violation of an express confidentiality agreement; and
- The defendant took information that it knew was confidential and used it to develop competing software.

---

[65] *Id.*
[66] 18 U.S.C. § 1836(b)(3)(C-D); MINN. STAT. §§ 325C.03(b) & 325C.04.
[67] *Scott Equip. Co.*, 2003 WL 21804868, *3 (management knowledge); *K-Sun Corp.*, 1998 WL 422182, *4 (continued solicitation and violation of express agreement); Zawels v. Edutronics, Inc., 520 N.W.2d 520, 524 (Minn. Ct. App. 1994) (knowing use to develop software).

PRACTICE POINTER: Nothing turns a problem into a catastrophe quicker than hiding, destroying, or altering evidence. Not only does this conduct constitute the independent tort of spoliation and risk serious sanctions, it also makes juries, judges, and arbitrators mad, which leads to findings of willful and malicious misappropriation and big damages.[68]

D. Bad Faith Adds Attorney's Fees

Attorney's fees may also be awarded if a claim of misappropriation is made in bad faith, or a motion to terminate an injunction is made or resisted in bad faith.[69] A party may be liable under this theory if it can be shown that there is a complete lack of evidence supporting the claim and the party had subjective misconduct in bringing or maintaining the claim.[70] However, courts have held that a trade secret claim is not brought in bad-faith if it survives summary judgment[71] or does not merit sanctions.[51]

PRACTICE POINTER: If there may be the potential for an award of fees for malicious/willful misappropriation or bad faith in bringing the claim, legal counsel should take care to differentiate the fees incurred to litigate the trade secret claim, verses other claims in the lawsuit.

---

[68] *In re* Adegoke, 632 B.R. 154 (N.D. Ill. 2021) (citing cases where courts infer misappropriation from spoliation of evidence).
[69] 18 U.S.C. 1836(b)(3)(D); MINN. STAT. § 325C.04.
[70] Norwood Operating Co. v. Beacon Promotions, Inc., Civ. No. 04-1390, 2006 WL 3103154, *1-2 (D. Minn. Oct. 31, 2006).
[71] *Id.* *3; Wixon Jewelers, Inc. v. Aurora Jewelry Designs, No. C0-01-2149, 2002 WL 1327014, *2 (Minn. Ct. App. June 18, 2002); Weaver v. Iverson, No. A12-0354, 2012 WL 3641358, *2 (Minn. Ct. App. Aug. 27, 2012).

V. COMMON CONTEXTS IN WHICH TRADE SECRET CLAIMS ARISE

A party's potential trade secret liability is determined in part by the relief the plaintiff is seeking. In order for a trade secret plaintiff to prevail on an injunction, the plaintiff must show the threat of misappropriation or actual misappropriation.[72] The threat of misappropriation is established if the party seeking the injunction can show there is "a high degree of probability of inevitable disclosure."[73] A party can establish actual misappropriation either by direct or circumstantial evidence.[74]

Although almost any business relationship can give rise to trade secret liability, several scenarios pose an especially high risk. The following examples are based on the scenarios most frequently presented by Minnesota case law.

A. Employment Relationships

Any new hire has the potential for bringing misappropriated trade secrets with them. The new employer might be held liable for misappropriation or theories of vicarious liability.[75] Moreover, even if a company has not used the information, it might still be subject to an injunction under the inevitable disclosure doctrine.[76] There are also a host of other companion claims that departing employees and their new employers should have on their radar screen including, for instance, tortious interference with business relationships, breach of fiduciary duty, and breach of duties of confidentiality and loyalty.[77]

---

[72] 18 U.S.C. 1836(b)(3)(A); MINN. STAT. § 325C.02.
[73] *Lexis-Nexis*, 41 F. Supp. 2d at 958 (citations omitted).
[74] *Wyeth*, 2003 WL 22282371, *21 (citing Pioneer Hi-Bred Int'l v. Holden Found. Seeds, Inc., 35 F.3d 1226, 1239 (8th Cir. 1994)).
[75] *Deluxe Fin. Servs.*, 2017 U.S. Dist. LEXIS 122795 at *10-11.
[76] *Lexis-Nexis*, 41 F. Supp. 2d at 959.
[77] *See, e.g., Bison Advisors*, 2016 U.S. Dist. LEXIS 88307; *Mid-Am. Bus. Sys.*, 2017 U.S. Dist. LEXIS 166463, 2017); Nilfisk, Inc. v. Liss, No. 17-cv-1902, 2017 WL 7370059, 2017 U.S. Dist. LEXIS 220970 (D. Minn. Jun. 15, 2017).

B. Business Acquisitions and Equity Funding

Trade secret claims commonly arise in the context of business acquisitions. The *K-Sun* case illustrates the dangers that a company can face in the context of an acquisition. Unsuccessful merger negotiations in *K-Sun* led to the defendant company being liable for attorneys' fees and punitive damages.[78] Other Minnesota cases illustrate that the bad feelings that often arise from a failed acquisition can give rise to trade secret claims.[79]

A business that is trying to raise capital also faces trade secret challenges. Despite the disclosure requirements imposed by securities law, a company must take steps to guard its trade secrets during the fundraising process. At a minimum, the capital-raising company should have non-disclosures in place with potential investors. Otherwise, the company faces the possibility that the potential investors will become competitors. Needless to say, this scenario presents a high litigation risk.

C. Manufacturing and Marketing Contracts

Contracts to manufacture complex goods that involve the exchange of technical information between the seller and buyer can give rise to trade secret claims. Likewise, trade secret liability can arise when one company offers another company the opportunity to market its product. If the other company refuses and then starts to market a similar product, that company faces a substantial litigation risk.

V. COMPANY ACTIONS TO AVOID TRADE SECRET CLAIMS

A. Employee Screening

Any new hire should be screened to see if that hire has any knowledge regarding her former employer's trade secrets. The level of screening should increase if the employee is going to be involved in a company's core business operations or research and development. The screening should focus on the employee's actual technical knowledge as

---

[78] *K-Sun*, 1998 WL 422182, *1-4.
[79] *See, e.g.*, Protégé Biomedical, LLC v. Z-Medica, LLC, 394 F. Supp. 3d 924, 939-40 (D. Minn. 2019); *Luigino's*, 2002 WL 122389.

opposed to general knowledge or skills that the employee gained at his previous job.[80]

New employees should be instructed not to disclose or use a former employer's trade secret information in connection with their employment with the company. Additionally, new employees should be required to attest something akin to the following in an offer letter or employment agreement:

> If Employee possesses any information that s/he knows or should know is considered by any third party, such as a former employer of Employee's, to be confidential, trade secret, or otherwise proprietary, Employee shall not disclose such information to Company or use such information to benefit Company in any way.

Similarly, new employees should attest to the following in an offer letter or employment agreement:

> Employee represents and warrants to Company that s/he is not under, or bound to be under in the future, any obligation to any person, entity, firm, or corporation that is or would be inconsistent or in conflict with, or would prevent, limit, or impair in any way Employee's employment by the Company.

Supervisors should monitor their supervisees to ensure that they are not using a former employer's trade secrets in connection with their

---

[80] *Lasermaster,* 931 F. Supp. at 636-37 ("The concept of a trade secret does not include a man's aptitude, his skill, his dexterity, his manual and mental ability, and such other subjective knowledge as he obtains while in the course of his employment … the right to use and expand these powers remains his property. …") (citation, internal quotation marks and alterations omitted); *Prime Therapeutics LLC,* 354 F.Supp.3d at 972 (denying preliminary injunction where departing employee was forthright about transition to new employer and there was no evidence that employee took documents containing trade secret information with her); Reliastar Life Ins. Co. v. KMG Am. Corp., No. A05-2079, 2006 Minn. App. Unpub. LEXIS 1018, 2006 WL 2529760, *5 (Minn. Ct. App. Sept. 5, 2006) ("[m]erely possessing trade secrets and holding a comparable position with a competitor does not justify an injunction" (citation and quotations omitted)).

work for their employer.[81] If such conduct is occurring, the company should take prompt action to put a stop to such conduct (including disciplinary action against the offending employee) and cease any and all use of the trade secret information.

B. Permission

Permission is the simplest way to avoid a trade secret claim. Generally, no misappropriation occurs where the defendant has received the plaintiff's express or implied consent to disclose the secret.[82] Moreover, requesting permission defeats the notion that the use was willful and malicious, unless the defendant is denied permission and proceeds anyway.

C. Clear Definitions

When a company enters into funding, acquisition, or marketing discussions, it should have an agreement in place that identifies precisely what information is being exchanged and who has access to the information. Conversely, the agreement should define what information is not covered. Finally, the agreement should provide for return of the information and reasonable restrictions on the information's use.

D. Honesty is the Best Policy

Often trade secret claims arise out of the frustration of a failed business relationship. That frustration is compounded if one party feels that it was led along so it could be mined for information. It is important to manage expectations during negotiations and clearly inform the other business when negotiations have reached an impasse. When a party accused of misappropriation, that party may be able to weaken an alleged

---

[81] *See, e.g., Mid-Am. Bus. Sys.*, 2017 U.S. Dist. LEXIS 166463 (denying temporary restraining order where there is not clear evidence that the departing employee is likely to use information in new position).

[82] 18 U.S.C. § 1839, subd. 5; MINN. STAT. § 325C.01, subd. 3.

misappropriation claim by committing to not use or disclose particular information.[83]

VI. COMPANY ACTIONS PROTECT ITS TRADE SECRETS

A trade secret owner must take *reasonable measures* to protect secrecy.[84] While the statute does not define reasonableness, courts will evaluate the particular trade secret and circumstances of the business.[85] The touchstone test for determining whether a company's security measures are adequate revolves around notice: "[i]f, under all the circumstances, the employee knows or has reason to know that the owner intends or expects the information to be secret, confidentiality measures are sufficient."[86]

Circumstances which may be reasonable at one time and under one set of circumstances may cease to be reasonable at another time or under other circumstances. Accordingly, it is appropriate for an enterprise to modify, typically by enhancing, its security procedures in order to respond to new challenges. The modifications are not evidence that prior procedures were inadequate, but rather are a legitimate exercise in imposing reasonable secrecy safeguards.

Techniques that can be employed to protect a secret are numerous. As a practical matter the care exercised tends to correspond to the economic value of the secret and its nature; some secrets are more readily protected with minimal effort than others can be with even extensive care. This means that a company's failure to employ the fullest range of protective techniques will not terminate the secrecy, provided that they were, in and of themselves, reasonably prudent.

Companies should, at minimum, conduct an audit of their intellectual property and trade secrets. They need to identify their trade secret information, implement procedures to reasonably protect the secrecy of the information, and assess and manage potential risks of misappropriation.

---

[83] Virtual Radiologic Corp. v. Rabern, No. 20-CV-0445, 2020 WL 1061465, 2020 U.S. Dist. LEXIS 37746, *9-10 (D. Minn. Mar. 5, 2020) (denying preliminary injunction where defendant hired outside firm to conduct forensic examination of computer and email accounts to confirm that it did not possess secret information).
[84] 18 U.S.C. 1839(3)(A); MINN. STAT. § 325C.01, subd. 5.
[85] *Id.*
[86] *Lasermaster*, 931 F. Supp. at 635.

A. Everything Means Nothing

As discussed throughout the rest of this section, there are a number of policies that a company can adopt to protect its trade secrets. But the adoption of the policies is not enough. A company must consistently follow its policies to make sure that it has not waived trade secret status on any particular information.[87] Remember that the defense in a trade secret case will focus on the defendant company's lapses.

Because these policies' expenses are related to the volume of information that a company is trying to manage, many companies would be better served if they identified their core trade secrets and only attempted to protect them. Moreover, because a larger volume of information creates a stronger potential for lapses, managing less information will probably make that core information more secure. Finally, if everything is defined as a trade secret, a company dilutes the notice it is providing on the information it is most interested in protecting. This potentially weakens a company's trade-secret claim.[88] It may be helpful to start with locking down protection for the company's crown jewels. Specifically identify and protect the core trade secrets, and then strategically assess whether and how to protect secondary and tertiary information.

B. Stamp Out Theft

Courts routinely consider whether documents used both in-house and those circulated to third parties are marked or stamped as "confidential" or "secret."[89] Moreover, a business must make sure that it follows its own procedures, or risk losing trade secret status. In one case, a business required the marking of trade secret documents as "confidential" but failed to stamp the information it sought to protect.[90]

---

[87] *Lexis-Nexis*, 41 F. Supp. 2d at 959.
[88] *See, e.g.*, Menzies Aviation (USA), Inc. v. Wilcox, 978 F. Supp. 2d 983, 995 (D. Minn. 2013).
[89] *CPI Card Grp., Inc.*, 294 F. Supp. 3d at 809 (denying injunction where alleged trade secrets were not marked as "confidential" or were not specifically defined); *AvidAir Helicopter Supply, Inc.*, 663 F.3d at 974 (citing *Wyeth*, 395 F.3d at 899-900 & n.4); *Oberfoell*, 2018 Minn. App. Unpub. LEXIS 74 at *9 (holding that secrecy requirement was not met where alleged trade secrets were not maintained in password protected systems or marked as confidential);
[90] *Lexis-Nexis*, 41 F. Supp. 2d at 959.

The court found that the business's failure to stamp the documents indicated that it had failed to take reasonable measures to protect them.[91]

Additionally, a business should have a policy in place for dealing with waste documents. Discarded plans or drawing should be shredded, not just thrown away.[92]

C. Non-Disclosure: An Ounce of Prevention

Employers seeking to provide their confidential and trade secret information are well-advised to enter into non-disclosure agreements with their employees. Employers should give special attention to how "confidential information" is defined in the agreement to ensure that the definition captures all of the company's secret information, including the information that is uniquely secret to the company. One benefit of a non-disclosure agreement is that it can protect a broader category of information than just trade secrets. Confidential information that does not qualify as a trade secret still qualifies for protection under a non-disclosure agreement.[93] Additionally, non-disclosure agreements should require employees not to disclose the company's confidential information during their employment and *for all time* following the end of their employment. Employers are encouraged to consult legal counsel in connection with drafting and implementing non-disclosure agreements.

Although a non-disclosure agreement is an important tool for protecting trade secrets, it, alone, is not enough.[94] A company's security measures will be deemed reasonable only if it follows the procedures outlined in the non-disclosure agreement and takes other steps to secure its trade secrets, including pursuing claims against employees who violate their non-disclosure obligations.[95] Moreover, where a company has a non-disclosure agreement, those contractual duties will define whether a misappropriation has taken place.[96] Thus, a company will want to

---

[91] *Id.*

[92] *Electro-Craft,* 332 N.W.2d at 902.

[93] Relco, LLC v. Keller, No. A13-1633, 2014 WL 2921895, *6 (Minn. Ct. App. June 30, 2014) (citing Cherne Indus., Inc. v. Grounds & Assocs., Inc., 278 N.W.2d 81, 90 (Minn. 1979)).

[94] Coyne's & Co., Inc. v. Enesco, LLC, Civ. No. 07-4095, 2010 WL 3269977, *16 (D. Minn. Aug. 16, 2010); Storage Tech. Corp. v. Cisco Sys., Inc., Civ. No. 00-2253, 2003 WL 22231544, *7 (D. Minn. Sept. 25, 2003) (citing Electro-Craft, 332 N.W.2d at 902).

[95] *See Id.*

[96] *Coyne's & Co.,* 2010 WL 3269977, *16.

carefully define what constitutes a permissible use; otherwise, a loose definition can effectively grant the other party permission to use a company's trade secrets.

D. Non-Competition Agreements

Most states, including Minnesota, will enforce reasonable employee non-competition agreements. Noncompetition agreements prohibit a former employee from working for a competitor in the company's trade area for a reasonable period of time following employment. Non-competition agreements may also prohibit a former employee from soliciting the company's customers and/or employees for a reasonable period of time following employment. While there is no bright-line rule with regard to the permissible duration of such agreements, most courts have held that post-employment restrictions lasting one year are reasonable. Non-competition agreements must be drafted as narrowly as possible so as to not unduly restrict the employee's ability to earn a livelihood. While Minnesota courts have the discretion to modify an overbroad agreement so as to make it reasonable, some states do not allow judicial modification and instead invalidate an overbroad agreement in its entirety.

Non-competition agreements must be supported by consideration. That is, the employee must be given something of value to which he or she is not otherwise entitled in exchange for his or her agreement to be bound by a non-competition agreement. In Minnesota, for new employees, the new employment itself is adequate consideration provided the employee was notified of the requirement and signed the noncompetition agreement prior to commencing employment. If an existing employee is asked to sign a noncompetition agreement under Minnesota law, the employer must give the employee something more than mere continued employment as consideration for the agreement. For example, the employer may elect to give the employee a pay raise, signing bonus, stock options, a new bonus plan or the like, provided the employee was not already entitled to such benefit in the normal course of employment.

There are two employment law trends that have weakened the enforceability of non-compete agreements. First, some major states have either refused to enforce non-competition agreements (*e.g.,* California,

North Dakota, Montana)[97] or have placed substantial limitations on their enforceability. For example, Illinois state courts have held that there must be at least two years or more of continued employment to constitute adequate consideration to enforce a restrictive covenant.[98] While one federal court has adopted this approach,[99] three federal judges in Illinois have rejected this line of reasoning, predicting that the Illinois Supreme Court would not adopt such a bright-line rule.[100] Second, there is at least one significant decision refusing to enforce a choice-of-law provision that would have avoided a jurisdiction's law that refused to enforce a non-compete agreement.[101]

Because non-competition agreements call into question additional drafting and enforceability issues, employers are encouraged to consult legal counsel in connection with such agreements.

E. Physical Security

Secret use protects an existing trade secret. In contrast, a purportedly secret process which is employed in a plant with little or no

---

[97] CAL. BUS. & PROF. CODE § 16600 ("Except as provided in this chapter, every contract by which anyone is restrained from engaging in a lawful profession, trade, or business of any kind is to that extent void."); MCA §28-2-704 and 705; N.D.C.C. § 9-08-06.

[98] See, e.g., Fifield v. Premier Dealer Servs., Inc., 993 N.E.2d 938, 943 (Ill. App. Ct. 2013) (collecting cases).

[99] Instant Tech., LLC v. DeFazio, No. 12 C 491, 2014 WL 1759184, *14 (N.D. Ill. May 2, 2014) ("This court, however, predicts the Illinois Supreme Court upon addressing the issue would not alter the doctrine established by the recent Illinois appellate opinions, which clearly define a 'substantial period' as two years or more of continued employment.").

[100] Cumulus Radio Corp. v. Olson, No. 15-CV-1067, 2015 WL 643345, *4 (C.D. Ill. Feb. 13, 2015) ("[T]the Court does not believe that the Illinois Supreme Court would adopt the bright-line test announced in *Fifield*."); Bankers Life & Cas. Co. v. Miller, No. 14 CV 3165, 2015 WL 515965, *4 (N.D. Ill. Feb. 6, 2015) ("The Illinois Supreme Court would . . . reject a rigid approach to determining whether a restrictive covenant was supported by adequate consideration; it would not adopt a bright-line rule requiring continued employment for at least two years in all cases."); Montel Aetnastak, Inc. v. Miessen, 998 F. Supp. 2d 694, 716 (N.D. Ill. 2014) ("Given the contradictory holdings of the lower Illinois courts and the lack of a clear direction from the Illinois Supreme Court, this Court does not find it appropriate to apply a bright line rule.").

[101] Ascension Ins. Holdings, LLC v. Underwood, C.A. No. CV 9897-VCG, 2015 WL 356002 (Del. Ch. Jan. 28, 2015) (holding that a Delaware choice of law and venue provision in an employment agreement, which purported to impose non-competition requirements, was not controlling because California law would otherwise apply to the agreement and California's interest in preventing the enforcement of a covenant not to compete—against a California resident, employed in California, and seeking to compete largely in California—was greater than Delaware's interest in freedom of contract).

measures to keep it from public view ceases to be a secret. A Minnesota court held that reasonable measures did not exist where the plaintiff had twice held an open house where the public was invited to observe the manufacturing process.[102]

Companies must take reasonable precautions to protect secret information from discovery by those outside the company, including implementing measures to physically protect the secret information. For example, a company's practice of keeping trade secret documents in locked rooms or files is frequently cited as a reasonable precaution.[103] Failure to keep sensitive drawings or documents in a central and locked location will often defeat a trade secret claim.[104]

Similarly, restricting visitors to sensitive areas of a plant or facility will protect trade secrets.[105] Additional security measures can include the following: requiring employee ID badges, requiring that visitors sign in with proper identification and questioning and removing unknown persons from the property.[106] Failure to restrict visitor access can defeat a trade secret claim.[107] Securing entrances to buildings and certain sensitive areas within facilities is also important.

> *PRACTICE POINTER:* Pride goes before the fall. Two relatively innocuous events—plant tours and seminar presentations—can place a company's trade secrets in danger. Although it is easy to understand a company taking pride in its accomplishments, company agents must be careful not to disclose trade secrets during these events. A company should segregate any sensitive processes or technology from a plant tour and carefully monitor employee presentations.[108]

---

[102] *Electro-Craft*, 332 N.W.2d at 903.
[103] *Surgidev*, 648 F. Supp. at 693-94 (citations omitted).
[104] *Electro-Craft*, 332 N.W.2d at 902.
[105] *Surgidev*, 648 F. Supp. at 693.
[106] *Id.*; *Electro-Craft*, 332 N.W.2d at 902.
[107] *Surgidev*, 648 F. Supp. at 693. 84 *Electro-Craft*, 332 N.W.2d at 902 85 *Id.*
[108] Defendants often assert that information that is available through tours and public presentations loses its trade secret status. *See, e.g.,* ACG, Inc. v. Bailageron, No. CV10601844S, 2011 Conn. Super. LEXIS 549. *45-48 (Sup. Ct. Conn. Mar. 9, 2011) (finding that company failed to take reasonable measures to protect secrecy of information when it gave tours of its facilities to competitors without taking additional confidentiality precautions); TWR Serv. Corp. v. Peterson, 2021 IL App (2d) 210208-U (Ill. App. Ct., 2nd Dist., *88-90 (Dec. 2, 2021).

F. Digital Security

Sensitive information is often stored on computers. Companies should limit access to computers and systems through passwords and keep magnetic tapes, flow charts, symbolics and source codes under lock and key when not in use.[109] Policies regarding employee use and travel with laptop computers containing trade secret information should also be in place. There may also be independent remedies under federal statute, discussed in further detail below.

G. Publication Policies

The policies may include a screening process for all outgoing publications and speeches to ensure that no confidential information is disseminated.[110] A trade secret may be lost through disclosure occurring in advertising, trade circulars, or in an analogous manner. For example, if the owner of proprietary data permits it to be published for government procurement purposes, absent express contractual or statutory protection, trade secret protection will be lost. Additionally, if a company publishes what it later claims to be confidential information on its website (e.g., customer names, pricing), the company will lose protection with regard to another's use of such information. Adherence to a screening process for all publications can prevent inadvertent disclosure.

H. Division of Information

Internal secrecy can be maintained by dividing a manufacturing or development process into steps or separating the various departments working on the several steps. Courts have found that separating sensitive departments or processes from the central facility or plant is a reasonable step in protecting secrets.[111]

---

[109] *Dexon Computer, Inc.*, 2016 Minn. App. Unpub. LEXIS 741 at *13-14. Password protections and confidentiality agreements are not, by themselves, sufficient to show reasonable efforts to maintain secrecy.

[110] *Id.* at 901-02.

[111] *Surgidev*, 648 F. Supp. at 693.

I. Need to Know

A trade secret does not lose its character by being confidentially disclosed to employees, without whose assistance it would be valueless. But a trade secret owner must be scrupulous in confidentiality strictures with its employees and disseminate trade secrets only to employees on a "need-to-know" basis—for example, providing field representatives with sales information for their assigned territory only and managers with information for those they supervise only.[112]

Employees having such access should be carefully cautioned as to the trade secret status of matters on which they work. Some companies require that employees meet with the legal department to discuss secrecy at the start of their employment.

J. Employee and Vendor Training and Follow-Through

Policies only go so far - employees and third parties need to be trained on the policies and know what steps they need to take to protect confidential information. Failure to take these simple steps - which can fall outside basic corporate training – has resulted in failed litigation and lost protections. Likewise, trade secret protections may be lost if employees routinely disregard confidentiality policies and security measures.[113]

K. Establish a Trade Secret Team – Implement Continual Improvement

Problems arise when no one within a company has overall responsibility for protecting trade secrets and other confidential information. Courts may look unfavorably on companies that fail to put a person or group in charge of protecting trade secrets. Consider establishing a cross-functional team with broad representation to establish trade secret polices and ensure that those policies are being followed.

Companies are also well-served to develop a plan to respond in the event of a breach. This may include vetting legal counsel who can respond on a dime.

---

[112] *Id.* at 694.
[113] *Berkley Risk Adm'rs Co.*, 2016 U.S. Dist. LEXIS 113421 (evidence that employees emailed confidential information to their personal email accounts cuts against requirement to reasonably protect trade secrets); *Lexis-Nexis*, 41 F. Supp. 2d at 959) (finding that polices which "were frequently disregarded in practice" raised a substantial question as to whether plaintiff made reasonable efforts to maintain secrecy).

VII. COMMON COMPANION CLAIMS

The Federal Defend Trade Secrets Act of 2016 ("FDTSA") does not affect "contractual remedies, whether or not based upon misappropriation of a trade secret" or "other civil remedies that are not based upon misappropriation of a trade secret."[114] The MTSA, meanwhile, displaces tort claims that do not allege additional factual allegations beyond the misappropriation of trade secrets or seek remedies beyond the MTSA.[115] Common companion claims include, for instance, breach of fiduciary duties and the duty of loyalty, tortious interference of business relations, and theft.

Beyond trade secret law, another popular avenue to protect companies' confidential information is a federal civil cause of action under the Computer Fraud and Abuse Act for unauthorized access to information. The Computer Fraud & Abuse Act ("CFAA"), 18 U.S.C. § 1030, is a federal statute that makes it unlawful for persons to engage in several forms of computer fraud and abuse, including:

- Accessing, without authorization, certain computer systems;
- Exceeding the scope of authorization; and
- Causing damage to computer systems or data maintained on those systems.

Employees who misappropriate trade secrets using computers may be in violation of the CFAA. The CFAA does not require proof of the elements of a trade secret. In contrast to trade secrets law, the CFAA only requires an employer to prove that the employee accessed the computer "without authorization" or that the employee exceeded authorized access. "[E]xceeds authorized access" is defined as accessing "a computer with authorization and [using] such access to obtain or alter information in the computer that the accessor is not entitled so to obtain or alter."[116]

---

[114] MINN. STAT. § 325C.07
[115] SL Montevideo Tech., Inc. v. Eaton Aerospace, LLC, 292 F. Supp. 2d 1173, 1179 (D. Minn. 2003); MINN. STAT. § 325C.07(a) (stating that the Act "displace[s] conflicting tort, restitutionary, and other law of this state providing civil remedies for misappropriation of a trade secret"); Micro Display Sys., Inc. v. Axtel, Inc., 699 F. Supp. 202, 205 (D. Minn. 1988) ("To the extent a cause of action exists in the commercial area not dependent on trade secrets, that cause continues to exist.").
[116] 18 U.S.C.A. § 1030(a)(4).

However, "without authorization" is not defined by the statute. There is a split among the federal circuits regarding what constitutes unauthorized access under the CFAA. Under the narrow view adopted by the Fourth and Ninth Circuits, an employee granted access to a computer in connection with his employment is "authorized" to access that computer under the CFAA regardless of his or her intent or whether internal policies limit the employee's use of the information accessed.[117] A majority of circuit courts have taken a broader view of "without authorization," concluding that an employee who is granted access to a computer in connection with his or her employment may exceed his or her authority by misusing the information on the computer, either by severing the agency relationship through disloyal activity, or by violating employer policies and/or confidentiality agreements.[118]

VIII. CONCLUSION

Failing to manage trade-secret information puts the very existence of a company at risk. A company can lose its investment in research and development, see its margins erode, and face large verdicts that include punitive damages and attorneys' fees. In the worst case, a court could issue an injunction that shuts down a critical product. Given the risks associated with mismanaging trade-secret information, a minimal upfront investment in establishing policies and procedures can prevent catastrophic damage to a business. Every company should have policies in place for managing trade-secret information.

---

[117] See Micro Display Sys. at 205-06; United States v. Nosal, 676 F.3d 854, 857-59 (9th Cir. 2012) (en banc); LVRC Holdings LLC v. Brekka, 581 F.3d 1127, 1132-35 (9th Cir. 2009).
[118] United States v. John, 597 F.3d 263, 271-73 (5th Cir. 2010); United States v. Rodriguez, 628 F.3d 1258, 1263 (11th Cir. 2010); Int'l Airport Ctrs. LLC v. Citrin, 440 F.3d 418, 420-21 (7th Cir. 2006); Ef Cultural Travel Bv v. Explorica, Inc., 274 F.3d 577, 582 (1st Cir. 2001)); see also Reliable Prop. Servs., LLC v. Capital Growth Partners, LLC, 1 F. Supp. 3d 961, 964 (D. Minn. 2014) ("When George used his access not to help maintain the SnowMaster software, but instead to analyze and compile customer data to further his own interests, George almost certainly 'exceed[ed] authorized access' for purposes of § 1030(a)(2).").

SEXUAL HARASSMENT CLAIMS IN FEDERAL COURT: AN EMPIRICAL ANALYSIS

ALIX VALENTI*

I. INTRODUCTION

The Supreme Court, in *Meritor v. Savings Bank v. Vinson*,[1] first recognized that a claim of hostile environment sexual harassment is form of sex discrimination actionable under Title VII. Twelve years later, the Supreme Court ruled that same-sex harassment can be a form of sexual harassment.[2] Nevertheless, plaintiffs face a formidable challenge in proving that offensive conduct in the workplace is actionable as sexual harassment. In a study of over 600 lawsuits filed in federal court, we find that the vast majority of sexual harassment claims are filed by women alleging harassment by male supervisors or co-workers. However, allegations of same sex harassment were more often raised by men. We also found that judgments for women were significantly higher than for men. In cases when judgments were rendered against a male plaintiff, the judgements were generally based on a finding that the conduct was not based on sex.

II. SEXUAL HARASSMENT DEFINED

Barnes v. Costle[3] was the first federal court case to address sexual harassment. In that case, the D.C. Circuit Court of Appeals held that the plaintiff had a valid Title VII claim when she was fired for rejecting the sexual advances of her supervisor. The court stated that she became the target of her superior's sexual desires because she was a woman, which is actionable as sex discrimination under Title VII.

The legal definition of sexual harassment is any unwelcome sexual advances, requests for sexual favors, or other conduct of a sexual nature that: (1) explicitly or implicitly are a condition of employment, (2) are used to make a hiring or other employment decision, or (3) unreasonably interfere with a person's performance or create an intimidating, hostile, or offensive work environment. Sexual harassment

---

*Professor of Legal Studies & Management, University of Houston - Clear Lake
[1] 477 U.S. 57 (1986).
[2] *Oncale v. Sundowner Offshore Services, Inc., 523 U.S. 75 (1998).*
[3] 561 F.2d 983, 990 (D.C. Cir. 1977).

can be verbal conduct, physical conduct, or both and generally must be severe and pervasive.[4]

The definition of sexual harassment as a psychological construct includes unwanted sex-related attention and sexualized harassment which includes sexual threats or bribes and sexual coercion.[5] Sexual harassment also includes gender harassment which is not aimed at sexual cooperation but rather involves the insulting, hostile, or degrading treatment of women, which includes sexist hostility as well as unwanted or humiliating sexual provocation.[6] Common to most behavioral definitions of sexual harassment is that the conduct is offensive and threatens the recipient's well-being.[7]

The courts recognize two types of sexual harassment: quid pro quo and hostile work environment. The court of appeals first coined the term "quid pro quo" in *Henson v. City of Dundee*,[8] where the court held that an employer may not require sexual consideration from an employee as a quid pro quo for job benefits. The court based the distinction between harassment that creates an offensive environment ("condition of work") and harassment in which a supervisor demands sexual consideration in exchange for job benefits ("quid pro quo") on an earlier book by McKinnon.[9] In fact, several earlier court decisions recognized that a Title VII violation occurred if an employee experienced a detrimental employment action because she rejected her supervisor's advances.[10]

Six elements must be established for a quid pro quo sexual harassment claim under Title VII: (1) the employee belongs to a protected group; (2) the employee was subject to unwelcome sexual harassment; (3)

---

[4] Meritor Savings Bank v. Vinson, 477 U.S. 57, 67 (1986).

[5] Louise F. Fitzgerald , Michele J. Gelfand & Fritz Drasgow, *Measuring Sexual Harassment: Theoretical and Psychometric Advances*, 17 BASIC AND APPLIED SOC. PSYCHOL. 425 (1995); Margaret S. Stockdale, Cynthia Gandolfo Berry, Robert Schneider & Feng Cao, *Perceptions of the Sexual Harassment of Men*, 5 PSYCHOL. OF MEN & MASCULINITY 158 (2004).

[6] Margaret S. Stockdale, Michelle Visio, & Leena Batra, *The Sexual Harassment of Men: Evidence for a Broader Theory of Sexual Harassment and Sex Discrimination*, 5 PSYCHOL., PUB. POL'Y & L. 630 (1999).

[7] Louise Fitzgerald, Suzanne Swan & Vicki Magley, *But Was It Really Sexual Harassment? Legal, Behavioral, and Psychological Definitions of the Workplace Victimization of Women*. In SEXUAL HARASSMENT: THEORY, RESEARCH, & TREATMENT 5-28 (William O'Donohue ed. 1997).

[8] 682 F.2d 897, 908 (9th Cir. 1982).

[9] Catherine MacKinnon, SEXUAL HARASSMENT OF WORKING WOMEN (1979).

[10] Barnes v. Costle, 561 F.2d 983, 990 (D.C. Cir. 1977); Miller v. Bank of America, 600 F.2d 211, 213 (9th Cir. 1979); Williams v. Saxbe, 413 F. Supp. 654, 657 (D.D.C. 1976).

the harassment complained of was based upon sex; (4) the acceptance or rejection of the harassment was an express or implied condition to the receipt of a job benefit or the cause of a tangible job detriment; (5) the effect of the harassment was on a tangible aspect of the employee's job, such as compensation, promotion, termination, or demotion; and (6) the employer either knew or should have known of the harassment and took no effective remedial action.[11] With respect to the fifth element, a plaintiff must show that he or she was deprived of a job benefit that the employee was otherwise qualified to receive.[12] The last element is automatically met when the harassment was alleged to have been perpetrated by a supervisor.[13] In addition, evidence that several complaints were made about a supervisor's conduct plus testimony that many co-workers were aware of the harassment is sufficient to put an employer on constructive notice that harassment was taking place.[14]

If a claim of "quid pro quo" cannot be sustained, the claim is often classified as a "hostile environment" case.[15] Many quid pro quo cases are often re-characterized by the courts as hostile workplace environment cases because the plaintiffs failed to allege any tangible employment action suffered as a result of the alleged discrimination.[16]

The Supreme Court, in *Meritor Savings Bank v. Vinson,*[17] first recognized that a claim of hostile environment sexual harassment is a form of sex discrimination actionable under Title VII. Sexual harassment based on a hostile work environment requires a showing of conduct that is so objectively severe or pervasive as to alter the conditions of employment.[18] The focus of the inquiry should be whether a reasonable person would find the environment objectively hostile and not whether the plaintiff subjectively found the conduct severe and pervasive.[19] For example, in *Hockman v. Westward Communications, LLC,*[20] the court of appeals did not find a supervisor's conduct sufficiently egregious where the plaintiff claimed her immediate supervisor commented on her body and

---

[11] *Brown v. Perry,* 184 F.3d 388, 393 (4th Cir. 1999).
[12] *Id.*
[13] *Spencer v. Gen. Elec. Co.,* 894 F.2d 651, 658 n. 10 (4th Cir. 1990).
[14] Delgado v. GGNSC Grand Island Lakeveiw LLC, 259 F. Supp. 3d 991, 1002 (N.D. Neb. 2017).
[15] Wyatt v. Hunt Plywood Co., 297 F.3d 405, 409 (5th Cir. 2002).
[16] Quinones v. Puerto Rico Hosp. Supply, Inc., 307 F. Supp. 2d 352, 359 (D.P.R. 2004).
[17] 477 U.S. 57 (1986).
[18] *Id.*
[19] Williams v. Gen. Motors Corp., 187 F.3d 553, 568 (6th Cir.1999).
[20] 407 F.3d 317, 321–22, 329 (5th Cir. 2004).

her buttocks, made comments to her about the bodies of other employees, slapped her behind with a newspaper, brushed up against her breasts and behind, attempted to kiss her, asked her to come in early so they could be alone together, and once stood in the doorway of the ladies' room to watch plaintiff wash her hands. Occasional touching and comments about an employee's body will not be treated as a hostile work environment sufficient to withstand a summary judgment motion by the employer.[21]

In examining whether a plaintiff has stated a claim for hostile environment harassment, the court will examine the totality of the circumstances, including: (1) the frequency of the discriminatory conduct; (2) the severity of the conduct; (3) whether the conduct is physically threatening or humiliating, or merely an offensive utterance; and (4) whether the conduct unreasonably interferes with an employee's work performance.[22] With regard to the first element, the court will look at both the number of incidents and the period of time during which they occurred. While no one single incident might be sufficient to support a hostile work environment claim, their cumulative effect might be sufficient to raise material issues of fact as to whether the conduct was so severe or pervasive to alter the conditions of the workplace.[23] Allegations of twenty sexually implicit remarks by a co-worker over eighteen months would not be sufficient to establish sexual harassment.[24] Conversely, fifteen incidents of unwelcome and inappropriate conduct over the course of four months, including sexually charged comments and gestures, "giving [the plaintiff] unwanted massages, standing so close to [her] that his body parts touched her from behind, and pulling his pants tight to reveal the imprint of his private parts" was frequent and severe enough to constitute harassment.[25] Similarly, evidence that, throughout a two-year period, the plaintiff was subjected on a daily basis to comments about her dress and underwear, interference with her work, name-calling and other insults, and criticisms of her work was sufficient to conclude that she was sexually harassed.[26]

---

[21] *Shepherd v. Comptroller of Pub. Accounts of Tex.,* 168 F.3d 871, 872 (5th Cir. 1999).

[22] Miller v. Kenworth of Dothan, 277 F.3d 1269, 1276 (11th Cir. 2002).

[23] Arizona ex rel. Horne v. Geo Group, Inc., 816 F.3d 1189, 1207 (9th Cir. 2016), *cert. denied sub nom;* Geo Group, Inc. v. EEOC, 137 S. Ct. 623 (2017).

[24] Williams v. United Launch Alliance, LLC, 5:16-CV-00335-HNJ, 2018 WL 723135, at *7 (N.D. Ala. Feb. 6, 2018).

[25] Johnson v. Booker T. Washington Broadcast Serv., Inc., 234 F.3d 501, 509 (11th Cir. 2000).

[26] Rosario v. Dep't of the Army, 607 F.3d 241, 247 (1st Cir. 2010).

Regarding the third and fourth elements, the standard is that the "sexually objectionable environment must be both objectively and subjectively offensive, one that a reasonable person would find hostile or abusive, and one that the victim in fact did perceive to be so."[27] A plaintiff's testimony that her supervisor made inappropriate comments to her "[e]very time he had a chance" together with questions about her personal life, making inappropriate gestures, and discussions of his sex life were ruled as conduct that was both subjectively and objectively offensive.[28] The Eleventh Circuit found that daily vulgar and gender-specific insults and office conduct that was humiliating and degrading to women "created a discriminatorily abusive working environment."[29] This was sufficient, said the court, that a jury could find that it subjected a female employee to disadvantageous terms or conditions of employment to which members of the other sex were not exposed.[30]

Where there is evidence of physical threats or assaults, even one incident may constitute sexual harassment. An isolated incident, if sufficiently egregious, can alter the terms and conditions of employment.[31] Deliberate and unwanted touching of intimate body parts can constitute severe sexual harassment.[32] In *EEOC v. Dillard's*[33] the court considered whether one act of a supervisor exposing his genitals and masturbating in front of a subordinate constituted "severe or pervasive" harassment. The court found that the conduct the plaintiff, who was nineteen years old, had witnessed was "humiliating," that he feared retaliation after the incident, and that he became uncomfortable and "paranoid" during the rest of his employment at Dillard's. This was sufficiently egregious, said the court, that a reasonable jury could find that the harassment altered the terms and conditions of the plaintiff's employment. In *Williams v. Silver Spring Volunteer Fire Department*,[34] the court held that a single incident where, at a fire department board meeting, the plaintiff's supervisor straddled and grinded on her lap in the presence of numerous colleagues was so degrading and humiliating that it satisfied the severe or pervasive element of the hostile work environment claim.

---

[27] Faragher v. City of Boca Raton, 524 U.S. 775, 787 (1998).

[28] Xiaoyan Tang v. Citizens Bank, N.A., 821 F.3d 206, 217(1st Cir. 2016).

[29] Reeves v. C.H. Robinson Worldwide, Inc., 594 F.3d 798, 811 (11th Cir. 2010).

[30] *Id.* at 813.

[31] *Royal v. CCC & R Tres Arboles, L.L.C.*, 736 F.3d 396, 403 (5th Cir. 2013).

[32] *Harvill* v. Westward Commc'ns, 433 F.3d 428, 436 (5th Cir. 2005).

[33] No. 6:07–cv–1496–Orl–19GJK, 2009 WL 789976, at *9 (M.D. Fla. Mar. 23, 2009).

[34] 86 F. Supp. 3d 398, 413 (D. Md. 2015).

III. DIFFERENCES IN SEXUAL HARASSMENT CLAIMS BY MEN AND WOMEN

In 2018, there were 7,609 complaints filed with the EEOC alleging sexual harassment, and in 2017 the number of complaints was 6,696. Of those, approximately 16% were filed by men.[35] Women are more likely than men to view certain social behavior as sexually harassing, not necessarily because they experienced sexual harassment more than men but because they evaluate such behaviors more negatively.[36] Rotundo and colleagues reported similar results although the distinction between men and women dissipated in the case of more serious quid pro quo harassment.[37] Several studies have concluded that males are more likely to find certain behaviors as merely annoying[38] and are more likely to accept sexual-based conduct in the workplace.[39] Women are more likely to experience gender harassment while males reportedly were more likely to be subject to unwanted sexual attention.[40] Males are significantly more likely to experience sexual harassment when they worked primarily with women and/or when they had a female supervisor.[41] In addition, men are likely to experience more same-sex sexual harassment than women.[42]

---

[35] EEOC, Charges Alleging Sexual Harassment FY2010-FY20168 (2019), https://www.eeoc.gov/eeoc/statistics/enforcement/sexual_harassment_new.cfm

[36] Jennifer L. Berdahl, *The Sexual Harassment of Uppity Women*, 92 J. OF APPLIED PSYCHOL. 425.

[37] Maria Rotundo, Dung Hanh Nguyen & Paul R. Sackett, *A Meta-Analytic Review of Gender Differences in Perceptions of Sexual Harassment*, 85 J. APPLIED PSYCHOL, 914 (2001).

[38] Stockdale, *supra* note 5, at 651.

[39] Camille Gallivan Nelson, Jane A. Halpert & Douglas F. Cellar, *Organizational Responses for Preventing and Stopping Sexual Harassment: Effective Deterrents or Continued Endurance?* 56 SEX ROLES 811 (2007).

[40] Julie Ann Cogin & Alan Fish, *An Empirical Investigation of Sexual Harassment and Work Engagement: Surprising Differences between Men and Women*, 15 J. MGMT. & ORG. 47 (2009).

[41] Robert A. Jackson & Meredith A. Newman, *Sexual Harassment in the Federal Workplace Revisited: Influences on Sexual Harassment by Gender*, 64 PUB. ADMIN. REV. 705 (2004).

[42] Cathy L.Z. DuBois, Deborah E. Knapp, Robert H. Faley & Gary A. Kustis, *An Empirical Examination of Same-and Other-Gender Sexual Harassment in the Workplace*, 39 SEX ROLES 731 (1998).

IV. ANTECEDENTS OF SEXUAL HARASSMENT IN THE WORKPLACE

Scholars suggest that sexual harassment is prevalent based on the context of the organization and/or the nature of the job.[43] Women in organizations which foster an "old boy" culture are more likely to experience sexual harassment. In these organizations, women are discouraged from making complaints of sexual harassment for fear of losing promotional opportunities or worse, for fear of being terminated. Complaints of sexual harassment are not taken seriously and investigations are cursory at best. Rarely is the offending party disciplined for the offending conduct. Thus, without any threat of repercussions, supervisors and co-workers are free to engage in harassing conduct.

The nature of the work may also encourage sexual harassment. Women in jobs traditionally held by men are more likely to experience harassment in the work place. These often include jobs in law enforcement, construction, oil and gas, firefighting, and manufacturing. Other studies suggest that women in lower paid jobs such as in the restaurant and hospitality industry are more likely to face sexual harassment.[44]

To exacerbate the situation, many employers require employees to sign an agreement that all employment-related disputes be submitted to arbitration, including claims of sexual harassment. This precludes employees from bringing their claims before the EEOC or in a court. One researcher estimates that this affects nearly 30 million women workers.[45] Other research has shown that employers tend to obtain more favorable results when employment disputes are determined through arbitration. In a study of 3,945 arbitration cases between 2003 and 2007, the employee win rate was 21.4% lower than reported win rates in court trials. In cases

---

[43] Louise F. Fitzgerald, Fritz Drasgow, Charles L. Hulin, Michele J. Gelfand & Vicki J. Magley,
Antecedents and Consequences of Sexual Harassment in Organizations: A Test of an Integrated Model, 82 J. APPLIED PSYCHOL. 578 (1997).

[44] Danielle Paquette, *The Industries with the Worst Sexual Harassment Problem*, THE WASH. POST (Nov. 24, 2017),
https://www.washingtonpost.com/news/wonk/wp/2017/11/24/the-industries-with-the-worst-sexual-harassment-problem/

[45] Debra S. Katz, *30 Million Women Can't Sue Their Employers over Harassment. Hopefully That Is Changing*, THE WASH. POST (May 17, 2018),
https://www.washingtonpost.com/opinions/companies-are-finally-letting-women-take-sexual-harassment-to-court/2018/05/17/552ca876-594e-11e8-b656-a5f8c2a9295d_story.html

won by employees, the amounts awarded were substantially lower than the amounts awarded after trials.[46]

The term sexual harassment suggests that all such behavior is based on sexual desire, and courts have stipulated that, to be actionable, the employee must demonstrate that his or her sex is the cause of the harassment. The sexual desire theory of sexual harassment assumes that such behavior is motivated solely by one's sex[47] and a carnal interest in another person.[48] Proponents of this view further suggest than since men are inherently more sexually aroused and promiscuous than women, sexual urges resulting in harassment are more prevalent among men.[49]

However, social science researchers argue that sex-based harassment recognizes that perpetrators mistreat other people based on their sex not because of sexual motivation but rather to protect or enhance their own sex-based social status.[50] In other words, sexual harassment is not about sex, but about power and the ability to dominate other people to one's own advantage, here to enhance the perpetrator's sense of control, especially when threatened.[51] Further, since power differentials exist within the workplace, typically with male dominance and female subordinance, sexual harassment of women by men can be anticipated as a means to further maintain the status quo.[52] Thus, sexual harassment may be driven, not by sexual attraction, but rather by the desire to reinforce socially constructed perceptions of identity and position in the gender hierarchy.[53] Even if women are in more senior positions, the power

---

[46] Alexander Colvin, *An Empirical Study of Employment Arbitration: Case Outcomes and Processes*, 8 J. EMPIRICAL LEGAL STUD. 1 (2011). https://doi.org/10.1111/j.1740-1461.2010.01200.x

[47] Katherine Franke, *What's Wrong with Sexual Harassment?* 48 STAN. L. REV. 691 (1997).

[48] Sandra S. Tangri & Stephanie M. Hayes, *Theories of Sexual Harassment.* In SEXUAL HARASSMENT: THEORY, RESEARCH, & TREATMENT 112-128 (William O'Donohue ed. 1997).

[49] Jennifer L. Berdahl, *Harassment Based on Sex: Protecting Social Status in the Context of Gender Hierarchy,* 32 ACAD. MGMT. REV. 641 (2007).

[50] *Id.*

[51] Jennifer L. Berdahl, Vicky J. Magley & Craig R. Waldo, *The Sexual Harassment of Men?: Exploring the Concept with Theory and Data,* 20 PSYCHOL. OF WOMEN Q. 527 (1997).

[52] Afroditi Pina, Theresa A. Gannon & Benjamin Saunders, *An Overview of the Literature on Sexual Harassment: Perpetrator, Theory, and Treatment Issues,* 14 AGGRESSION AND VIOLENT BEHAVIOR 126 (2009).

[53] Mary Ann C. Case, *Disaggregating Sex from Gender: The Effeminate Man in the Law and Feminist Thought,* 105 YALE L. J. 1 (1995).

balance in society at large lies with men, and women are made to feel more vulnerable by the mere fact that they are women.[54]

In support of the power theory, Berdahl notes that female to male harassment is relatively rare because men generally occupy more powerful positions in organizations; conversely, other women are more likely to be the target to harassment by women because they are perceived as less powerful.[55] McLaughlin and colleagues argue that the power-threat theory explains why women in authority are more frequently targets of sexual harassment.[56] Women who hold positions of authority not only pose a threat to male superiority but also challenge the presumptive order of male dominance in the workplace. As a result, sexual harassment is a form of "masculine overcompensation," which is used to explain men's reactions to threats to their manhood. Vogt and colleagues further note that sexual harassment is prevalent in highly male-dominated industries such as law enforcement and construction, because there is a high value placed on masculine qualities of power, dominance, competitiveness, and aggressiveness, which are threatened by female presence.[57]

Because women have been traditionally viewed as the victims of sexual harassment, mostly perpetrated by men, but sometimes by other women, courts tend to be more sympathetic towards women plaintiffs than male plaintiffs. This will be more prevalent when the harasser is a supervisor. Thus, we hypothesize:

Hypothesis 1a: The percentage of judgments in favor of female plaintiffs will be higher than the percentage of judgments in favor of male plaintiffs.

Hypothesis 1b: Judgment for plaintiffs will be more likely when the harasser is a supervisor.

---

[54] Harriet Samuels, *Sexual Harassment in the Workplace: A Feminist Analysis of Recent Developments in the UK*, 26 WOMEN'S STUD. INT'L FORUM 467 (2003).
[55] Berdahl, *supra* note 47.
[56] Heather McLaughlin, Christopher Uggen & Amy Blackstone, *Sexual Harassment, Workplace Authority, and the Paradox of Power*, 77 AM. SOC. REV. 625 (2012).
[57] Dawne Vogt, Tamara A. Bruce, Amy E. Street & Jane Stafford, *Attitudes toward Women and Tolerance for Sexual Harassment among Reservists*, 13 VIOLENCE AGAINST WOMEN 879 (2007).

V. SEXUAL HARASSMENT MUST BE BECAUSE OF SEX

An essential requirement of any sexual harassment claim, including quid pro quo, is that the misconduct occurred "because of sex." In early quid pro quo cases, the courts concluded that a male supervisor's heterosexuality supplied the inference that his advances toward a female employee was because of sex.[58] This resulted in a sexual desire-dominance paradigm which has influenced court decisions regarding whether conduct is in fact sexual harassment.[59] A defense that the conduct is not based on sex has been more effective in hostile environment claims. For example, in *King v. Board of Regents of the University of Wisconsin System*, the court dismissed claims against defendants whose behaviors were characterized as nonsexual mistreatment, but upheld the claim against the plaintiff's supervisor because his conduct was driven by sexual desire.[60]

From a legal perspective, behavior is considered sexual harassment only if it is motivated by the gender of the victim and has a detrimental effect on job performance. However, courts have interpreted Title VII's "because of" language to mean that harassment is discrimination only if "but for" the plaintiff's sex, he or she would not have been subjected to the harassment treatment.[61] As noted by Justice Ginsberg in *Harris v. Forklift Systems*, sex discrimination requires that "members of one sex are exposed to disadvantageous terms or conditions of employment to which members of the other sex are not exposed."[62]

Because a claim of sexual harassment requires that the harassment must be triggered by the sex of the plaintiff, courts have ruled that an employee cannot prove that the harassment was "based on sex" when the harasser was an "equal opportunity" abuser and treated men and women with equal hostility or that coarse and vulgar language was prevalent throughout the workplace. The Supreme Court stated in *Oncale v. Sundowner Offshore Services, Inc.,* that Title VII prohibits "discriminate[tion] ... because of ... sex" in the "terms" or "conditions" of employment.[63] Harassment is not necessarily sex discrimination. The

---

[58] Vicki Schultz, *Reconceptualizing Sexual Harassment.* 107 YALE L. J. 1683 (1998).
[59] *Id.*
[60] 898 F.2d 533 (7th Cir. 1990).
[61] Christopher Deering, *Same-Gender Sexual Harassment: A Need to Re-Examine the Legal Underpinnings of Title VII's Ban on Discrimination because of Sex*, 27 CUMB L. REV. 231 (1996).
[62] *510 U.S. 17, 25 (J. Ginsberg, concurring, 1998).*
[63] *523 U.S. 75, 80 (1998).*

critical issue "is whether members of one sex are exposed to disadvantageous terms or conditions of employment to which members of the other sex are not exposed."[64] In *Campbell v. Meredith Corp.*, the plaintiff argued that he was subjected to a hostile work environment in which employees posted news clippings and photos containing hand-written captions that the plaintiff found distasteful.[65] The court held that the graffiti was not gender-based and was equally offensive to all employees, and perhaps more offensive, to women.[66]

Legal theorists argue that Title VII should be interpreted more broadly as a remedial statute to address a more expansive social purpose.[67] The United States Court of Appeals for the Sixth Circuit has recognized that harassing behavior that is not sexually explicit but is directed at women and motivated by discriminatory animus against women satisfies the "based on sex" requirement.[68] Courts have acknowledged that in the context of male-female sexual harassment, involving more or less explicit sexual proposals, it is easy to infer discrimination because of sex since it is reasonable to believe those proposals would not have been made to someone of the same sex.[69] Based on the courts' reading of Title VII, we surmise that it will be more difficult for men to prove that harassment at work was but for their sex. Accordingly, we hypothesize:

Hypothesis 2: In cases alleging sexual harassment by a male plaintiff, courts are more likely to rule in favor of the defendant based on a finding that the harassment was not based on sex.

VI. SAME-SEX HARASSMENT

In 1998 the Supreme Court ruled that same-sex harassment is actionable as a form of sexual harassment. In *Oncale v. Sundowner Offshore Services, Inc.*, the Court ruled that nothing in Title VII bars a claim of discrimination because of sex merely because plaintiff and the harasser are the same sex.[70] However, the Court was careful to point out that Title VII does not prohibit all verbal or physical harassment in the

---

[64] *Id.*

[65] 260 F. Supp. 2d 1087, 1102 (D. Kan. 2003).

[66] *Id.*

[67] Deborah Zalesne, *When Men Harass Men: Is It Sexual Harassment?*, 7 TEMP. POL. & CIV. RTS. L. REV. 395 (1997-1998).

[68] *Williams v. Gen. Motors Corp.*, 187 F.3d 553, 565 (6th Cir. 1999).

[69] *Simonton v. Runyon*, 232 F.3d 33, 37 (2d Cir. 2000).

[70] 523 U.S. 75, 79 (1998).

workplace, but only discrimination because of sex.[71]   Workplace harassment, whether or not between men and women, is not automatically treated as unlawful discrimination merely because the words used have sexual content or connotations.[72] Title VII protects members of one sex who are exposed to disadvantageous terms or conditions of employment to which members of the other sex are not.[73]

Writing for the majority, Justice Scalia listed three circumstances when same-sex harassment would be actionable under Title VII: first, where the employee or supervisor makes explicit or implicit proposals of sexual activity to an employee of the same sex; second, where the harasser is motivated by general hostility to the presence of persons of a certain gender in the workplace; and third, where an alleged harasser treats members of one sex differently than members of the opposite sex in a mixed-sex workplace.[74]

Since *Oncale,* courts have been split as to whether the examples provided by Justice Scalia are exhaustive.[75] In several cases of same sex harassment, plaintiffs have relied on the first circumstance by presenting evidence that the harasser was homosexual.[76] The Supreme Court indicated that the inference of discrimination in same sex cases is easy to make if the harasser is proven to be homosexual.[77] In cases where the workplace is composed solely of employees of the same sex, the first evidentiary route is the only way the plaintiff can prove discrimination. Under a narrow reading of Oncale, courts have held that sexual harassment based on sexual desire is discrimination only if the plaintiff can prove that the harasser was homosexual.[78] Two kinds of evidence provide credible proof that a harasser may be homosexual: (1) the alleged harasser intended to have some kind of sexual contact with the plaintiff rather than merely to humiliate, for reasons unrelated to sexual interest; or (2) alleged harasser made same-sex advances to others, especially to other

---

[71] *Id.* at 81.

[72] *Id.*

[73] *Id.* at 80 (citing *Harris v. Forklift Systems, 510 U.S. 17, 25 (1998)* (Ginsberg, J., concurring)).

[74] *523 U.S.* at 80-81

[75] Kaitrin Vohs, *I Don't Know the Question, But Sex Is Definitely the Answer*, 40 WM. MITCHELL L. REV. 1611 (2014).

[76] Clare Diefenback, *Same-Sex Sexual Harassment after* Oncale: *Meeting the "Because of . . .Sex" Requirement*, 22 BERKELEY J. GENDER L. & JUST. 42 (2007).

[77] *Oncale v. Sundowner Offshore Services, Inc., 523 U.S. at 80.*

[78] *Wasek v. Arrow Energy Servs., 682 F.3d 463, 468 (6th Cir. 2012).*

employees.[79]   Statements by the harasser that he was jealous of the plaintiff's girlfriend plus sexual touching was sufficient to find that the harasser was homosexual under the first condition.[80] Even if the harasser denied being homosexual and claimed that the harassing actions were merely intended to "taunt" the plaintiff, summary judgment for the employer will be denied if the evidence is sufficient to conclude that the harasser was homosexual and intended to make advances toward the plaintiff.[81]

Absent proof of sexual desire, a same-sex harassment suit can be brought on the basis of gender stereotyping. The Supreme Court recognized gender stereotype as a form of sex-based discrimination in *Price Waterhouse v. Hopkins.*[82] In that case, the Court found that Title VII applied not only to discrimination because of biological sex, but also to gender stereotyping—failing to act and appear according to expectations defined by gender.[83] This theory was applied by the Fifth Circuit in *EEOC v. Bohs Brothers Construction Co.*[84] Humiliation which is sufficiently severe and based on gender stereotyping against employees who were deemed less manly from other employees is actionable.[85] In such cases, the plaintiff must present sufficient proof that he or she in fact deviated from expected gender norms which were the basis of the harassment.[86]

While *Oncale* requires proof of homosexual behavior only under the first circumstance enumerated by Justice Scalia, some commentators have notated that when harassers are openly homosexual, the courts will infer that same sex harassment is based on sexual desire and thus based on sex.[87] Thus, we expect that plaintiffs in same-sex cases will be more successful in proving that the harassment was based on sex when the harasser is homosexual.

---

[79] LeDay v. Catalyst Tech., Inc., 302 F.3d 474, 480 (5th Cir. 2002).
[80] *Id.*
[81] Guadalajara v. Honeywell Int'l, Inc., 224 F. Supp. 3d 488, 500 (W.D. Tex. 2016).
[82] *490 U.S. 228, 250 (1989).*
[83] *Id.* at 272.
[84] *731 F.3d 444, 454 (5th Cir. 2013) (en banc).*
[85] Arredondo v. Estrada, 120 F. Supp. 3d 637, 646 (S.D. Tex. 2015).
[86] Roberts v. Archbold Med. Ctr., 220 F. Supp. 3d 1333, 1349 (M.D. Ga. 2016).
[87] Jessica A. Clarke, *Inferring Desire*, 63 DUKE L.J. 525 (2013); Vohs, *supra* note 69.

Hypothesis 3: In cases alleging same-sex harassment, judgment for the plaintiff is more likely if the harasser is homosexual.

Courts had previously applied the power theory, as discussed above, as grounds to deny relief in same-sex harassment claims. For example, in *Goluszek v. H.P. Smith*, decided before *Oncale*, the court rejected a male employee's claim of harassment, noting that Title VII was meant to remedy an imbalance of power which exploits unwilling and less powerful victims.[88] Thus, the court reasoned that only those forms of sexual harassment that makes a person feel inferior because of the person's gender were actionable and no such imbalance could exist between persons of the same gender.[89]

Goluszek has been deemed overruled by *Oncale*. Nevertheless, the power argument still suggests that same-sex cases will more often than not involve dominant males harassing other males deemed less powerful or less threatening. Connell's theory of hegemonic masculinity suggests that society favors a single normative ideal of male behavior and provides a broad sociological framework for understanding harassment, gender, and power.[90] Men are vulnerable to harassment if they are perceived as not meeting the expectations of male behavior.[91] When men are targeted by other men, harassers aim to prove their own manhood by undermining their targets' masculinity.[92] Thus, we expect to find the following:

Hypothesis 4: In cases alleging same-sex harassment, the plaintiff and harasser are more likely to be males.

VII. QUID PRO QUO SEXUAL HARASSMENT

In a quid pro quo case, the two issues that generally receive the most attention are whether the complaining employee suffered a tangible

---

[88] 697 F. Supp. 1452, 1456 (N.D. Ill 1988).

[89] *Id.*

[90] RAEWYN CONNELL, GENDER AND POWER: SOCIETY, THE PERSON, AND SEXUAL POLITICS (1987).

[91] Eros DeSouza & Joseph Solberg, *Women's and Men's Reactions to Man-to-Man Sexual Harassment:*
Does the Sexual Orientation of the Victim Matter? 50 SEX ROLES 23 (2004); Craig Waldo, Jennifer L. Berdahl & Louise F. Fitzgerald, *Are Men Sexually Harassed? If So, by Whom?* 22 LAW & HUM. BEHAV. 59 (1998).

[92] McLaughlin et al., *supra* note 54.

employment action and whether that action was causally related to unwelcome sexual advances or behaviors. The Court of Appeals for the District of Columbia Circuit noted that the gravamen of a *quid pro quo* claim is that a tangible job benefit or privilege is conditioned on an employee's submission to sexual black-mail and that adverse consequences follow from the employee's refusal.[93] The court further ruled that, in order to prove *quid pro quo* sexual harassment, a plaintiff must demonstrate that "the supervisor wielded the authority entrusted to him [or her] to subject the victim to submit to unwelcome sexual advances."[94] Thus, only a supervisor of an employee may commit quid pro quo sexual harassment under Title VII, because only a supervisor has the authority to alter the terms and conditions of an employee's employment.[95] Tangible employment actions fall within the special province of a supervisor who can, for example, dock a worker's pay or demote a worker.[96] Without the authority to make direct hiring decisions, a person will not be considered a supervisor for purposes of *quid pro quo* sexual harassment claims.[97] However, even if the ultimate decision to fire an employee is not made by his or her immediate supervisor, if that supervisor has significant input into the decision or partnered with the manager on the decision, the court will consider the role to be supervisory.[98]

A. Tangible Employment Action

A tangible employment action must cause a substantial detriment to the plaintiff's employment relationship.[99] The Supreme Court has defined a "tangible employment action" as a "significant change in employment status such as hiring, firing, failure to promote, reassignment, or a decision causing a significant change in benefits."[100] A tangible employment action normally inflicts direct economic harm; physical

---

[93] *Gary v. Long,* 59 F.3d 1391, 1395 (D.C.Cir. 1995).
[94] *Id.* at 1396.
[95] McPherson v. HCA-Health One, LLC, 202 F. Supp. 2d 1156. 1169 (D. Co. 2002).
[96] Burlington Indus., Inc. v. Ellerth, 524 U.S. 742, 760, 672 (1998).
[97] McCain v. CCA of Tenn., 254 F. Supp. 2d 115, 123 (D.D.C. 2003).
[98] Langley v. Dolgencorp, LLC, 972 F. Supp. 2d 804, 823 (D.S.C. 2013).
[99] Burlington Indus., Inc. v. *Ellerth,* 524 U.S. at 761.
[100] *Id.*

touching or sexual remarks do not constitute tangible employment actions.[101]

Depriving an employee of training critical to career advancement may be considered a tangible job detriment.[102] Issuance of a disciplinary notice that did not result in any adverse consequences to the plaintiff is not an adverse employment action.[103] Similarly, where a supervisor tells an employee that he would tear up her first negative job performance memo if she would have a drink with him, his implied threat is not proof of quid pro quo if he destroyed the memo in spite of the plaintiff's refusal to accede to his request.[104] According to the court, there was no actionable change in the plaintiff's employment, and thus no sexual harassment, based on quid pro quo although the facts might be sufficient to establish a hostile work environment.[105]

Reduced hours for one week will not be considered a tangible employment action absent a claim of any lost wages or other economic harm.[106] Reassignment to a comparable office is neither sufficiently adverse nor significant.[107] More favorable treatment given to a co-worker who had sex with a supervisor is not a tangible employment action.[108]

An interesting issue arises when the employee gives into the sexual demands of a supervisor and thus does not experience any tangible employment action. The Second Circuit held that although the plaintiff suffered no economic harm, the fact that she was required to submit to her supervisor's sexual abuse in order to retain her job amounted to tangible employment action.[109] The court distinguished these facts from those in the seminal Supreme Court decision in *Burlington Industries, Inc. v. Ellerth*, because in the case before it, the plaintiff was required to submit to sexual acts that her supervisor used as a basis for granting her a job benefit, namely continued employment.[110] This was "substantially different from the type of unfulfilled threat alleged in *Ellerth*, where no job benefit was granted or denied based on the plaintiff's acceptance or

[101] *Jackson v. Ark. Dept. of Educ.*, 272 F.3d 1020 (8th Cir. 2001).
[102] *Henson v. Dundee*, 682 F.2d 897, 900 (11th Cir. 1982).
[103] Mormol v. Costco Wholesale Corp., 364 F.3d 54, 58 (2d Cir. 2004).
[104] Henthorn v. Capital Commc'ns, Inc., 359 F.3d 1021, 1027 (8th Cir. 2004).
[105] *Id.*
[106] Mormol v. Costco Wholesale Corp., 364 F.3d 54, 58 (2d Cir. 2004).
[107] *Savino v. C.P. Hall Co.*, 199 F.3d 925, 932 n. 8 (7th Cir. 1999).
[108] *Candelore v. Clark Cty. Sanitation Dist.*, 975 F.2d 588, 590 (9th Cir. 1992).
[109] *Jin v. Met. Life*, 310 F.3d 84, 98 (2d Cir. 2002).
[110] 524 U.S. 742, 748 (1998)

rejection of her supervisor's advances."[111]   Conversely, the Eighth
Circuit's decision in *Newton v. Cadwell Laboratories* took the position,
contrary to that of the Second Circuit, that absent a tangible job detriment,
no "tangible employment action" can be shown.[112] Following *Newton*, the
district court in Iowa found for the employer, stating that that a tangible
employment action must be "adverse" even in a "submission" case
because no tangible job detriment had been suffered.[113] Such cases, said
the court, are distinguishable from the typical *quid pro quo* claim, where
the employee who refuses to submit to her supervisor's advances actually
suffers a job-related detriment or is denied a job benefit.[114] Instead, the
court held that such cases should be treated as involving only unfulfilled
threats and thus should be categorized as a hostile work environment claim
as in *Ellerth.*[115]

B. Causation

The second part of the quid pro quo analysis is whether there is a
nexus between a work-related event and sexual requests to establish the
existence of an implicit condition.[116] The facts must establish that a
reasonable person in the employee's position would believe that his or her
continued employment was dependent upon providing a supervisor with
sexual favors.[117]
Establishing causality between the rejection of sexual advances
and a tangible employment action often presents a challenge. While the
plaintiff may rely on both direct and circumstantial evidence, proving the
causal connection becomes difficult where the acceptance of harassment
was purportedly an implied condition, rather than an explicit condition of
an employment benefit.[118] The time period between the two actions is
critical. When less than two months passed between when the plaintiff
specifically voiced her rejection to her supervisor of his sexual advances

---

[111] 310 F.3d at 97.
[112] 156 F.3d 880, 883 (8th Cir.1998),
[113] Fisher v. Elec. Data Sys., 278 F. Supp. 2d 980, 988 (D. Iowa 2003).
[114] *Id.* at 989.
[115] 524 U.S. at 754.
[116] Nichols v. Frank, 52 F.3d 503, 512 (9th Cir. 1994).
[117] Holly D. v. Cal. Inst. of Tech., 339 F.3d 1158, 1175 (9th Cir. 2003).
[118] *Briggs v. Waters,* 484 F. Supp. 2d 466, 479 (E.D. Va. 2007).

and her termination, the **temporal proximity** was sufficient to establish causation.[119]

A plaintiff may introduce evidence that a supervisor's behavior created a hostile environment to demonstrate that his motivation for firing her was her rejection of his crude advances.[120] In an Eleventh Circuit decision, the court appeals reversed a district court's grant of summary judgment and held that the plaintiff stated a claim under quid pro quo because, if a jury believed her, she would "have established a paradigm case for holding her employer vicariously liable for sexual harassment on a tangible employment action theory."[121] Further, the supervisor's conduct amounted to creating a hostile working environment.[122] It was frequent, occurring at least eighteen times during a two- to two-and-a-half-week period.[123] The conduct was severe, involving many direct as well as indirect propositions for sex.[124] It included following her into the restroom, and repeated attempts to touch her breasts, grope her, and pull off her pants.[125] The court stated that any "reasonable employee in [the plaintiff's] position likely would perceive this behavior to be physically threatening and humiliating, especially coming as it did from an immediate supervisor."[126]

In *Carter v. State of New York*, the court found that the plaintiff's' supervisor never promised any benefit or threatened any harm in exchange for his romantic advances; there was no nexus between his attempts to kiss her and any retaliatory acts.[127] Moreover, with regard to the plaintiff's claim that she was denied travel and overtime, the court found that the supervisor was simply following a nondiscriminatory policy against overtime, unrelated to the kissing or any other harassing incident. Similarly, in *Fisher v. Electronic Data Systems*, the court noted that while a jury could reasonably conclude that the plaintiff received job benefits because the supervisor had a sexual interest in the plaintiff, there was no genuine issue of fact as to whether the benefits were tied to her

---

[119] Langley v. Dolgencorp, LLC, 972 F. Supp. 2d 804, 823 (D.S.C. 2013).
[120] Hulsey v. Pride Restaurants, LLC, 367 F.3d 1238, 1247 (11th Cir. 2004).
[121] *Id.*
[122] *Id.* at 1248.
[123] *Id.*
[124] *Id.*
[125] *Id.*
[126] *Id.* at 1248.
[127] 310 F. Supp. 2d 468, 477-78 (N.D.N.Y 2004).

submission.[128] According to the court, the plaintiff was unable to allege any explicit threats to condition her job benefits on her submission, and while she avoided and repeatedly complained to her harasser about it throughout the time she worked for him, she received these job benefits regardless.[129]

If the plaintiff agreed to the employment action, it will be difficult to show that the action was related to the harassing conduct of a supervisor.[130] On the other hand, a prior relationship will not prevent plaintiff from relief for quid pro quo sexual harassment discrimination.[131]

Based on the case law regarding quid pro quo sexual harassment, we posit the following:

Hypothesis 5: In quid pro quo cases where judgment is for the defendant, the court will most likely base its decision on a finding that there was no tangible employment action or that the plaintiff cannot prove causation.

VIII. RESEARCH DESIGN AND RESULTS

Using the Thompson Reuters WestLaw database, we coded every case between 2000 and 2018 listed under the Key Number for sexual harassment workplace cases where the plaintiff was male. Several cases were eliminated because the plaintiff was not in fact a male, the case was reversed by the appellate court, the case was decided on a procedural issue (*e.g.*, failure to comply with a limitation period) or because the case was decided solely under state law. The resulting list yielded 221 cases. Using matched pair technique, we randomly chose 221 cases under the Key Number for workplace sexual harassment where the plaintiff was a female. We matched cases both with respect to the year of the decision and whether the case was decided by a district court or a court of appeals. Similar to the process followed for the male-plaintiff cases, we did not include any case that was reversed by the appellate court, was decided on a procedural issue (*e.g.*, failure to comply with a limitation period) or was decided solely under state law.

To test Hypothesis 1A, the McNemar's statistical test was used to compute the difference in means between men and women who obtained

---

[128] 278 F. Supp. 2d 980, 989 (D. Iowa 2003).
[129] *Id.*
[130] Speaks v. City of Lakeland, 315 F. Supp. 2d 1217, 1227 (M.D. Fla. 2004).
[131] Perks v. Town of Huntington, 251 F. Supp. 2d 1143, 1156-57 (E.D.N.Y. 2003).

favorable judgments and whether such difference was significant. The McNemar test is suitable to determine whether there are significant differences in the likelihood of a result between two variables. This test is designed for use on paired nominal data and is thus appropriate to test the differences in means of variables in this study.[132]

Our study revealed that of the 221 cases where the plaintiff was male, judgment was awarded to the plaintiff in only 20 cases. Where the plaintiff was female, judgment was awarded in 79 cases. The difference was significant at $p<.000$ requiring us to reject the null hypothesis that the results would be equally likely regardless of sex. Hypothesis 1a was supported.

Since Hypothesis 1b posited that judgments would be more likely in a plaintiff's favor when the harasser was his or her supervisor, with no distinction based on the sex of the plaintiff, we used a binary logistic regression model to test all 442 observations. In the model, the dependent variable was dichotomous equal to 1 if judgment was for the plaintiff, otherwise 0. The predictor variables reflected whether the harasser was the plaintiff's supervisor, whether the harasser was male, and whether the plaintiff was male. The results shown in Table 1 below reveal that the coefficient on the supervisor variable was positive at a marginally significant level ($p<.064$). The coefficient for male harasser was not significant, but the coefficient was negative and at the $p<.000$ level for cases where a male was the plaintiff. Thus, Hypothesis 1b was marginally supported.

---

[132] Omolola A. Adedokun & Wilella D. Burgess, *Analysis of Paired Dichotomous Data: A Gentle Introduction to the McNemar Test in SPSS*, 8 J. MULTIDISCIPLINARY EVALUATION 125 (2011).

Table 1: Results of the Logistic Regression on the Likelihood that Judgment Would Be for the Plaintiff if the Harasser Was His or Her Supervisor

Variable	Coefficient	Wald Statistic	df	Significance	Exp(B)
Male Plaintiff	-1.839	40.076	1	.000	.186
Male Harasser	0.338	.832	1	.362	.159
Supervisor Harasser	0.463	3.425	1	.064	1.589

While our Hypothesis 1b did not make any predictions regarding the sex of the plaintiff or the supervisor harasser, our findings are worth mentioning. First, there was little difference between men and women in the percentage of claims involving their supervisor, with 138 claims by men (mean=1.28; s.d.=.48) and 131 claims by women (mean=1.21; s.d.=.49). This means that in over 50% of the lawsuits by both men and women, the claim was that the plaintiff was harassed by his or her supervisor. Further, in the case of female plaintiffs, it was much more likely that the supervisor harasser was male (121 out of 131 cases or 92%). In the case of male plaintiffs, 79 of the 138 claims involved female supervisor harassers or 57%. Thus, same sex harassment by a supervisor is more likely for men than for women, supporting our Hypothesis 4, discussed more fully below.

Hypothesis 2 predicted that the basis for a judgment against the plaintiff based on a finding that the conduct complained of was not based on sex would be more likely when a man was the plaintiff. Of the 195 judgments against male plaintiffs, 191 were because the court found that the conduct was not based on sex. With respect to female plaintiffs 46 of the 134 judgments were because the conduct was not based on sex. Using the McNemar's statistical test, the difference was significant at the p<.000 level. Thus, Hypothesis 2 was supported.

Our Hypothesis 2 did not distinguish between cases based on a claim of quid pro quo and those based on hostile work environment. As noted above, claims based on quid pro quo are generally decided by looking at whether there was a tangible employment action or whether the causation element was proven. When only those cases where hostile work environment was the primary basis for the lawsuit are considered, 33% of the judgments against women were because the court found that the conduct was not based on sex, while 90% were because the court found that the conduct was not sufficiently severe or pervasive (in many cases both grounds were the bases for the ruling). Compare these results to those for male plaintiffs where over 90% of the judgments against men were because the court found that the conduct was not based on sex.

To test Hypothesis 3, we examined the cases listed in the WestLaw database that characterized the lawsuit as same sex workplace harassment. The total of such cases, eliminating any cases which were not in fact same sex harassment, were reversed by the appellate court, were decided on procedural grounds, or were decided solely on the basis of state law, was 164. Of those cases, fewer than 15% alleged that the harasser was homosexual. Further, the results of a binomial logistic regression revealed no relationship between a finding that the harasser was homosexual and judgment for the plaintiff (p<.566). Thus, Hypothesis 3 was not supported.

Hypothesis 4 predicted that claims for same-sex sexual harassment would be more prevalent for men than for women. Our study revealed that of the 221 cases where the plaintiff was male, the harasser was a male in 94 cases. Where the plaintiff was female, the harasser was female in 29 cases. Using the McNemar's statistical test, we found the difference to be significant at p<.000 requiring us to reject the null hypothesis that the harasser would be the same sex as the plaintiff is equally likely regardless of sex of the sex of the plaintiff. Hypothesis 4 was supported.

The last hypothesis posited that, in quid pro quo cases, where judgment was for the defendant, the basis for the decision would be either a lack of tangible employment action or plaintiff's failure to prove causation. Of the total number of cases in our data base, 167 contained an allegation of quid pro quo. Of these, 120 were decided in favor of the defendant, and all of them were based on the tangible employment action or causation issue. Thus, Hypothesis 5 was supported.

IX. DISCUSSION

Based upon the events of the past few years, including numerous allegations of sexual harassment by famous men and men in positions of great power and the emergence of the "me too" movement, the focus on sexual harassment as a relevant issue requiring employers' attention is evident. The fact that more sexual harassment claims were filed with the EEOC in 2018 than in the eight prior years underscores the change in attitude when viewing conduct in the workplace. While many of the allegations raised might not make an employer liable in court, they go far to damage an organization's reputation.

Discrimination of any kind is bad for business. Research findings show that discriminatory practices including sexual harassment, negatively affect a company's reputation in the community it serves, resulting in customers taking their business elsewhere.[133] Claims of sexual harassment also has a negative effect in recruiting job candidates and lowering employee satisfaction.[134] Even when corrective action is taken, negative publicity can linger on the internet for years, discouraging future potential customers, employees, or investors. Thus, employers cannot ignore the complaints of sexual harassment and must take action regardless of against whom the complaint is made.

An interesting finding, contrary to our suppositions, is that courts are not more likely to rule in favor of a plaintiff when the complaint alleges that a supervisor was the harasser. This somewhat negates the power theory but also supports a competing argument that women in positions of power are often the victims of sexual harassment. The power-threat theory posits that women supervisors are more prone to be subject to harassment because they threaten men's power in the workplace. Women supervisors hold power over their male subordinates, directly challenging the presumptive authority of men. "Masculine overcompensation" through sexual harassment is an extreme reaction attempting to demean or humiliate the "powerful woman."[135]

Our findings did not support the contention that plaintiffs in same sex cases would be more successful if they could prove that the harasser was homosexual (and thus satisfying Justice Scalia's first condition of same sex sexual harassment). In several cases where the plaintiff alleged that the harasser was homosexual, he or she failed to meet the burden of proof that the conduct was motivated by sexual desire. Occasional remarks about the plaintiff's body and underwear did not constitute sufficient credible evidence of sexual desire.[136] Rumors about the sexual orientation of the harasser are not sufficient, especially where he testified that he was not gay and was in fact married.[137]

---

[133] Joseph Cohen, *Ways That Gender Discrimination Impacts a Company*, CHRON (2019), https://smallbusiness.chron.com/ways-gender-discrimination-impacts-company-2848.html

[134] *Id.*

[135] McLaughlin *et al.*, *supra* note 54.

[136] Wade v. Automation Personnel Servs, Inc., 612 F. App'x 291, 297 (6th Cir. 2015).

[137] Stancombe v. New Process Steel, LP, 652 F. App'x 729, 733 (11th Cir. 2016).

In addition, a review of the cases shows that the vast majority of same-sex cases were hostile work condition claims by co-workers or a combination of co-workers and supervisors that were decided under Justice Scalia's third basis of same sex sexual harassment. The Seventh Circuit's decision in *Smith v. Rosebud Farm, Inc.*, is instructive on the mixed-gender condition.[138] In that case, the male plaintiff claimed that his male coworkers groped him, grabbed him, and even reached down his pants.[139] They repeatedly mimed oral and anal sex on both the plaintiff and on each other.[140] The plaintiff's supervisor not only knew about the harassment, but also participated once or twice.[141] The court ruled in favor of the plaintiff because he was able to prove through direct evidence that only men, and not women, experienced the kind of treatment described above.[142]

The employer relied on two prior cases decided by the Seventh Circuit, where the court distinguished between sexual horseplay and sexual discrimination. In those cases, the court ruled that sexual touching and taunting was not enough, standing alone, to prove that the plaintiffs had been harassed because they were male,[143] especially where there was evidence that women were subjected to the same objectionable treatment.[144] In contrast, the plaintiff in *Smith* provided ample testimony that established that only men were groped, taunted, and otherwise tormented.[145] Witnesses recounted the numerous times they saw men grabbing the genitals and buttocks of other men.[146] No witness recalled seeing female employees subjected to the same treatment.[147]

The court in *Smith* also rejected the employer's argument that only men worked behind the meat counter where the plaintiff worked and, thus, the third condition could not apply in a non-mixed gender environment. The court noted that the defendant employed six to seven women and fifteen to sixteen men who often interacted with each other both in the meat department and in other areas of its store.[148]

---

[138] 898 F.3d 747 (7th Cir. 2018).
[139] *Id.* at 749.
[140] *Id.*
[141] *Id.*
[142] *Id.* at 752.
[143] *Lord v. High Voltage Software Inc.*, 839 F.3d 556, 561-62 (7th Cir. 2016).
[144] *Shafer v. Kal Kan Foods, Inc.*, 417 F.3d 663, 666 (7th Cir. 2005).
[145] Smith, 898 F.3d at 752.
[146] *Id.*
[147] *Id.*
[148] *Id.*

These cases underscore the need for the plaintiff to prove unequivocally that his or her sex was the motivating factor behind the harassment in same-sex cases. Even when the actions can be characterized as assaults, clearly satisfying the severe and pervasive standard, the plaintiff cannot prove Title VII discrimination without showing that the conduct was motivated by sexual desire or was limited exclusively to members of one sex.

X. CONCLUSION

Legal protections against sexual harassment have been in place for over thirty years. Nevertheless, current events demonstrate that little has changed in preventing or discouraging sexual harassment in the workplace. Courts often apply a narrow interpretation of the "because of" sex requirement to rule in favor of the employer. Social science researchers suggest a broader view, recognizing that sexual desire is often not the motive for harassment, but the discriminatory effect is just as damaging. This paper presents empirical evidence that summarizes the likelihood of plaintiffs' success in various sexual harassment cases. Overall, our findings support the conclusion that, despite the social norms against sexual harassment, employees face significant challenges in redressing their claims in federal court.

THE NEED FOR COMPREHENSIVE FEDERAL LEGISLATION TO REGULATE FACIAL RECOGNITION TECHNOLOGY

WINSTON SPENCER WATERS[*]

I. INTRODUCTION

Each day, as Americans embark on their daily commutes to work or drives to the supermarket or shopping mall, or even to the airport for work or for a summer vacation, they are being identified by facial recognition technology, in most cases without their knowledge or consent. Likely due to the absence of widespread knowledge about this type of biometric technology, the federal government has been reticent in promulgating national legislation as to when and how it should be used and for what purposes. Due to the lack of uniform state regulation or comprehensive federal legislation in this area, biometric data is, in some instances, being used in a manner inconsistent with our basic civil liberties.

Biometrics is "the automatic recognition of a person using distinguishing traits."[1] A more expansive definition of biometrics is "any automatically measurable, robust and distinctive physical characteristic or personal trait that can be used to identify an individual or verify the claimed identity of an individual."[2] Examples of physical characteristics measured by biometrics include: (1) iris; (2) retina; (3) face; (4) voice; (5) fingerprint; (6) hand /finger geometry; (7) gait; (8) ear; and (9) odor. Other esoteric biometrics include signature verification and keystroke dynamics. Biometrics can be any automatically measurable, robust, and distinctive physical characteristic or personal trait used to identify an individual or verify the claimed identity of an individual.[3]

Referential of the more expansive definition of biometrics, "measurable" means that the characteristic or trait can be easily presented to a sensor, located by it, and converted into a quantifiable, digital format.[4] This measurability allows for matching to occur in a matter of seconds in an automated process.[5] The robustness of a biometric refers to the extent

---

*M.B.A., J.D., Associate Professor of Law, Robert B. Willumstad School of Business, Adelphi University.
[1] JOHN D. WOODWARD, Jr. et al., BIOMETRICS: A LOOK AT FACIAL RECOGNITION, 3, RAND Public Safety and Justice (2003).
[2] Id.
[3] Id.
[4] Id.
[5] Id.

to which the characteristic or trait is subject to significant changes over time.[6] These changes can occur as a result of age, injury, illness, occupational use, or chemical exposure.[7] A highly robust biometric does not change significantly over time, while a less robust biometric will change.[8] For example, the iris, which changes very little over person's lifetime, is more robust than one's voice.[9] Distinctiveness is a measure of the variations or differences in the biometric patterns among the general population.[10] The higher the degree of distinctiveness, the more unique the identifier.[11] In comparison, a low degree of distinctiveness indicates a biometric pattern found frequently in the general population.[12] For example, the iris and the retina have higher degrees of distinctiveness than hand or finger geometry.[13]

Biometric technologies allow for the automated recognition of individuals based on their behavioral and biological characteristics.[14] Any human physiological and/or behavioral characteristic can be used as a biometric characteristic as long as it satisfies the following requirements: (1) universality: each person should have the characteristic; (2) distinctiveness: any two persons should be sufficiently different in terms of the characteristic; (3) permanence: the characteristic should be sufficiently invariant (with respect to the matching criterion) over a period of time; and (4) collectability: the characteristic can be measured quantitatively.[15] In a practical biometric system (i.e., a system that employs biometrics for personal recognition), there are a number of other issues that should be considered, including: (1) performance, which refers to the achievable recognition accuracy and speed, the resources required to achieve the desired recognition accuracy and speed, as well as the operational and environmental factors that affect the accuracy and speed; (2) acceptability, which indicates the extent to which people are willing to accept the use of a particular biometric identifier (characteristic)

---

[6] *Id.*
[7] *Id.*
[8] *Id.*
[9] *Id.*
[10] *Id.*
[11] *Id.*
[12] *Id.*
[13] *Id.*
[14] Joseph N. Pato & Lynette I. Millett, eds., *National Research Council, Biometric Recognition: Challenges and Opportunities 1*, (2010).
[15] Anil K. Jain et al., *An Introduction to Biometric Recognition*, 14 IEEE Transactions on Cir. Sys. Video Tech. 4, 4 (2004).

in their daily lives; (3) circumvention, which reflects how easily the system can be fooled using fraudulent methods.[16]

II. FACIAL RECOGNITION TECHNOLOGY

Unlike conventional identification methods, such as a card to gain building access or a password to log on to a computer system, biometric technologies measure things that are generally distinct to each person and cannot easily be changed.[17] There are four basic components to a facial recognition technology system: a camera to capture an image, an algorithm to create a faceprint, a database of stored images, and an algorithm to compare the captured image to the database of images or a single image in the database.[18] The higher the quality of each of these components, the more effective the system. In addition, the more similar the environments in which the images are compared—such as the background, lighting conditions, camera distance, and size and orientation of the head—the better a facial recognition technology system will perform.[19]

Facial recognition technology (hereinafter referred to as "FRT") uses a database of photos, such as mugshots and driver's license photos to identify people in security photos and videos.[20] FRT uses biometrics to map facial features and help verify identity through key features of the face.[21] FRT records the spatial geometry of distinguishing features of the face, such as the distance between a person's eyes and the distance from their forehead to their chin.[22] This creates a "facial signature," also called a faceprint or facial template.[23] A faceprint or facial template is essentially a digital code that a facial recognition algorithm creates from an image.[24] Faceprints generally are unique to a particular company because different

---

[16] *Id.*

[17] *Id.*

[18] *See* U.S. Gov't Accountability Office, GAO-15-621, Facial Recognition Technology Report 33,3 (2015), http://www.gao.gov/assets/680/671764.pdf [https://perma.cc/3LVE-YFLG]

[19] *Id.*

[20] N. Martin, *The Major Concerns Around Facial Recognition Technology*, FORBES (September 2019), https://www.forbes.com/sites/nicolemartin1/2019/09/25/the-major-concerns-around-facial-recognition-technology/?sh=738a8bf14fe3.

[21] *Id.*

[22] Woodward, et al., *supra* note 1.

[23] *Id.*

[24] *Id.* at 8.

companies use different facial recognition algorithms, according to industry sources.[25] A single server computer can search over 10 million records in less than 10 seconds.[26]

While different vendors use different methods of facial recognition, all focus on measures of key features of the face.[27] Because a person's face can be captured by a camera from some distance away, facial recognition has a clandestine or covert capability (i.e., the subject does not necessarily know he has been observed).[28] For this reason, facial recognition has been used in projects to identify card counters or other undesirables in casinos, shoplifters in stores, and criminals and terrorists in urban areas.[29]

As a biometric, FRT is a form of computer vision that uses faces to attempt to identify a person or verify a person's claimed identity.[30] Regardless of specific method used, facial recognition is accomplished in a five step process.[31] First, an image of the face is acquired.[32] This acquisition can be accomplished by digitally scanning an existing photograph or by using an electro-optical camera to acquire a live picture of a subject.[33] As video is a rapid sequence of individual still images, it can also be used as a source of facial images.[34] Second, software is employed to detect the location of any faces in the acquired image. This task is difficult, and often generalized patterns of what a face looks like (two eyes and a mouth set in an oval shape) are employed to pick out the faces.[35] Third, once the facial detection software has targeted a face, it can be analyzed.[36]

Because different vendors use a variety of methods to extract the identifying features of a face, the specific techniques are proprietary.[37]

---

[25] *Id.*
[26] *See* Michael Petrov, *Law Enforcement Applications of Forensic Face Recognition*, MORPHOTRUST USA, 12 (September 2012), http://www.planetbiometrics.com/creo_files/upload/ article-files/whitepaper_facial_recognition_ morphotrust.pdf [https://perma.cc/UJ6M-DH4B].
[27] *Id.*
[28] *Id.* at 4.
[29] *Id.*
[30] *Id.*
[31] *Id.*
[32] *Id.*
[33] *Id.*
[34] *Id.*
[35] *Id.*
[36] *Id.*
[37] *Id.*

The most popular method is called Principle Components Analysis (PCA), which is commonly referred to as the *eigenface method*.[38] PCA has also been combined with neural networks and local feature analysis in efforts to enhance its performance.[39] Template generation is the result of the feature extraction process.[40] A template is a reduced set of data that represents the unique features of a subject's face.[41] It is important to note that, because the systems use spatial geometry of distinguishing facial features, they do not use hairstyle, facial hair, or other similar factors.[42] The fourth step is to compare the template generated in step three with those in a database of known faces.[43] In an identification application, this process yields numerical scores that indicate how closely the generated template matches each of those in the database.[44] When using FRT to verify a person's identity, the generated template is only compared with one template in the database—that of the claimed identity.[45] The final step is determining whether any scores produced in step four are high enough to declare a match.[46] The rules governing the declaration of a match are often configurable by the end user, so that he or she can determine how the facial recognition system should behave based on security and operational considerations.[47]

Using the biometric database, faceprints allow for: (1) facial classification, by classifying the face into categories such as an estimation of gender, age or race; (2) verification, by comparing the similarity of previously stored faceprints of any particular individual to a new faceprint and establishing a confidence score that the two individuals are the same; and (3) identification.[48] A multimedia database contains various types of information: text, image, video clip, sound, diagram, and graphical animation. The material in multimedia databases is generated by the system and populated from a variety of sources. Once facial segments have been successfully detected and verified, the derived information is

---

[38] *Id.*
[39] *Id.*
[40] *Id.*
[41] *Id.*
[42] *Id.* at 9.
[43] *Id.*
[44] *Id.*
[45] *Id.*
[46] *Id.*
[47] *Id.*
[48] Fed. Trade Comm'n, *Facing Facts: Best Practices for Common Uses of Facial Recognition Technologies* 4-5 (2012).

exploited, including numbers of face segments, scale and average chrominance components.[49] This information is stored in a multimedia database and employed for content-based indexing and retrieval purposes, leading to new types of indexing criteria in a query-by-example framework.[50] Input images are analyzed in real-time, and features obtained from the face segments detected are employed for face matching and retrieval in the database.

In recent years, massive amounts of identified and unidentified facial data have become available—often publicly so—through Web 2.0 applications.[51] So too have the infrastructure and technologies necessary to navigate through the data in real time, matching individuals across online services, independent of their knowledge or consent.[52] In the literature on statistical re-identification, an identified database is pinned against an unidentified database in order to recognize individuals in the latter and associate them with information from the former.[53] Many online services make available to visitors identified images of third parties: social networks such as Facebook and LinkedIn, online services such as Amazon.com profiles, or organizational rosters.[54] Consider Facebook, for example. Most active Facebook users (an estimated 1.35 billion monthly active users worldwide with, combined, over 250 billion photos uploaded) use photos of themselves as their primary profile image.[55] These photos are often identifiable: Facebook has pursued a *real identity* policy, under which members are expected to appear on the network using their real names, under penalty of account cancellation.[56] Using tagging features and login security questions, Facebook has encouraged users to associate their and their friends' names to uploaded photos. Facebook photos are also frequently publicly available.[57]

---

[49] N. Tsapatsoulis, et al., *Facial Image Indexing in Multimedia Databases*, 4 PATTERN ANALYSIS & APPLICATIONS 93, 99 (2001).

[50] *Id.*

[51] *See* Alessandro Acquisti et al., *Face Recognition and Privacy in the Age of Augmented Reality*, 6 J. PRIVACY & COMM. 1, 1 (2014) (demonstrating through research the capability to reliably reidentify individuals offline using Facebook reference photos); *see also* Fed. Trade Comm'n, *supra* note 49, at 8 ("[The FTC] is not aware of companies currently using data in these ways, if they begin to do so, there would be significant privacy concerns.").

[52] *Id.*

[53] *Id.*

[54] *Id.*

[55] *Id.*

[56] *Id.*

[57] *Id.*

Even individuals with preexisting criminal records cannot escape FRT. At a time when personal information is often found online and can rocket around the globe in seconds, the estimated 78 million Americans with criminal records are a rich target for websites that collect mugshots from police departments and sheriffs' offices across the country and typically charge hundreds or thousands of dollars to have the photos removed.[58] Even individuals who are arrested but never charged have their photos on these sites.[59]

Face recognition systems are capable of matching faceprints with individuals' names at times when consumers' identities are known, such as when using CCTV to monitor store checkouts or returns when credit cards are used.[60] Additionally, geo-fencing and passive Wi-Fi tracking may allow identification by matching a smartphone's Device ID with a face scan.[61] By collecting signals from a smartphone's Wireless Positioning System (WPS) and Global Positioning System (GPS) connecting with a Wi-Fi network access point, a system may identify a user profile that has been created using the same phone.[62] The system then could identify an individual's faceprint by combining automated CCTV data with device information from Wi-Fi positioning.[63]

While this field is still developing, as facial recognition gains more widescale adoption, market forces likely will improve and expand upon automated identification techniques.[64]

III. USES OF FACIAL RECOGNITION TECHNOLOGY

Basic FRT has been used for some time now, and its potential uses appear to be endless. However, within the last five years there has been a proliferation in technological advances which have resulted in enormous

---

[58] Rebecca Beitsch, *Fight Against Mugshot Sites Brings Little Success*, PEW RES. CTR. (December 2017), https://www.pewtrusts.org/en/research-and-analysis/blogs/stateline/2017/12/11/fight-against-mugshot-sites-brings-little-success [https://perma.cc/R9E9-XNF5].

[59] *Id.*

[60] Elias Wright, *The Future of Facial Recognition Is Not Fully Known: Developing Privacy and Security Regulatory Mechanisms for Facial Recognition in the Retail Sector*, 29 Fordham Intell. Prop. Media & Ent. L.J. 611, 622–23. (2019).

[61] *Id.*

[62] *Id.*

[63] *Id.*

[64] *Id.*

interest and advancement within the field. Biometrics are increasingly being used in business organizations, residential and commercial security applications, online banking transactions, electronic devices, and motor vehicles.[65]

A. *Aid to the Blind*

Mouthwash brand Listerine has released an app that causes a phone to vibrate when it detects a smile.[66] J. Walter Thompson designed and built Listerine Smile Detector, which uses FRT to help the blind and partially sighted know when someone is smiling at them.[67]

B. *Airline Flights*

The Transportation Security Administration (TSA) started piloting FRT in late 2018.[68] Now, in conjunction with various airlines, the use of FRT is growing considerably. It is being used for everything from identifying passengers at gates to full *biometric terminals* where you only need your face to check in, check baggage, traverse security and board the plane.[69] Airlines believe that facial recognition technology will make life simpler for passengers who will no longer have to juggle identification documents along with carry-on bags and other travel *accoutrements* as they move through the airport.[70] FRT also makes boarding airplanes up to 10% faster, not to mention that the use of this technology will be cost effective for the airlines.[71] One photo taken at the gate will be matched against a Customs and Border Protection (CBP) gallery of photos of others on the same flight.[72] According to CBP, the system is more accurate than a human can be, and works 97% of the time—although some suggest that

---

[65] Kelsey Sherman, *Biometrics: The Future Is in Your Hands*, 50 Loy. L.A. L. Rev. 663, 668 (2017).

[66] *Listerine—Feel every smile,* (September 2015), https://www.adweek.com/agencyspy/jwt-london-helps-the-blind-feel-every-smile-for-listerine/92468/.

[67] *Id.*

[68] Jackson Lewis P.C., *Facial Recognition Technology in Use for Air Travelers*, JD SUPRA (August 2019), https://www.jdsupra.com/legalnews/facial-recognition-technology-in-use-54137/.

[69] *Id.*

[70] *Id.*

[71] *Id.*

[72] *Id.*

the accuracy rate is a bit lower than that.[73] The photos in the gallery come only from public sources such as passport and visa photographs and the photos taken at the gate are apparently only stored for 12 to 24 hours.[74]

Raising privacy concerns, the U.S. House of Representatives has questioned TSA and Federal Bureau of Investigations (FBI) use of facial recognition technology.[75] At hearings, lawmakers have criticized the FBI for not meeting the standards set by the Government Accountability Office (GAO) for testing and auditing privacy protocols and for the accuracy of the data.[76] Critics also have concerns about TSA's standards.[77] Although facial recognition may seem unavoidable at airports today, TSA's FRT program is voluntary for U.S. citizens, who can opt out when travelling.

JetBlue airlines has tested facial recognition check-ins for flights from Boston to Aruba in the latest attempt by the industry to streamline boarding.[78] Passengers will step up to a camera, and the kiosk will compare their facial scan to passport photos in the U.S. customs database to confirm the match.[79] A screen above the camera will let passengers know when they're cleared to board.[80] Despite the technology, passengers are required to have their passport available. JetBlue is collaborating with SITA, a technology company that specializes in air travel, and is responsible for cutting edge products like robotic check-in kiosks that autonomously rove around airports, sensing where they are needed.[81] JetBlue says it will be the first airline to use facial recognition for boarding.[82] To preventatively assuage consumer fears about privacy violations, the airline stated that it will not have access to the photos; only SITA will, and SITA has asserted that it will not store the photos.[83]

C. Banking

As global financial transactions transition to digital, many banks are incorporating the use of biometric technologies into their service

---

[73] Id.
[74] Id.
[75] Id.
[76] Id.
[77] Id.
[78] Aaron Smith, *Jet Blue will Test Facial Recognition for Boarding,* CNN BUSINESS (May 31, 2017, 11:01 AM), https://money.cnn.com/2017/05/31/technology/jetblue-facial-recognition/index.html.
[79] Id.
[80] Id.
[81] Id.
[82] Id.
[83] Id.

platforms.[84] For example, Bank of America customers can use the fingerprint scanner on their mobile phones to sign into the Bank of America mobile banking application.[85] Further improving the accessibility of banking services, Citibank also uses voice biometrics authentication.[86] This authentication service automatically identifies a customer while he or she explains an issue to a customer service representative over the phone, eliminating the process of verifying a customer's identity through identification numbers and personal details.[87] Commercial banks are already using such biometric signatures to enable secure remote account access.[88] Many commercial uses of facial verification, such as the Face ID on an Apple iPhone or user verification in mobile banking applications, rely on one-to-one matching. In contrast, a "one-to-many" search compares a photograph or a live scan of someone's face to an existing database of thousands or millions of faces to attempt to find a match.[89]

D. *Casinos*

Casinos around the country have started to employ facial recognition technology. Though the possible applications of machine learning and facial recognition in casinos are many, they largely fall into the customer service realm, allowing a casino operator to automatically recognize who you are and adjust service in real time.[90] Las Vegas, Nevada, has long been known as "America's playground" due in large part to the casino and gaming business that thrives within this desert city. Along with the glitz, glamour, and sparkling lights of the casinos come the hopes of hitting the jackpot-whether through the luck of an honest wager or from cheating the house. Because of the large amount of money handled by Las Vegas casinos, casinos are continually seeking ways to protect and

---

[84] *Id.*

[85] *Id.*

[86] *Id.*

[87] *Id.*

[88] Aziz Z. Huq, *Constitutional Rights in the Machine-Learning State*, 105 Cornell L. Rev. 1875, 1878 (2020).

[89] Lindsey Barrett, *Ban Facial Recognition Technologies for Children-and for Everyone Else,* 26 B.U. J. Sci. & Tech. L. 223, 232 (2020).

[90] *See* Jacob Solis, *How AI and Facial Recognition Could Reshape Las Vegas Casinos*, THE NEV. INDEP. (January 2020), https://thenevadaindependent.com/article/how-new-ai-and-facial-recognition-tech-could-reshape-las-vegas-casinos [https://perma.cc/ZGN2-HYHJ].

increase their profits through various security measures-which has made Las Vegas a technology innovator. This innovation in technology makes Sin City's slogan of "[w]hat happens here, stays here" take on an additional meaning when one considers the amount of personal information collected in Las Vegas."[91] Because of the large amount of money handled by Las Vegas casinos, casinos are continually seeking ways to protect and increase their profits through various security measures—which has necessarily made Las Vegas a technology innovator. [92] As early as 1997, casinos began integrating facial recognition technology as part of their overall surveillance system, together with security cameras, and cross-referencing this information with the Nevada State Gaming Control Board's database of "excluded persons."[93]

This technological innovation makes Sin City's slogan of "[w]hat happens here, stays here" take on an additional meaning when one considers the amount of personal information collected in Las Vegas.[94]

Information is shared with other casinos for a variety of purposes. For example, for a nominal monthly fee, casinos can join a data-sharing network managed by Biometrica.[95] Biometrica's Surveillance Information Network (hereinafter, "SIN") allows casinos to share and retrieve information about patrons gathered at any member casino.[96] Biometrica's SIN service enables the sharing (both sending and receiving) of information between all of its casinos and law enforcement agencies. By using its private network, their clients can identify patrons, suspects, and persons of interest to greatly reduce potential losses. SIN offers a broad network of more than 200 casino and gaming agencies located in the United States, Canada, Puerto Rico, Bahamas and Aruba.[97] This information sharing has become "crucial" in both identifying potential cheats as well as alerting the casino to high-

---

[91] Gregory H. Gunn, *Las Vegas Is America's Playground . . . and Its Security Lab: How the Technology Developed to Protect Casinos' Earnings Is Also Helping to Protect Against Terrorism and Why We Should Be Concerned*, 84 UMKC L. Rev. 897 (2016).
[92] *Id.*
[93] *Id.* at 898.
[94] *Id.*
[95] *Id.* at 900.
[96] *Id.*
[97] *Id.* at 901.

rollers who are on the gaming floor.[98] Biometrica's SIN program is able to record a variety of information including: a digital facial scan, a person's height and weight, name, race, sex, aliases, known associates, type of games played, and even a mathematical profile of the individual's win/loss probability.[99]

Casinos use many forms of technology to gather data.[100] For example, if you play baccarat at the Mirage, the cards are printed with invisible ink that the dealing shoe can instantly read before the cards are dealt, informing the dealer of any discrepancies between a winning hand and the actual cards dealt.[101] And at The Wynn, "chips contain radio-frequency identification devices allowing the casino to verify a chip's legitimacy, track an individual throughout the casino, and create a rating profile of an individual based upon how much and how often they wager—focusing on those that bet and lose the most.[102] Also, Treasure Island uses RFID [radio-frequency identification] technology on its beer taps and liquor bottles allowing it to measure, transmit, and record the amount of alcohol being served."[103] The Bellagio also employs FRT to identify known criminals, while the Venetian uses FRT to deliver targeted advertisements to its patrons.[104]

E. *Concert Venues*

Concert venues around the country have been using FRT for years. For example, Madison Square Garden has quietly used facial-recognition technology to bolster security and identify those entering the building, according to multiple people familiar with the arena's security procedures.[105] In 2018, Ticketmaster and its parent company, Live Nation, announced plans to deploy facial recognition at its concerts, allowing patrons to walk past facial recognition cameras instead of presenting their

---

[98] *Id.*

[99] *Id.* at 901.

[100] *Id. at* 898.

[101] *Id.* at 898. A dealing shoe is a gaming device used to hold multiple decks of playing cards.

[102] *Id.* at 899.

[103] *Id.*

[104] *Id.* at 898.

[105] *See* Kevin Draper, *Madison Square Garden Has Used Face-Scanning Technology on Customers*, N.Y. TIMES
(March 2018), https://www.nytimes.com/2018/03/13/sports/facial-recognition-madison-square-garden.html.

tickets for entry.[106] Ticketmaster quietly revealed plans to use FRT in venues to facilitate admission to live shows and more.[107] The rollout was part of a trial that followed the ticketing giant's investment in Blink Identity, an Austin, Texas-based startup.[108] Blink Identity's platform allows a venue to identify people using their facial biometrics without requiring them to stop and stand in front of a lens.[109] This is a potential game-changer that elevates the service above most of the consumer-focused facial recognition technology that exists today.[110] Blink Identity claims it can capture people walking past at full speed at a rate of more than sixty people each minute.[111] For a venue that may hold tens of thousands of people, such efficiency is key.[112] More than that, Blink Identity cites various potential use cases for its technology once the attendee is inside the venue.[113] They can buy merchandise and drinks, for example, assuming the user has a valid payment card attached to their Ticketmaster profile. Facial Recognition could also be used to regulate access to VIP zones.[114] Ticketmaster alleges that the technology will boost safety and security, as well as enabling venues to know "exactly who is in attendance."[115] The FRT will be integrated into Ticketmaster Presence, the company's e-ticketing platform unveiled last year that is slated to replace paper tickets with digital passes and other forms of proximity-based access keys.[116]

F. *Governmental Uses*

Biometric technologies are used mostly by federal, state and local governments to identify criminals and to ensure national security. Most

---

[106] Janus Rose, *Musicians Demand Ticketmaster Ban Facial Recognition at Concerts*, VICE MOTHERBOARD (SEPTEMBER 2009), https://www.vice.com/en/article/59n9yb/musicians-demand-ticketmaster-ban-facial-recognition-at-concerts.
[107] Paul Sawers, *Ticketmaster to trial facial recognition technology at live venues,* VENTUREBEAT (May 2018), https://venturebeat.com/ai/ticketmaster-to-trial-facial-recognition-technology-at-live-venues/.
[108] *Id.*
[109] *Id.*
[110] *Id.*
[111] *Id.*
[112] *Id.*
[113] *Id.*
[114] *Id.*
[115] *Id.*
[116] *Id.*

people equate biometrics with fingerprints.[117] This is because fingerprints have been used for more than a hundred years and automated recognition systems have been commercially available since the 1970s.[118] In fact, the FBI has 110 million fingerprint records, the Department of Defense has 9.5 million, and the Department of Homeland Security has 156 million fingerprints in their respective databases.[119] The use of FRT by local governments is often even more coercive and surreptitious than commercial uses, often fraught with more severe implications due to the authority of the governmental entity, and the context in which the technology is used.[120]

The uses in the criminal law arena are quite significant and helpful to law enforcement. For example, some cities, like Detroit, have attempted to deploy facial-recognition cameras widely specifically to "deter crime," including in public housing.[121] Simply walking around in Detroit, or being in an economic circumstance that requires you to rely on public housing, could be enough for your face to be added to a database, available for perusal by the police.[122]

The use of FRT by police departments has spread rapidly, with one estimate placing the facial recognition market for federal, state and local law enforcement at $375 million by 2025, up from $136.9 million in 2018.[123] A landmark report by the Center on Privacy & Technology at Georgetown Law in 2016 placed its "conservative" estimate for how many police departments were using facial recognition at one in four.[124] Law enforcement agencies use FRT for both investigation and surveillance, including searching video footage, monitoring or tracking people in real time, tracking specific individuals in real time, and attempting to identify suspects.[125]

State and local police departments also are not the only government agencies relying on FRT. Federal agencies like Immigrations

---

[117] *The Current and Future Applications of Biometric Technologies: Hearing Before the Subcommittee on Research and Technology of the H. Comm. on Science, Space and Technology*, 113th Cong. 1 (2013) (statement of John Mears, Board Member, International Biometrics & Identification Association). The International Biometrics & Identification Association is a trade association representing providers and users of biometric technologies.

[118] *Id.*

[119] *Id.*

[120] Lindsey Barrett, *Ban Facial Recognition Technologies for Children-and for Everyone Else*, 26 B.U. J. Sci. & Tech. L. 223, 236 (2020).

[121] *Id.*

[122] *Id.*

[123] *Id.*

[124] *Id.*

[125] *Id.* at 237.

and Customs Enforcement have searched for immigrants to deport using state driver's license databases, including states that permit immigrants to obtain those licenses regardless of immigration documentation.[126] The GAO reported in 2019 that 21 states and the District of Columbia allow federal agents to scan their driver's license databases, and the FBI collectively has access to more than 641 million face photographs across a range of government databases.[127]

The United States has also made significant investments in facial recognition technology. In 2017, the government used FRT at nine airports for its Biometric Entry-Exit Program.[128] Biometric e-Gates are currently operating at U.S. airports, including LAX in California, MIA and MCO in Florida, and JFK in New York.[129] The TSA is also testing programs at other airports including LAS in Nevada.[130] Customs and Border Protection (hereinafter, "CBP") claims that this pilot program was able to confirm passenger identities with exceptional speed and accuracy by logging photos for over 98% of passengers in internal databases.[131] Yet, due to both technical and operational problems, the actual match rate may be closer to 85%.[132] The current goal is to have the accuracy rate at 98% by 2021 for identification of all foreign departures.[133] This biometric system was not only funded as part of the Consolidated Appropriations Act of 2016 but also ordered to be implemented by Executive Order 13,780.[134]

Facial recognition technology is used for administrative purposes (the State Department, for example, uses it to process visa applications).[135] The CBP published a notice of proposed rulemaking (NPRM) in the Federal Register on November 19, 2020, concerning collection of facial images and other biometrics from aliens entering and departing the United States. The proposed rule sought to enable the CBP to make the process

---

[126] *Id.*

[127] *Id.*

[128] Jonathan Turley, *Anonymity, Obscurity, and Technology: Reconsidering Privacy in the Age of Biometrics*, 100 B.U. L. Rev. 2179, 2187 (2020).

[129] *Id.* at 2188.

[130] *Id.*

[131] *Id.*

[132] *Id.*

[133] *Id.*

[134] *Id.*

[135] Megan Garber, *Of Course Gas Stations Will Use Facial Recognition Tech to Serve 'Relevant' Ads*, ATLANTIC ONLINE, (November 2013). https://www.theatlantic.com/technology/archive/2013/11/of-course-gas-stations-will-use-facial-recognition-tech-to-serve-relevant-ads/281118/.

for verifying the identity of aliens more efficient, accurate, and secure by using facial recognition technology.[136]

But the landscape for biometric technologies is changing and other technologies are being rapidly deployed in other countries.[137] For example, India is in the process of collecting biometric information for every single resident.[138] They have already enrolled more than 300 million people, collecting both fingerprints and iris scans.[139] Efforts such as these could help combat fraud and waste, but also raise significant civil liberties concerns.[140]

Most countries are currently investing in some form of biometric technology, particularly at airports and border entry points.[141] China, Russia, and the United States have been the most prominent investors in this technology.[142] The result is a market that is expected to exceed $7 billion per year by 2022.[143] Some estimates predict an increase in market share for FRT alone as high as $10.9 billion by 2025.[144] Given that the estimate for this market was $3.85 billion in 2017, these projections

---

[136] Collection of Biometric Data From Aliens Upon Entry to and Departure From the United States, 85 FR 74162-01 (November 19, 2020). The Department of Homeland Security (DHS) is required by statute to develop and implement an integrated, automated entry and exit data system to match records, including biographic data and biometrics, of aliens entering and departing the United States. Although the current regulations provide that DHS may require certain aliens to provide biometrics when entering and departing the United States, they only authorize DHS to require certain aliens to provide biometrics upon departure under pilot programs at land ports and at up to 15 airports and seaports. To advance the legal framework for DHS to begin a comprehensive biometric entry-exit system, DHS is proposing to amend the regulations to remove the references to pilot programs and the port limitation to permit collection of biometrics from aliens departing from airports, land ports, seaports, or any other authorized point of departure. In addition, to enable U.S. Customs and Border Protection (CBP) to make the process for verifying the identity of aliens more efficient, accurate, and secure by using facial recognition technology, DHS is proposing to amend the regulations to provide that all aliens may be required to be photographed upon entry and/or departure. U.S. citizens may voluntarily opt out of participating in CBP's biometric verification program. The NPRM also makes other minor conforming and editorial changes to the regulations.

[137] *Id.*

[138] *Id.*

[139] *Id.*

[140] *Id.*

[141] Jonathan Turley, *Anonymity, Obscurity, and Technology: Reconsidering Privacy in the Age of Biometrics*, 100 B.U. L. Rev. 2179, 2184 (2020).

[142] *Id.*

[143] *Id.*

[144] *Id.*

exemplify the impressive growth that FRT is expected to have in the near future.[145]

The extensive use of FRT in both commercial and security applications is already on display in many countries, especially in China. Shanghai Hongqiao International Airport has already deployed self-service kiosks for flight and baggage check-in.[146] Passengers will be cleared through security clearance and boarding with FRT programs that confirm their identities within seconds.[147] Even some vending machines in China now operate using FRT.[148]

China's investment, however, has an even greater political design.[149] The Chinese government has openly tried to create the very fishbowl society abhorred in dystopian novels and movies.[150] The behavioral impact of FRT has long been a draw for authoritarian countries for obvious reasons.[151] Individuals will be reluctant to attend protests or meetings if government can ascertain their identity.[152] Individuals are also unlikely to associate with others, or businesses, that are deemed problematic by the government, particularly when the Chinese government is expanding its "citizen score" system by tying travel and other privileges to an individual's conduct.[153]

With the world's largest network of cameras in public spaces, China has incorporated FRT to create a fearsome surveillance system.[154] Not surprisingly, much of the FRT efforts in China have been directed at minority communities, including Uighurs and other populations viewed as a threat to the authoritarian regime.[155] In one month alone, officials in the city of Sanmenxia screened 500,000 images of Uighur people.[156] Police called it "minority identification," a system that has been denounced for its ability to categorize and identify people based on their ethnicity.[157] Indeed, Chinese companies are now selling programs with a

---

[145] *Id.*
[146] *Id.*
[147] *Id.*
[148] *Id.*
[149] *Id.* at 2185.
[150] *Id.*
[151] *Id.*
[152] *Id.*
[153] *Id.*
[154] *Id.*
[155] *Id.*
[156] *Id.*
[157] *Id.*

"minority recognition function."[158] China is currently completing the largest FRT system in the world, aimed at identifying any one of its 1.3 billion citizens within three seconds with a 90% accuracy rate.[159] Once completed, the already limited ability of citizens in China to engage in protests or reform activities will be sharply reduced.[160] Notably, the greatest concern voiced by protesters in the 2019 protests in Hong Kong was evading FRT systems.[161]

China's interest in FRT is not only political; it is also economic. China and Russia are quickly dominating this expanding international market. YITU Technology in Shanghai, China, and other Chinese companies have produced seven of the ten highest performing algorithms in the world.[162] Interestingly, Microsoft is also believed to be using a Chinese algorithm.[163]

Russia also seems eager to deploy FRT and is combining its own algorithms with its massive public surveillance system.[164] In January 2020, Moscow deployed a new live facial recognition system throughout the city.[165] In Moscow alone, there are more than 160,000 cameras that will now sweep the streets with FRT to identify individuals and track their movements.[166]

G. *Hotels*

Hotels are using FRT for security reasons.[167] Enhanced guest security is made possible by state-of-the-art fingerprint door locks, facial recognition technology, and other new and impressive means of controlling an individual's safety now available on the market. NEC Global is the worldwide leader of facial recognition technology in the hospitality industry, installing cameras throughout a property to recognize the faces of guests, check registered guest information, identify guests and alert hotel staff of VIP or undesirable visitors. Hoteliers are now beginning to understand that, although a safe environment for guests should be a basic and given element and condition, situations can arise which cannot

---

[158] *Id.*
[159] *Id.*
[160] *Id.* at 2186.
[161] *Id.*
[162] *Id.*
[163] *Id.*
[164] *Id.*
[165] *Id.*
[166] *Id.*
[167] Lindsey Barrett, *Ban Facial Recognition Technologies for Children-and for Everyone Else*, 26 B.U. J. Sci. & Tech. L. 223, 235 (2020).

be determined or pre-planned. The available FRT has now reached a level of maturity and accuracy allowing for its use in real-life situations of varying levels of security threat. Terrorism, theft, violence and other security threats can now be monitored more closely and accurately. VIPs, as well as undesirable guests including wanted criminals, can be detected as soon as they arrive on a hotel property.

H. *Human Trafficking*

Law enforcement agencies are using facial recognition technology to locate missing persons, including victims of kidnapping and human trafficking. By including such missing person databases in other mainstream databases, if a victim is located at an airport, a retail store, bus station or any other public place, law enforcement can be notified. For example, Emily Kennedy, the founder and CEO of Marinus Analytics, a startup that licenses technology to law enforcement to fight human trafficking, created a program called Traffic Jam that uses AI tools to identify victims.[168] According to Marinus' website: "[w]e find crucial evidence where others don't, and save detectives hundreds of investigative hours by pointing them to the high-value targets. Culling data from publicly-available websites—such as websites where you might find escort ads ... Traffic Jam builds a database of images, phone numbers, and location data which can help identify patterns and evidence."[169] It examines websites every few minutes, which means that even removed or edited ads can still be studied.[170] Kennedy stated that Traffic Jam does work that is nearly impossible for humans: "This is an extremely slow and tough manual process that would not for most cases show you all of the ads. One, because of human error, but also because traffickers delete old ads, so they are not on Google and can't be found."[171] The company last year added a feature to Traffic Jam called Facesearch, which combs through online photographs and identifies specific victims with the help of facial recognition software. Law enforcement officials can take a photo of the person in question and match it to other photos in Traffic Jam's

---

[168] Rachel Kaser, *This Company is Using Facial Recognition to Fight Human Trafficking,* THENEXTWEB.COM, (June 2018), https://thenextweb.com/news/this-company-is-using-facial-recognition-to-fight-human-trafficking.

[169] *Id.*

[170] *Id.*

[171] *Id.*

databases, which will help them find the victim if their picture is being used to advertise them online.[172]

I. *Law Enforcement*

Retail stores are vulnerable to shoplifting and other criminal activity and these circumstances threaten citizen safety and businesses nationwide. FaceFirst, a facial recognition software system, recently partnered with a nationally renowned Fortune 500 company to deploy hundreds of cameras in store entrances across the nation in order to curb shoplifting incidents and other criminal activity in the retail market.[173] FaceFirst's national deployment is the industry's largest retail deployment of FRT and the software company anticipates securing additional retailers in the future.[174] FaceFirst markets its advanced facial recognition technology as boosting customer loyalty by providing shoppers with a peace of mind knowing their shopping experience can be enjoyed without the threat of criminal activity.[175] Additionally, FaceFirst released "Fraud-IQ," the first facial recognition product built specifically to combat retail return fraud.[176] Using face recognition surveillance, Fraud-IQ provides brick-and-mortar stores with an added layer of intelligence that helps them better assess whether returns are fraudulent.[177] While many iconic retail brands have generous return policies, abuse is surprisingly rampant.[178] Retail return fraud often involves dishonest customers taking merchandise directly off shelves and presenting it as returned merchandise.[179] According to the National Retail Federation, 10.8 percent of returns made each year are fraudulent, costing the retail industry $9.6 billion a year.[180] Fraud-IQ uses the power of FRT to instantly locate video of people entering the store within the context of returns.[181] Customer service reps can instantly determine whether people are returning goods that they did not enter the store with.

---

[172] *Id.*
[173] *Id.*
[174] *Id.*
[175] *Id.*
[176] *FaceFirst Launches Fraud-IQ to Solve $9.6B Retail Return Fraud Problem with Facial Recognition,* Global Data Point, (June 2018), https://www.prweb.com/releases/2018/06/prweb15550963.htm.
[177] *Id.*
[178] *Id.*
[179] *Id.*
[180] *Id.*
[181] *Id.*

FaceFirst's system also provides facial recognition and initiates queries to perform statistical analysis and produce measurable reports.[182] These results improve field officer identification processes and enhance resolution of outstanding wants/warrants.[183] Fugitives may not have proper identification, making the job of law enforcement agents much more difficult, so the technology and integration with Tactical Identification System helps agents quickly and accurately identify wanted persons when only limited information on suspects is available and often times identifiable.[184] The ARJIS network that employs the Tactical Identification System is used by 82 local, state, and federal agencies in two California counties that border Mexico.[185] ARJIS currently integrates with more than 6,000 workstations and 9,000 authorized users, which generate 35,000 transactions daily.[186] Officers are given contextual data that tells them who they are dealing with and whether they need to proceed with caution. FRT also aids law enforcement in criminal investigations. During forensic evaluations, for example, trace material may consist of facial images extracted from CCTV footage taken at a crime scene and reference material may be (high quality) mugshots or 3D scans.[187]

J. Medicine

In June 2014, researchers from Oxford reported that they had developed computer software that uses facial feature recognition to look for similarities from a database of photos of facial structures that have similar genetic conditions, such as Down syndrome.[188] At the time of the report, the software correctly predicted a genetic disorder, on average, ninety-three percent of the time.[189] The concept of using facial feature recognition to diagnose diseases is not new because many rare disorders do not have an accompanying genetic test and specialists rely on analysis of facial features to help in diagnosis.[190] However, doctors with the

---

[182] *FaceFirst(TM) Secures New Business with ARJIS (Automated Regional Justice Information System); FaceFirst Keeps Citizens Safe: Providing Technology Behind Accurate Criminal Identification*, Business Wire, (May 2013).
[183] *Id.*
[184] *Id.*
[185] *Id.*
[186] *Id.*
[187] Chris G. Zeinstra, et al., *ForenFace: a unique annotated forensic facial image dataset and toolset*, IET Biometrics, (November 2017).
[188] Seema Mohapatra, *Use of Facial Recognition Technology for Medical Purposes: Balancing Privacy with Innovation*, 43 Pepp. L. Rev. 1017 (2016).
[189] *Id.* at 1022.
[190] *Id.*

requisite skill set for such diagnoses are scarce. There are over 17,000 genetic disorders that have been diagnosed, of which about 700 can be diagnosed with the assistance of abnormal facial characteristic recognition.[191] The program developed by the scientists at Oxford currently can help identify ninety individual disorders, and the hope is that it will be used where specialists are unavailable.[192] The software is not currently used as a sole test for diagnosis but is used for assisting pediatricians in the process.[193] In the future, this program could be used to identify those born with a detectable disorder, allowing for earlier treatment.[194] According to the study, previous work has established that thirty to forty percent of all rare genetic disorders impact how the face forms in some way and thus should be detectable with the assistance of FRT.[195]

   In such exceptional times as the Covid-19 pandemic, one could argue that fever checks offer substantial population health benefits with limited long-term impacts on personal privacy.[196] Several private companies have integrated thermal imaging with facial recognition technology.[197] Collectively, these companies' claims, which have yet to be systematically evaluated in the empirical literature, suggest clear benefits of combining thermal detection with facial recognition capabilities to detect and track potentially infected individuals. For example, police in China are currently using devices from Hanwang Technology that claim to identify an individual's name within a second upon detecting a temperature over 99.5°F/37.5°C.[198] The company claims that the technology is 95 per cent accurate, even in a group of 30 individuals or among people wearing masks.[199] China-based firms Sense Time and Sunell are also selling similar technology.[200] Sunell recently unveiled a body temperature detection network camera that they assert is able to identify individuals, collect real-time biometric data, and trigger a warning system upon detecting an unusual temperature.[201] Additionally, Chinese startup Rokid has developed multimodal biotechnology that

---

[191] *Id.*
[192] *Id.*
[193] *Id.*
[194] *Id.*
[195] *Id.*
[196] Meredith Van Natta, et al., *The Rise and Regulation of Thermal Facial Recognition Technology During the Covid-19 Pandemic*, 7 J.L. & Biosciences 1, 5 (2020).
[197] *Id.*
[198] *Id.*
[199] *Id.*
[200] *Id.*
[201] *Id.*

includes thermal-imaging wearable glasses, a technology they are currently marketing to American hospitals and local municipalities.[202] These smart glasses, which Rokid suggests can be paired with facial recognition software, use an infrared sensor that Rokid claims can detect temperatures of up to 200 people as far away as three meters, and they are already being used in China in national parks, schools, and by national authorities.[203]

In Singapore, Ramco Innovation Lab is promoting its integrated thermal imaging and facial recognition technology to launch an attendance tracking system that will ostensibly enable organizations to track employees and visitors with elevated temperatures.[204] This multimodal technology includes contact tracing that sends notifications to event attendees if any person exhibits COVID-19 symptoms and uses facial recognition to capture both an employee's presence and their temperature.[205] When a visitor with an elevated temperature enters the premises, a notification is sent to management.[206] The company touts that this contactless tracking system can be integrated with sliding doors, kiosks, and turnstiles to mitigate SARS-CoV-2 exposure by restricting access based on temperature range, recommending testing of flagged individuals, and sharing contract-tracing data with health agencies if mandated by the government.[207]

According to the Kaiser Family Foundation, 82% of large firms and 53% of small firms offer some form of workplace wellness program.[208] These programs commonly incentivize workers to stop or reduce smoking, join a gym, exercise more often, eat healthier foods, try meditation programs, or lose weight.[209] Workplace wellness programs are, according to one estimate, an $8 billion industry in the United States.[210] Employers use workplace wellness programs for at least two reasons. First, there is a widespread belief that healthy workers are more productive, and productivity benefits the business.[211] This belief is bolstered by research including one recent study showing that workers who improved their health by eating better, exercising more and reducing

---

[202] Id.
[203] Id.
[204] Id. at 6.
[205] Id.
[206] Id.
[207] Id.
[208] Elizabeth A. Brown, *A Healthy Mistrust: Curbing Biometric Data Misuse in the Workplace*, 23 Stan. Tech. L. Rev. 252, 258 (2020).
[209] Id.
[210] Id.
[211] Id.

their stress levels increased their productivity by approximately ten percent.[212] These workplace wellness programs often reward the use of wearable devices such as Apple Watches or Fitbits that track employees' biometric data and physical activity.[213] Workers are also more accustomed to wearables, many of which employers can leverage for data. According to one study, the global market for wearable technology grew nearly 30% in 2018.[214] The success of the Apple Watch is a key driver of this industry growth.[215] Another study shows that the market has grown from eighty-four million units shipped in 2015 to a projection of 245 million units shipped in 2019.[216] Analysts predict that greater adoption of wearables different from fitness bands like the Fitbit, including "smart hearables and smart shoes," will lead to sales of 260 million units in 2023, resulting in a market worth almost $30 billion.[217]

The Apple Watch is a perfect example of the ease with which people have accepted the presence of wearable technology. It allows the user to access texts, emails, and other data that she would previously have used her phone to collect.[218] The watch has "powerful sensors" that collect data from the user as well, notifying her of unusually high or low heart rates and irregular rhythms that may suggest atrial fibrillation (AFib), and the sensors may even be able to take an electrocardiogram reading.[219] It is easy to imagine an employer's interest in gathering such data about its workforce and using that data to make decisions about individual workers.

While employers have been using wearables for some time, wearable makers are now catering more expressly to their needs. Fitbit, for example, appeals directly to employers to "invest in healthy behavior change" and help those many employees who "struggle to get and stay healthy, which can drive higher rates of chronic conditions and disease."[220] Underscoring the expense of health insurance, it notes that "the associated healthcare costs—especially for those employees living with or at risk for chronic disease—are unsustainable."[221] Its dedicated corporate health platform, Fitbit Care, promises to "get employees moving" through devices and apps.[222] Fitbit facilitates the entire employer

---

[212] *Id.* at 259.
[213] *Id.* at 263.
[214] *Id.*
[215] *Id.*
[216] *Id.*
[217] *Id.* at 264.
[218] *Id.*
[219] *Id.*
[220] *Id.*
[221] *Id.*
[222] *Id.*

monitoring process.[223]   The Fitbit Care division offers employers a "customized, online storefront" where employees can choose an incentive for getting a tracking device.[224]   The employee is directed to join the employer's workplace wellness program while setting up their device.[225]   Then the reporting begins. Fitbit Care's program dashboard provides the employer with reports on data collected from employees' devices and helps the employer motivate employees directly.[226]   The dashboard helps the employer see "[c]ontinuous program participation levels and engagement data," "[a]ctivity level trends" and "[c]hallenge results and activity level changes."[227]   Some of this activity may be generalized to groups of employees, as employers can monitor "group reporting on steps, floors climbed, active minutes and distance."[228]   Other data is, however, collected and transmitted at the individual employee level, as Fitbit promises that both "individual and group data is also available for export."[229]   Fitbit also developed special models of their devices that workers can only get via their employers. The Fitbit Inspire and Inspire HR, introduced in early 2019, were first described as only being available through employers and health plans as part of workplace wellness programs.[230]   In announcing them, Fitbit's CEO noted that its revenue was increasingly linked with its corporate customers, and that 6.8 million people were in wellness programs incorporating Fitbit devices.[231]

K. *Restaurants*

Like casinos, concert venues, hotels, and sports arenas are also adopting facial recognition systems, out of a desire to spot high-paying customers, make providing their service more efficient, or to identify "persons of interest."[232]   Fast food restaurants have started using facial recognition technology to expedite order preparation.[233]   Similarly,

---

[223] *Id.* at 265.

[224] *Id.*

[225] *Id.*

[226] *Id.*

[227] *Id.*

[228] *Id.*

[229] *Id.*

[230] *Id.*

[231] *Id.*

[232] Lindsey Barrett, *Ban Facial Recognition Technologies for Children-and for Everyone Else*, 26 B.U. J. Sci. & Tech. L. 223, 235 (2020).

[233] *See* Kate Bernot, *Restaurants are Using Facial Recognition Software to Remember How You Like Your Burger,* THE TAKEOUT (June

various customer experience metrics from entry to pick-up and exit can be obtained, leveraging FRT for fast food restaurants.[234]   CLEAR, a biometric identification company known especially for its air-traveler identification service, recently introduced a system called Health Pass for office buildings, restaurants, retailers, cruise ships and sports arenas.[235] It will use facial recognition to confirm employees' identities and vet worker-provided health information—such as symptom data and verified test results—so they can be cleared to enter workplaces. Caryn Seidman-Becker, CLEAR's chief executive, said this kind of multilayered approach to entry screening could help reduce risk for employers and create a safer working environment.[236]

L. *Retail*

A person walks into a shopping mall, and, unbeknownst to them, a camera scans their face, identifies them, collects information about their gender, age, and other characteristics, and tracks their movements.[237] Certain stores implement this technology to better target and advertise to their loyal customers while others, such as NewMark Merrill, utilize this technology to determine customer reactions to certain displays and adjust the displays to attract new customers.[238] Facial recognition is a rapidly growing biometric technology used in the retail sector.[239] A recent study found that facial recognition is likely to generate revenue of $9.78 billion

---

2018), https://thetakeout.com/restaurants-are-using-facial-recognition-software-to-re-1827237920

[234] Abhijit Shanbhag, *Facial Recognition Technology is the Future of Safety and Security in India*, EXPRESS COMPUTER (April 2021).

[235] Natasha Singer and Julie Creswell, *A Multibillion-Dollar Opportunity: Virus-Proofing the New Office*, THE NEW YORK TIMES - INTERNATIONAL EDITION (June 2020), https://www.nytimes.com/2020/06/22/business/virus-office-workplace-return.html

[236] *Id.*

[237] *See* Esther Fung, *Shopping Centers Exploring Facial Recognition in Brave New World of Retail*, WALL ST. J. (July 2019) https://www.wsj.com/articles/shopping-centers-exploring-facial-recognition-in-brave-new-world-of-retail-11562068802 (describing how shopping center owners use facial scans to accurately identify customers and track their movements to gain insights on their behaviors, which could involve gathering information about gender, age, and other identifying characteristics).

[238] Ye-Eun Sung, *The Case for the Use of Facial Recognition Technology*, B.C. Intell. Prop. & Tech. F., August 3 2020, at 1, 1.

[239] Elias Wright, *The Future of Facial Recognition Is Not Fully Known: Developing Privacy and Security Regulatory Mechanisms for Facial Recognition in the Retail Sector*, 29 Fordham Intell. Prop. Media & Ent. L.J. 611, 634 (2019).

by 2023, growing at a projected compounded annual growth rate of 16.81% between 2017 and 2023.[240] The market for facial recognition is increasing, with large investments of up to $1.6 billion in start-ups from China, a country that has been an open environment for testing the technology.[241] Intel, and Chinese internet company Tencent, have announced a collaboration on products that use artificial intelligence (AI) and facial recognition to "gain new insights about their customers to both elevate the users' experience and drive business transformation."[242] Decreases in the associated costs of the technology have made facial recognition software a viable tool for retailers.[243] Services such as FaceFirst offer facial recognition specifically targeted to retailers using "surveillance . . . and an underlying software platform that leverages artificial intelligence to [prevent] theft, [fraud,] . . . and . . . violence."[244] Additionally, facial recognition can be used by retailers to connect online with offline behaviors, provide more in-depth demographics, and track in-store product engagement.[245]

FRT is being used throughout the retail industry. Gas stations have installed screens at fuel pumps with FRT,[246] advertising firms are exploring the use of this technology in the form of "omni-present advertising", and Virgin Mobile USA released an interactive YouTube video where viewers could change scenes by blinking.[247] AdAge notes that the video combined 25 different films, "leading to a total of more than two million different combinations."[248] These ads are notable, in large part, in that they treat facial recognition capabilities not as means to data-gathering, but as ends in themselves.[249] They focus on fun and quirk, on the amusing serendipity that can result when you interact with a computer using not your finger, but your face.[250] Tesco's adaptation of the technology to a more utilitarian purpose targeting customers, rather than

---

[240] *Id.*

[241] *Id.* at 635.

[242] *Id.* at 635.

[243] *Id.*

[244] *Id.*

[245] *Id.*

[246] Megan Garber, *Of Course Gas Stations Will Use Facial Recognition Tech to Serve 'Relevant' Ads*, ATLANTIC ONLINE, (November 2013). https://www.theatlantic.com/technology/archive/2013/11/of-course-gas-stations-will-use-facial-recognition-tech-to-serve-relevant-ads/281118/.

[247] *Id.*

[248] *Id.*

[249] *Id.*

[250] *Id.*

delighting them, suggests the other side of the technology: the side that has more in common with stores' efforts to mine customers' phone data using Wi-Fi signals.[251]

Retailers are using facial recognition to identify past or potential shoplifters.[252] Vendors like FaceFirst promote their wares with splashy taglines like "ready to reduce your in-store violence by up to 91%?" and promises to "prevent retail crime" by comparing shoppers' images against "vast databases of criminals."[253] FaceFirst refused to reveal its clients, but stores like Walmart, Macy's, Lowes, and Saks Fifth Avenue have reportedly deployed facial recognition systems in their stores at various points in time, and the use of facial recognition in the retail sector remains widespread.[254] Drugstores and grocery stores are also deploying facial recognition systems along with shopping malls and boutiques.[255]

M. *Security*

Many retailers, casinos, financial institutions, and apartment buildings use facial recognition technology for safety and security purposes. According to the National Retail Federation,[256] some retailers in the United States are testing systems that use facial recognition technology with CCTV for theft prevention.[257] According to one vendor, security cameras in a retail location compare images of individuals who walk into a store against a database of images of known shoplifters, members of organized retail crime syndicates, or other persons of interest.[258] If a match is found, security personnel or management are alerted and provided whatever information is known about the individual.[259] FRT has also been incorporated into the security systems of some financial institutions to identify robbery suspects or accomplices.

---

[251] *Id.*

[252] Lindsey Barrett, *Ban Facial Recognition Technologies for Children-and for Everyone Else*, 26 B.U. J. Sci. & Tech. L. 223, 233 (2020).

[253] *Id.* at 234.

[254] *Id.*

[255] *Id.*

[256] The National Retail Federation is a retail trade association that represents discount and department stores, home goods and specialty stores, grocers, wholesalers, chain restaurants, and Internet retailers from the United States and more than 45 countries.

[257] *Id.*

[258] *Id.*

[259] *Id.*

According to a vendor of this technology, these systems deter crime and help identify suspects much faster than traditional means, which require staff to spend hours reviewing video recordings. Facial recognition systems have also been used in large apartment buildings to help identify perpetrators of crimes or other known persons of concern who seek to enter the property.[260]

N. *Sporting Events*

Facial recognition is also making its way into the stadiums, arenas, and ballparks of professional sports franchises nationwide.[261] Biometrics is nothing new to professional sports teams and their home stadiums, arenas, and ballparks.[262] Currently, the most common form of biometrics used at sports venues is fingerprint biometrics.[263] This is driven in large part by the recent partnership between Major League Baseball (MLB) and biometrics technology vendor CLEAR.[264] This partnership has brought dedicated biometric security lanes which use fingerprints to verify ticketed fans for a frictionless fan entry process—to most MLB ballparks. At the same time, other professional sports franchises have started to integrate facial recognition systems into the operations of their home venues as well.

Sports venues employ facial recognition to identify criminals and criminal suspects.[265] Facial recognition systems help minimize security risks by scanning crowds to identify criminals and criminal suspects before an attack occurs.[266] Venues also use facial recognition to identify, eject, and ban unruly fans.[267] Incidents warranting eviction range from pouring beers to throwing punches at other spectators.[268] Thus, keeping these problematic fans out of the stadium can not only improve the

---

[260] *Id.*

[261] Jeffrey N. Rosenthal and David J. Oberly, *Facial Recognition at Sports Venues: Enhancing the Gameday Experience While Minimizing Liability,* JD SUPRA (November 2020), https://www.jdsupra.com/legalnews/facial-recognition-at-sports-venues-54419/.

[262] *Id.*

[263] *Id.*

[264] *Id.*

[265] Kirsten Flicker, *The Prison of Convenience: The Need for National Regulation of Biometric Technology in Sports Venues*, 30 Fordham Intell. Prop. Media & Ent. L.J. 985, 1001 (2020).

[266] *Id.* at 1002.

[267] *Id.* at 1003.

[268] *Id.*

spectator experience, but also keep fans safe. Violence is a proven issue for teams such as the San Francisco 49ers; in a single season, over two hundred fights and twenty-three felony arrests occurred at home games.[269] From Madison Square Garden for the New York Knicks and New York Rangers to CenturyLink Field for the Seattle Seahawks, sports venues around the country use biometrics such as fingerprints and facial recognition to reimagine the sports spectator experience.[270] Ticketing and concession sales are powered by fingerprinting, and advertisements and music are selected using facial recognition.[271] As biometric technology continues to advance, sports venues continue to find innovative ways to integrate the technology into the game-going experience.[272] Many of these uses may seem glamorous, such as reduced time spent waiting in lines, and enhanced security.[273] A music festival or sporting arena using facial recognition for ticketing could offer discounts or shorter lines for those who consent. MLB has pioneered biometric ticketing through the use of fingerprinting.[274] CLEAR operates biometric security checkpoints at thirteen out of the thirty MLB ballparks.[275] CLEAR lanes expedite the check-in process by using fingerprints to identify ticketed fans.[276] CLEAR also expanded its biometric ticketing to three Major League Soccer arenas, two National Football League stadiums, and four National Basketball Association arenas.[277] CLEAR aims to provide "frictionless fan entry," and, according to its website, serves as a safe, simple, and secure alternative to traditional paper ticketing.[278]

In the spectator sports market, CLEAR has higher aspirations than just arena entry: it is expanding to concession sales.[279] In 2018, the Seattle Seahawks, Mariners, and Sounders FC implemented CLEAR for concession purchases.[280] Fingerprints serve as a means both to pay and to

---

[269] Id.
[270] Id. at 988.
[271] Id.
[272] Id.
[273] Id.
[274] Id. at 991.
[275] Id.
[276] Id.
[277] Id. at 992.
[278] Id.
[279] Id.
[280] Id.

verify age.[281] The goal is to optimize time spent watching the game and to reduce time spent waiting in lines by creating a fully wallet-less experience."[282] Seattle fans' positive reception of biometric concessions has laid the groundwork for biometric concessions in stadiums around the country, starting with the Mets' Citi Field.[283] Citi Field took this technology a step further by opening a "Walk Thru Bru" store that eliminates the need for both wallets and cashiers.[284] Fans select their items, place them on an AI-powered self-checkout kiosk, and pay using CLEAR's fingerprinting machine.[285] Similarly, the New York Jets, the San Francisco 49ers, and Barclays Center (home of the Brooklyn Nets) all partner with IDEMIA, the company behind TSA PreCheck.[286] IDEMIA's IdentoGO strives to use biometric data to provide "fast pass" entrance for "trusted fans."[287]

IV. LEGAL ISSUES WITH FRT TECHNOLOGY

In the computer science and data analytics fields, ethical use of artificial intelligence is now a topic of serious conversation.[288] Hard questions about error, bias, fairness, and transparency are increasingly part of the ongoing conversation about how to build "better" facial recognition technologies.[289] This is all for the good, because correcting the naive assumption that big data policing systems will not replicate human bias is a necessary first step.[290] Just like humans, algorithms used for facial recognition technology can only match images based on the information available.[291] Therefore, algorithmic biases occur when the datasets used to program facial recognition algorithms do not contain a plethora of diverse images.[292] If the images input into the dataset are not diverse, then the algorithms will not be able to match all individuals

---

[281] *Id.*

[282] *Id.*

[283] *Id.*

[284] *Id.* at 993.

[285] *Id.*

[286] *Id.*

[287] *Id.*

[288] Andrew Guthrie Ferguson, *Facial Recognition and the Fourth Amendment*, 105 Minn. L. Rev. 1105, 1167 (2021).

[289] *Id.*

[290] *Id.*

[291] Rachel S. Fleischer, *Bias in, Bias Out: Why Legislation Placing Requirements on the Procurement of Commercialized Facial Recognition Technology Must Be Passed to Protect People of Color*, 50 Pub. Cont. L.J. 63, 69 (2020).

[292] *Id.*

equally.[293] As a result, FRT can disproportionately misidentify individuals who are not properly represented in the dataset.[294]

The majority of facial recognition systems in use are developed and sold by private companies.[295] This means that, even in discussions that focus on government use, we need to examine commercial systems and the incentive structures driving their development. It also means that we need to challenge claims of corporate secrecy that prevent scrutiny and accountability. Amazon's Ring, a surveillance doorbell system installed by individuals and businesses, provides a significant and troubling example of the complex interconnections between government and private use of AI-enabled surveillance systems.[296] Ring enables persistent surveillance of homes and neighborhoods, and while it does not currently include facial recognition, Amazon has filed a facial recognition patent in this space,[297] and appears to be planning to connect facial recognition capabilities to a "neighborhood watch list" database of people deemed suspect.[298] Amazon has partnered with at least 400 local police departments, enlisting officers as Amazon spokespeople to convince residents to install Ring systems.[299] In exchange, police get access to a dashboard of Ring surveillance footage, either directly from users who opt-in to share, or by submitting a request to Amazon.[300] Amazon Ring offers a clear example of the way that private deployments of surveillance technology, including facial recognition, enable a backdoor to police and government surveillance.[301] This is particularly troubling when it extends law enforcement monitoring into spaces previously inaccessible to them without a warrant - such as commercial properties or personal residences.[302] Data sharing between private companies and governments is a problem that extends beyond Ring.[303] In many places, there is total lack of statutory, case law, or agency rules governing the sharing of biometric data with governmental agencies, third parties, or law

---

[293] *Id.*

[294] *Id.* at 70.

[295] House Oversight and Reform Committee Hearing, "Facial Recognition Technology (Part III): Ensuring Commercial Transparency and Accuracy." Testimony by Meredith Whittaker, Co-Founder and Co-Director, AI Now Institute, New York University, https://docs.house.gov/Committee/Calendar/ByEvent.aspx?EventID=110380.

[296] *Id.*

[297] *Id.*

[298] *Id.*

[299] *Id.*

[300] *Id.*

[301] *Id.*

[302] *Id.*

[303] *Id.*

enforcement.[304] There are many cases of behind-the-scenes data sharing arrangements that allow data collected by the private sector to be transferred and used by law enforcement, and due to a lack of transparency, it is likely that there are many more instances the public is not yet aware of.[305]

The use of FRT and other biometric technology by governments is only a small fraction of its use in the private industry, with dozens of companies in the United States alone producing products for private and law enforcement use.[306] The exponential growth of FRT applications and other biometric technology has led to some legislative proposals, but much of this industry remains largely unregulated.[307]

The common thread of these critiques is that the perceived objectivity arising from computer code is both false and dangerous, and computer models can be as biased as any other human enterprise.[308] Further, without oversight, artificial intelligence systems could similarly reify existing structural bias or exacerbate inequalities, all the while claiming to be data-driven, neutral, and objective.[309] In the specific context of facial recognition technology, the questions become even more pointed.[310] For example, on the morning of April 25, 2019, Brown University student Amara K. Majeed awoke to death threats.[311] Majeed's photo had been associated with the name of a suspected terrorist, tied to an attack in Sri Lanka that killed more than 250 people.[312] Because of an error in the facial recognition software used to investigate the attack, Majeed's photo was connected to the suspected terrorist's name, ultimately putting both Majeed and her family in danger for a crime she never committed.[313]

Despite the lack of legislative restraints, private companies have faced pressure over the use of FRT. And companies like IBM, Amazon, and Microsoft have halted or scaled back on the production of FRT products for law enforcement uses.[314] Several musicians and festivals are coming   together   to   call   to   an   end   to concert promoters

---

[304] Id.
[305] Id.
[306] Turley, *supra* note 141, at 2189.
[307] Id. at 2190.
[308] Andrew Guthrie Ferguson, *Facial Recognition and the Fourth Amendment*, 105 Minn. L. Rev. 1105, 1167 (2021).
[309] Id. at 1168.
[310] Id.
[311] Id.
[312] Id.
[313] Id.
[314] Turley, *supra* note 141, at 2190.

using facial recognition at venues and music festivals.[315] Tom Morello of Rage Against The Machine, Glitch Mob's Speedy Ortiz, and a growing number of dozens of other artists and festivals have teamed up with digital rights activist group, Fight For the Future, in a campaign to call out Ticketmaster and its parent company, Live Nation, as well as other venues for using facial recognition on concert goers.[316] The group of artists cite "dangers to their fans in the form of police harassment including—misidentification, deportation, arrests for outstanding charges during an event and drug use during an event, discrimination at their concerts, and fans in a permanent government database"—all very valid concerns.[317]

A growing body of research points to systematic inaccuracy and bias issues in biometric technologies, which pose disproportionate risks to non-white individuals.[318] A recent report by the National Institute of Standards and Technology on facial recognition tools found that Black, Brown, and Asian individuals were up to 100 times more likely to be misidentified than white male faces.[319] At a time when Americans are demanding that we address systemic racism in law enforcement, the use of facial recognition technology is a step in the wrong direction.[320]

Another underlying issue in most FRT applications is the lack of consent. Currently, there is a class action lawsuit involving Microsoft and Amazon.[321] According to the plaintiffs, both companies did not seek consent from Illinois residents before using facial recognition technology to store and analyze biometric information.[322] Specifically, Amazon is accused of scanning the faces of users who upload images to Prime Photo.[323] This is a photo storage application that allows users to store their

---

[315] Aaron Smith, *Jet Blue will Test Facial Recognition for Boarding,* CNN BUSINESS (May 31, 2017, 11:01 AM), https://money.cnn.com/2017/05/31/technology/jetblue-facial-recognition/index.html.

[316] *Id.*

[317] *Id.*

[318] https://www.markey.senate.gov/news/press-releases/senators-markey-merkley-lead-colleagues-on-legislation-to-ban-government-use-of-facial-recognition-other-biometric-technology.

[319] *Id.*

[320] *Id.*

[321] *Microsoft and Amazon Sued over Facial Recognition Technology,* ICT Monitor Worldwide, (May 2021), https://www.reuters.com/article/dataprivacy-facialrecognition/microsoft-amazon-must-face-facial-recognition-data-suits-idUSL1N2LE215.

[322] *Id.*

[323] *Id.*

personal images in the cloud.[324] As for Microsoft, the company is said to have used facial recognition technology on residents in Illinois through a partnership with ride-sharing giant Uber.[325] Plaintiffs allege that Microsoft took data from bio authentication for the Uber application.[326] The suit alleges, however, that Ubers Real Time ID Check, unbeknownst to drivers, works by providing a picture of the individual to Microsoft's API,[327] which then extracts the drivers' facial biometrics to build a geometric template that is then compared against the template from their original picture.[328] Per the suit, Microsoft failed to obtain proper consent and provide required disclosures to Illinois Uber drivers before collecting and storing their biometric data.[329]

V. Existing State Laws

Throughout the nation there is total lack of comprehensive legislation in the area of FRT. Only a very small number of states have enacted FRT legislation. In 2018, Illinois, Washington, and Texas enacted privacy laws impacting biometric technologies.[330] More recently, California enacted privacy laws impacting biometric technology.[331] And, each state with privacy laws limiting biometric technology classify "biometric identifiers" differently. Illinois, for example, describes "biometric identifiers" as a retina or iris scan, fingerprint, voiceprint, or scan of hand or face geometry.[332] Surprisingly, Illinois excludes commonly used biometric identifiers including basic demographic information; physical descriptors such as height, weight, and eye color; photographs; and most information collected from patients in a healthcare setting.[333] Washington State's exclusions are similar to Illinois', but specifically exclude information generated from photographs and videos, such as the facial geometry data collected by Facebook from uploaded user

---

[324] *Id.*
[325] *Id.*
[326] *Id.*
[327] "API" is application programming interface. This is a web service which allow developers to add functionality to client applications.
[328] *Id.*
[329] *Id.*
[330] 740 Ill. Comp. Stat. 14/15 (2022); Tex. Bus. & Com. Code Ann. § 503.001 (2022); Wash. Rev. Code § 19.375.010 (2022).
[331] Cal. Civ. Code § 1798.100 (2022).
[332] 740 Ill. Comp. Stat. 14/10 (2022).
[333] *Id.*

photos.[334] New Hampshire also has a bill pending which would prohibit the use of facial recognition technology.[335]

Some States without facial recognition technology statutes have established commissions to review the need for such legislation. For example, in March 2020, the Maryland legislature created a task force on Facial Recognition Privacy Protection.[336]

VI. LITIGATION

Unlike its European counterpart, the United States lacks regulation at the federal level and has only a few states laws regulating the use of facial recognition technology. What is curious is that this difference in existing regulation of facial recognition technology has an inverse relationship with each country's appetite for development of the facial recognition systems. In 2016, the European Union invested €3.2 billion and Asia invested €6.5 billion into developing AI while, in comparison, the United States invested a staggering €12.1 billion. Yet, the United States is far behind in creating or enacting sufficient regulation or laws to guide the ethical development of facial recognition.[337]

In *Patel v. Facebook,*[338] the Court found that the invasion of privacy by facial recognition technology is a concrete harm. The plaintiffs in *Patel* argued that the collection of their biometric data, specifically photographs, without their consent or knowledge violated BIPA.[339] While Facebook initially vehemently denied that there was any harm, the company subsequently chose to settle a separate class-action lawsuit that alleged that the company had violated BIPA by collecting biometric data without the consent or knowledge of its users, and by failing to provide any notice to its users.[340] Soon after settlement of the Facebook lawsuit, Google was also sued for violating BIPA's requirement that a company

---

[334]Wash. Rev. Code Ann. § 19.375.010 (2021).

[335] 2021 Bill Text NH H.B. 499 (January 2021).

[336] 2021 Bill Text MD S.B. 587 (March 2021).

[337] *Id.*

[338] Patel v. Facebook Inc., 290 F. Supp. 3d 948 (N.D. Cal. 2018).

[339] *Id.* at 950.

[340] Sarah Chun, *Facial Recognition Technology: A Call for the Creation of A Framework Combining Government Regulation and A Commitment to Corporate Responsibility*, 21 N.C. J. L. & Tech. 99, 119–20 (2020).

must obtain written consent from users to collect, store, and use their personal data.[341]

VII.   THE NEED FOR FEDERAL LEGISLATION

With respect to federal law, there is currently no regulation of commercial use of facial recognition technology nor governmental use of technology. The current federal comprehensive act that has been proposed   is   the *Commercial Facial Recognition Privacy Act of 2019* (CFRPA),[342] which like state law, only regulates commercial use of facial   recognition   technology. The   CFRPA   specifically   exempts governmental use of this technology.[343]

On March 14, 2019, the United States Senate introduced the Commercial Facial Recognition Privacy Act, which would, among other things, require companies to first obtain explicit user consent before collecting   any facial recognition data.[344]   Interestingly,   even   some companies that are themselves developers of facial recognition software are encouraging regulation.[345]   Most notable among these is Amazon, which has proposed and drafted a bill that it has lobbied Congress to adopt. Other   organizations,   including   the   ACLU,   oppose   the   very   use of facial recognition technology because of what they believe to be inherent biases.[346]

Another federal law that could potentially cover some aspects of biometric   data   is   the   Stored   Communication   Act.[347]   The Stored Communications   Act   (SCA),[348]   a   component   of   the   broader

---

[341] *Id.*

[342] Commercial Facial Recognition Privacy Act of 2019, S. 847, 116th Cong. (2019), https://www.congress.gov/bill/116th-congress/senate-bill/847/text [https://perma.cc/G46D-MUVJ].

[343] Tate Ducker, *Orwell's 1984 "Big Brother" Concept and the Governmental Use of Facial Recognition Technology: A Call to Action for Regulation to Protect Privacy Rights*, 8 Belmont L. Rev. 600, 610 (2021).

[344] Elizabeth A. Rowe, *Regulating Facial Recognition Technology in the Private Sector*, 24 Stan. Tech. L. Rev. 1, 7 (2020).

[345] *Id.*

[346] *Id.*

[347] *Id.*

[348] Electronic Communications Privacy Act of 1986, Pub. L. No. 99-508, § 201, 100 Stat. 1848, 1860-68 (codified as amended at 18 U.S.C. §§ 2701-2711); *see also* Orin S. Kerr, *A User's Guide to the Stored Communications Act, and a Legislator's Guide to Amending It*, 72 GEO. WASH. L. REV. 1208, 1208 n.1 (2004) (noting the common reference to Title II of the Electronic Communications Privacy Act as the "Stored Communications Act ").

Electronic Communications Privacy Act (ECPA),[349] is the primary federal source of online privacy protections, but it is more than twenty years old. The Stored Communication Act mandates that "a person or entity providing an electronic communication service [("ECS")] to the public shall not knowingly divulge to any person or entity the contents of a communication while in electronic storage by that service."[350] Classification of an ECS is "context sensitive: the key is the provider's role with respect to a particular copy of a particular communication, rather than the provider's status in the abstract."[351]

While it is not clear that the statute would apply, an argument can be made that it does cover biometric data because of its "any transfer of . . . data" language.[352] On the other hand, one could argue that the "transfer" is not being made as part of a "communication."[353] For example, the data is simply being collected and stored by the company (e.g., Facebook) and is not used for communication between users in the same sense that Facebook Messenger works (i.e., a chat room).[354] There are, however, some scenarios where facial recognition allows users to simply communicate. The iPhone has a feature, for example, called Animoji that creates a cartoon animal/figure that mirrors your voice and facial expressions.[355] Further, Snapchat allows users to send photos back and forth to communicate.[356]

Congressional interest in passing biometric regulation has been high. On March 14, 2019, the United States Senate introduced the Commercial Facial Recognition Privacy Act, which, if passed, would require companies to first obtain explicit user consent before collecting

---

[349] Electronic Communications Privacy Act of 1986, Pub. L. No 99-508, 100 Stat. 1848 (codified as amended at 18 U.S.C. §§ 2510-2522, 2701-2712, 3121-3126).
[350] Electronic Communications Privacy Act of 1986, Pub. L. No. 99-508, § 201, 100 Stat. 1848, 1860-68 (codified as amended at 18 U.S.C. §§ 2701-2711); *see also* Orin S. Kerr, *A User's Guide to the Stored Communications Act, and a Legislator's Guide to Amending It*, 72 GEO. WASH. L. REV. 1208, 1208 n.1 (2004) (noting the common reference to Title II of the Electronic Communications Privacy Act as the "Stored Communications Act ").
[351] Republic of the Gambia v. Facebook, Inc., 567 F. Supp. 3d 291 (D.D.C. 2021), *vacated in part sub nom*, Republic of Gambia v. Facebook, Inc., 575 F. Supp. 3d 8 (D.D.C. 2021), *reconsideration denied sub nom*, Republic of Gambia v. Meta Platforms, Inc., No. MC 20-36 (JEB), 2022 WL 621397 (D.D.C. Mar. 3, 2022).
[352] Elizabeth A. Rowe, *Regulating Facial Recognition Technology in the Private Sector*, 24 Stan. Tech. L. Rev. 1, 35 (2020).
[353] *Id.*; 18 U.S.C. § 2510(12).
[354] *Id.* at 36.
[355] *Id.*
[356] *Id.*

any facial recognition data. It would also require notice that the technology is being utilized while informing about its capabilities and limits.[357]

On June 26, 2020, Oregon's U.S. Senator Jeff Merkley, along with U.S. Senator Edward J. Markey (D-MA) and Representatives Pramila Jayapal (D-WA-07), Ayanna Pressley (D-MA-07), Rashida Tlaib (D-MI-13), and Katherine Clark (D-MA-05), have announced the introduction of bicameral legislation to stop government use of biometric technology, including facial recognition tools. The Facial Recognition and Biometric Technology Moratorium Act[358] responds to reports that federal and local law enforcement entities have engaged with facial recognition companies and follows recent pledges by leading technology companies to pause their sale of facial recognition tools to law enforcement.[359] Specifically, the Act would (1) place a prohibition on the use of facial recognition technology by federal entities, which can only be lifted with an act of Congress; (2) place a prohibition on the use of other biometric technologies, including voice recognition, gait recognition, and recognition of other immutable physical characteristics, by federal entities, which can only be lifted with an act of Congress; (3) condition federal grant funding to state and local entities, including law enforcement, on those entities enacting their own moratoria on the use of facial recognition and biometric technology; (4) prohibit the use of federal dollars for biometric surveillance systems; (5) prohibit the use of information collected via biometric technology in violation of the Act in any judicial proceedings; (6) create a private right of action for individuals whose biometric data is used in violation of the Act and allow for enforcement by state Attorneys General; and (7) allow states and localities to enact their own laws regarding the use of facial recognition and biometric technologies.

The proposed legislation includes a handful of provisions restricting federal law enforcement's use of facial recognition technologies, new tools that combine complex algorithms with a broad database of faces often scraped from social media without the user's consent to identify potential suspects. The bill would place a prohibition on the use of facial recognition technology by federal entities, which can only be lifted with an act of Congress; place a prohibition on the use of other biometric technologies, including voice recognition, gait

---

[357] Id.
[358] Facial Recognition and Biometric Technology Moratorium Act of 2020, S. 4084, 116th Cong. (2020).
[359] Id.

recognition, and recognition of other immutable physical characteristics, by federal entities, which can only be lifted with an act of Congress; condition federal grant funding to state and local entities, including law enforcement, on those entities enacting their own moratoria on the use of facial recognition and biometric technology; prohibit the use of federal dollars for biometric surveillance systems; prohibit the use of information collected via biometric technology in violation of the Act in any judicial proceedings; create a private right of action for individuals whose biometric data is used in violation of the Act and allow for enforcement by state Attorneys General; and allow states and localities to enact their own laws regarding the use of facial recognition and biometric technologies.[360]

Unfortunately, to date, there remains no comprehensive federal legislation on this issue.

IX. CONCLUSION

Piecemeal state-by-state regulations for companies that do business nationally are, at the very least, inefficient and burdensome. Consequently, leaders of some of America's largest businesses are advocating for federal privacy legislation to govern the collection, use and sharing of personal data across industry sectors in order to preempt state legislation. The proposed Consumer Privacy Legislation Framework, drafted by the Business Roundtable on behalf of the CEOs of some of America's largest companies, would encompass consumer data that is held by the organization and identifies or is identifiable to a natural, individual person. This information may include but is not limited to name and other identifying information, such as government-issued identification numbers, and personal information derived from a specific device that reasonably could be used to identify a specific individual. Like the California Consumer Privacy Act, the legislation would provide consumers with a right of access, a right to opt out, and a right to deletion over their personal data that is collected and stored by companies.

With the vast number of concerns and privacy issues surrounding facial recognition software and its use, cities around the U.S. will face more dilemmas as they attempt to tackle these issues. The use of facial recognition technology is only increasing around the world, and in almost all areas of our society. It can be a powerful and helpful tool when used correctly, but it can also cause harm when with privacy and security issues

---

[360] https://www.merkley.senate.gov/news/press-releases/merkley-colleagues-introduce-legislation-to-ban-government-use-of-facial-recognition-and-other-biometric-technology-2020.

arise. Thus, federal lawmakers will have to balance this and determine when and how facial technology should be used and when and if limitations should be placed to protect issues of consent and reliability.

STRIVING FOR PIZZA FOR EVERYONE OR JUST MORE CALIFORNIA VAMPIRES?

CHRISTOPHER L. THOMPSON*

I. BACKGROUND AND HISTORY: A MAN WANTED A PIZZA

In 2016, a blind individual named Guillermo Robles sued Domino's Pizza LLC (hereinafter "Domino's") under the Americans with Disabilities Act for failing to design its website and mobile app to be compatible with the screen-reading software Robles uses to access the internet. Prior to filing his suit, Robles made several attempts to order pizza via Domino's online and app-based ordering systems. However, neither the app nor the online system was compatible with Robles' screen reader and his attempts proved unsuccessful.[1]

Robles' suit was filed in the United States District Court for the Central District of California.[2] Subsequently, Domino's filed a motion to dismiss which was granted by the Court and Robles appealed to the United States Court of Appeals for the 9th Circuit.

The Ninth Circuit overturned the lower court's decision and ruled in Robles' favor, reinstating his lawsuit against Domino's. Domino's then filed a petition for certiorari with the United States Supreme Court, setting the stage for one of the more important Supreme Court "accessibility" cases in recent times.

That stage would remain empty. For reasons that will never be wholly understood, given the significance of the issue, the Court denied certiorari on October 7, 2019. Now, instead of a concrete answer, businesses are left to speculate to what extent the ADA applies to their internet and application-based endeavors. This is because the Court's denial carries zero precedential value.[3] It is merely a manifestation of the "at-will" nature of the Court's jurisdiction. What follows will surely be years of waiting as Robles' suit meanders its way through the court system while businesses are now left in the wilderness to discern what the ADA

---

* J.D., Assistant Professor, Sam Houston State University.
[1] Robles v. Domino's Pizza, LLC, 2017 WL 1330216 (C.D. California) (citing Robles' Complaint).
[2] Robles v. Domino's Pizza, LLC, 2017 WL 1330216 (C.D. California) (citing Robles' Complaint); David Raizman, *Federal Court in Los Angeles Dismisses Website Accessibility Claims*, National Law Review, March 24, 2017, https://www.natlawreview.com/article/federal-court-los-angeles-dismisses-website-accessibility-claims.
[3] *See U.S. v. Shubert*, 75 S.Ct. 277, 348 U.S. 222 (U.S., 1955).

requires of their websites and mobile applications. However, the Ninth Circuit's opinion provides some degree of guidance— as does the Supreme Court's decision to not review the case.

A. The Americans with Disabilities Act

The Americans with Disabilities Act ("ADA"), enacted in 1990, acts as continuing force for inclusion and mechanism for eradicating "discrimination against individuals with disabilities."[4] The Act requires business and governmental entities to make accommodations rendering their facilities accessible to those with disabilities.[5] However, the application of the Act to technologies that did not exist in their present form in the late 1980's when the Act was drafted is a continuing legal issue with an immeasurable impact on business and entrepreneurship.[6] This is further complicated by the role the United States Department of Justice ("DOJ") occupies as the body charged with issuing any and all regulations necessary to fully implement the ADA.[7]

There should be little doubt that the DOJ was handed a tough assignment by Congress when it made the Attorney General responsible for promulgating any regulations necessary to wholly implement the ADA. Title III of the Act is concerned with what it terms "public accommodations" consisting of businesses open to the public and their accessibility to disabled persons. The Act charges the DOJ with assisting those required to comply with the act and enforcing Title III.[8] However burdensome it might be, those responsibilities do belong to the DOJ and its total failure to adopt and publish web accessibility regulations has left business owners and other places of public accommodation to their own devices.

The DOJ's failure to act regarding potential internet discrimination is rather puzzling for many reasons, but foremost among them is that over a decade ago, in 2010, it recognized the need to act and adopt regulations establishing online accessibility standards.[9] What followed was years of inaction before the proposed rulemaking notice was

---

[4] 42 U.S.C. § 12101 (b)(1); *Olmstead v. L.C. ex Rel. Zimring*, 527 U.S. 581, 589 (1999).
[5] 42 U.S.C. § 12101 (b) (1-4).
[6] *E.g.* Cullen v. Netflix, 880 F. Supp. 2d 1017 (N.D. Cal., 2012); *National Federation of the Blind v. Scribd, Inc.*, 97 F. Supp. 3d 565 (D. Vt., 2017).
[7] *See* 42 U.S.C. 12186 (b).
[8] 42 U.S.C 126, Subchapter III (Title III); *United States v. AMC Entertainment, Inc.*, F.3d 760 (9th Cir. 2008).
[9] U.S. DEPARTMENT OF JUSTICE, 28 C.F.R. parts 35-36, https://www.ada.gov/anprm2010/web%20anprm_2010.htm

withdrawn altogether in 2017.[10] Even more puzzling is that this years-long span of inaction covered parts of two different presidential administrations and spanned four different Attorneys General.[11]

In the absence of clear rules and standards, the only avenue available to provide any guidance to businesses and consumers are consumer lawsuits challenging the level of accessibility of a business's internet endeavors. As one can easily imagine, this is a very costly method of learning. In 2019, over 2,200 of these lawsuits were filed in Federal courts nationwide.[12] These lawsuits are made possible, as a practical matter, because the ADA has a several features which, for better or worse, can encourage litigation.

First, the ADA does not require any type of pre-suit demand or notice be given to the alleged violator.[13] It is not uncommon for an ADA defendant to first learn of their alleged failure to comply with the Act when they are served with a suit that has been brought against them.[14]

Second, the ADA provides for the potential recovery of attorney's fees by successful plaintiffs.[15] Critics allege that this encourages attorneys to bring cases on behalf of clients over even the most minor deviations or shortcomings under the Act.[16]

Third, an ADA compliance suit only requires a plaintiff to prove one instance of non-compliance to prevail.[17] Further, because the nature of a violation is often tangible or measurable, non-compliance can be simple to prove.[18] In an online accessibility suit, the lack of any tangible measure of compliance prevents businesses from offering evidence in its defense.

---

[10] *Id.* (includes notice of withdrawal).

[11] U.S DEPARTMENT OF JUSTICE, https://www.justice.gov/ag/historical-bios; https://www.whitehouse.gov/about-the-white-house/presidents.

[12] Kristina M. Launey and Minh N. Vu, *The Curve Has Flattened for Federal Website Accessibility Lawsuits,* SEYFARTH (April 29, 2020), https://www.adatitleiii.com/2020/04/the-curve-has-flattened-for-federal-website-accessibility-lawsuits.

[13] James O'Brien J.D., *What Businesses Need to Know When Defending Against ADA Lawsuits,* RETAIL MINDED (June 28, 2017), https://www.retailminded.com/what-businesses-need-to-know-when-defending-against-ada-lawsuits/#.YBrzT3dFyiM

[14] *Id.*

[15] 42 U.S.C. 12205.

[16] Jason Grant, *"Curve Flattens" for ADA Website-Accessibility Lawsuit Filings, Seyfarth Report Says,* NEW YORK LAW JOURNAL (May 6, 2020), https://www.law.com/newyorklawjournal/2020/05/06/curve-flattens-for-ada-website-accessibility-lawsuit-filings-seyfarth-report-says/?slreturn=20200522135947.

[17] James O'Brien J.D., *What Businesses Need to Know When Defending Against ADA Lawsuits,* RETAIL MINDED (June 28, 2017), https://retailminded.com/what-businesses-need-to-know-when-defending-against-ada-lawsuits/#.YBrzT3dFyiM.

[18] *Id.*

Finally, there is no requirement that a suit be filed by a good-faith plaintiff, or even someone who has ever visited or would normally even attempt to visit the place of public accommodation they are suing. For example, New York City is home to a rather notorious serial ADA plaintiff named Zoltan Hirsch who, as of 2017, had filed almost two hundred suits against businesses in his home state.[19] Mr. Hirsch is a double amputee who goes "street by street and block by block, looking for places that can't let him inside."[20] Hirsch claims he is merely fighting for the rights of disabled Americans.[21] However, it is hard to not doubt the sincerity of a man who makes it a practice to avoid suing businesses near his home while seeking out potential defendants in wealthier neighborhoods.[22] For some, their doubt as to Hirsch's sincerity is redoubled by the fact that, as a practicing Hasidic Jewish man without feet, he has sued a strip club, a seafood restaurant, and even a spa over the accessibility of one of its pedicure stations.[23]

B. Websites and the ADA

For over two decades the DOJ has maintained the position that the ADA applies to the websites of public accommodations.[24] What it has not done is adopt any standard of compliance or promulgate any rules to be used when designing web-based elements.

Advocates for the disabled maintain website accessibility is a continuing issue faced by visually impaired people as they attempt to use the internet and internet-based applications.[25] At least one survey of websites seems to bear that out. Web Accessibility In Mind (WebAim), an organization devoted to increasing web accessibility for the disabled,

---

[19] Aiden Pink, *"Disabled New Yorker has Sued 195 Businesses Since 2010"*, FORWARD (Sept. 18, 2017), https://forward.com/fast-forward/383097/disabled-new-yorker-has-sued-195-businesses-since-2010/.

[20] Isabel Vincent and Melissa Klein, *Amputee's Sue Spree Against Businesses that Aren't Handicapped Accessible*, N.Y. POST (June 5, 2011) https://nypost.com/2011/06/05/brooklyn-amputees-sue-spree-against-businesses-that-arent-handicapped-accessible/.

[21] *Id.*

[22] *Id.*

[23] *Id.*

[24] *See e.g., Applicability of the Americans with Disabilities Act to Private Internet Sites: Hearing before the House Subcommittee on the Constitution of the House Committee on the Judiciary,* 106th Cong. 2d Sess. 65-010 (2000); 75 Fed. Reg. 43460-01 (July 6, 2010).

[25] *See e.g. Hugo Martin, Lawsuits Targeting Business Websites Over ADA Violations are on the Rise*, LOS ANGELES TIMES (Nov. 11, 2018), https://www.latimes.com/business/la-fi-hotels-ada-compliance-20181111-story.html (quoting Jeff Thom, former president of and government affairs director for the California Council of the Blind).

began an annual accessibility analysis of the top 1 million home pages on the internet in 2019.[26] The premise of these studies is to compare the aforementioned 1 million pages along with a sampling of some interior pages of the same sites with the World Wide Web Consortium's (W3C) Web Content Accessibility Guidelines 2.0 Level AA Success Criteria better known as WCAG 2.0.[27] WCAG 2.0 is often put forth as a potential standard for web accessibility under the ADA and was, for a time, the actual standard proposed under the DOJ's Notice of Proposed Rulemaking prior to its withdrawal in 2017.[28]

The results of the two annual surveys were eye opening because the sites sampled were, on the whole, riddled with "errors" under WCAG 2.0 standards.[29] In 2019, the first year the survey was completed, 97.8 % of the sampled home pages had "errors" running afoul of WACG 2.0.[30] Perhaps more disturbing to those fighting for web accessibility should be that the next year that percentage had increased to 98.1 %.[31] Equally disturbing should be that, on average, each page had more than sixty errors.[32]

C. Golden State for Plaintiffs and Lawyers?

There is at least some validity to claims that "professional plaintiffs" and the firms representing them are targeting California at a higher rate than other states. However, California is far from the only state experiencing a high volume of these suits. The total number of ADA suits filed in federal courts in 2017 bears this out. In 2017, there were 2,933 ADA suits filed in California, 1,614 in Florida, and 1,265 in New York.[33] There were only 4,961 total ADA suits filed in the rest of the country combined that year.[34]

The high proportion of suits filed in these three states have been attributed to a few different factors. California state law allows for two

---

[26] WEBAIM, *The WebAIM Million* (Mar 31, 2022), https://www.webaim.org/projects/million/#intro. (It is worth noting that sites surveyed are drawn in large part from the *Majestic Million* which includes prominent sites such as Google.com, Facebook.com, and Apple.com).
[27] *Id.*
[28] U.S. Department of Justice, 28 C.F.R. parts 35-36.
[29] WEBAIM, *supra*, note 26.
[30] *Id.*
[31] *Id.*
[32] *Id.*
[33] United States Courts, *Just the Facts: Americans with Disabilities Act* (July 12, 2018), https://www.uscourts.gov/news/2018/07/12/just-facts-americans-disabilities-act.
[34] *Id.*

additional avenues for accessibility claims to be levied against a public accommodation. In California, any violation of the ADA is also a violation of the Unruh Act and section 54 of the California Civil Code.[35] These claims may be brought in conjunction with an ADA accessibility suit in federal court and a successful plaintiff is automatically entitled to recover at least $4,000 in damages and up to treble the plaintiff's actual damages plus attorney's fees under the Unruh Act and $1,000 plus attorney's fees under section 54.[36] New York, on the other hand, only allows for an award of $500 in damages, however, due to the advanced age of many of the buildings in the state, there is the possibility of one plaintiff successfully recovering multiple awards.[37] Florida's number of suits has been explained as the result of laws which authorize "tester" standing— allowing individuals to sue multiple defendants even absent any intent to patronize the business."[38]

California remains especially fertile ground and examples of professional plaintiffs and the attorneys who represent them are not difficult to find. [39] This fertility is at least partially due to the previously mentioned section 54 and the Unruh Act and their statutory minimum damages.[40] The Unruh Act makes any ADA violation a violation of the Unruh Act. An Unruh Act carries a minimum award of $4,000 and the possibility of treble damages, "plus attorney's fees for each ADA violation."[41] Plaintiffs are allowed to bring alleged section 54 violations

---

[35] Cal. Civ. Code §§ 51, 51.5, 52, 54.

[36] *Id.*; *see also,* Martin, *supra* note 25.

[37] Aiden Pink, *Disabled New Yorker has Sued 195 Businesses Since 2010*, FORWARD (Sept. 18, 2017), https://www.forward.com/fast-forward/383097/disabled-new-yorker-has-sued-195-businesses-since-2010/; Isabel Vincent and Melissa Klein, *Amputee's Sue Spree Against Businesses that Aren't Handicapped Accessible*, N.Y. POST (June 5, 2011) https://www.nypost.com/2011/06/05/brooklyn-amputees-sue-spree-against-businesses-that-arent-handicapped-accessible/.

[38] *See* Katie Lagrone, "Federal Judge: Florida's Most Prolific ADA Plaintiff did not Sue in Bad-Faith", ABC ACTION NEWS (January 17, 2017), https://www.abcactionnews.com/news/florida-investigative-team/federal-judge-floridas-most-prolific-ada-plaintiff-did-not-sue-in-bad-faith (story of a small business owner's litigation with a plaintiff who, as a self-described "tester," brought over 1,000 accessibility suits in Florida in a three-year span). In contrast, the Tenth Circuit does not allow "tester" standing, holding that "testers" suffer no injury in fact, and therefore lack standing to sue; *Laufer v. Looper,* 22 F. 4th 871 (10th Cir. 2022).

[39] *See e.g. Cullen v. Netflix*, 880 F. Supp. 2d 1017 (N.D. Cal., 2012); *National Federation of the Blind v. Target Corp.,* 452 F. Supp. 2d 946 (N.D. Cal., 2006); *Weyer v. Twentieth Century Fox Film Corp.,* 198 F.3d 1104 (9th Cir., 2000).

[40] Cal. Civ. Code §§ 51, 51.5, 52.

[41] Martin, *supra* note 25.

and Unruh violations in conjunction with their federal ADA suits.[42] Attorney Thomas Frankovich, who has been described as a master of accessibility litigation, and his legal practice, are often held up as examples of the predatory nature of California's ADA plaintiff's bar and professional plaintiffs.[43] As of 2017, Frankovich had filed over 2,000 ADA suits on behalf of his clients.[44] However, critics point to the fact that over 1,000 of those case were filed on the behalf of approximately twelve clients as proof of the predatory nature of Frankovich and his clients.[45] A client with 100 different suits who only received the state minimum of $4,000 would bring in $400,000 while Frankovich would receive his normal billing rate of $500 per hour.[46] Over fifteen years ago a federal judge took Frankovich and two of his "professional plaintiffs" to task and found that the "[p]laintiffs and their attorneys ha[d] participated in a pattern of abusive litigation, bordering on extortionate shysterism" necessitating action by the Court to protect the judicial system and the public at large from the plaintiffs and their counsel.[47]

In defense of attorneys like Mr. Frankovich, they do represent real clients. At least one California attorney has been accused of filing hundreds of accessibility suits on behalf of fictional persons known as "ghost clients."[48] Also deeply troubling to critics is the fact that over 80%

---

[42] Tom McNichol, *Targeting ADA Violators*, CALIFORNIA LAWYER (Jan. 2012) http://www.cabaretdesigners.com/ wp-content/uploads/2021/06/Targeting_ADA_Violators_April_30_2012.pdf

[43] Katherine Prankow, *Advocates for the Disabled, or Extortionist Vampires? Chapter 383 Attempts to Prevent Plaintiffs' Attorneys from Bleeding Small Businesses Dry*, 44 MCGEORGE L. REV. 559 (2013) (citing Ron Russell, *Wheelchairs of Fortune*, S.F. WEEKLY (July 25, 2007), http://www.sfweekly.com/2007/07/25/news/wheelchairs-of-fortune).

[44] Glenda Anderson, *Numerous Businesses in Willits, Ukiah Face New Legal Threats Over Disabled Access*, THE PRESS DEMOCRAT (July 27, 2017), https://www.pressdemocrat.com/article/news/numerous-businesses-in-willits-ukiah-face-new-legal-threats-over-disabled/?sba=AAS.

[45] Prankow, *supra* note 43.

[46] Tom McNichol, *Targeting ADA Violators*, Cal. Law., Jan. 2012 at 20. (Frankovich's stated billing rate as of 2012 when McNichol's work was published. One can likely assume it has increased, however, for illustration purposes the 2012 rate was used).

[47] Molski v. Mandarin Touch Restaurant, 359 F. Supp. 2d 924, 937-38 (C.D. Cal., 2005).

[48] Scott Schwebke, *These "Ghost" Legal Clients Are Shaking Down Mom-and-Pop Businesses Under the Guise of Disability Rights*, ORANGE COUNTY REGISTER (July 21, 2019), https://www.ocregister.com/2019/07/21/these-ghost-legal-clients-are-shaking-down-mom-and-pop-businesses-under-the-guise-of-disability-rights/.

of the 2,258 accessibility cases filed in the state in 2018 were filed by attorneys from only ten law firms.[49]

D. Drive-by Suits Morph into Surf-by Suits

"Drive-by lawsuits" wherein a disabled person or their attorney literally drive around looking for businesses to file suit against have existed for years.[50] These hit-and-run lawsuits under the ADA are nothing new; they have existed for decades, however, they have morphed into what are now known as "surf-by" suits. In these new "surf-by suits" no one even has to leave their home to find a defendant. Instead, all a potential plaintiff need do is visit websites and use apps until he or she locates a possible accessibility shortcoming that will support a Title III claim.[51]

The crux of most website and app accessibility suits can be found in Title III of the ADA, which includes the general rule that:

> No individual shall be discriminated against on the basis of disability in the full and equal enjoyment of the goods, services, facilities, privileges, advantages, or accommodations of any place of public accommodation by any person who owns, leases (or leases to), or operates a place of public accommodation.[52]

Title III goes on to give specific definitions of discrimination, including what is known as the "auxiliary aids and services" section.[53] This title makes any failure by a place of public accommodation to ensure that no disabled person is excluded or treated differently from other people "because of the absence of auxiliary aids and services" is an act of discrimination under the Act. Courts have held that this provision requires owners and operators of places of public accommodation to actually provide any auxiliary aid or device necessary for persons with disabilities

---

[49] *See* Jason Taylor, *2018 ADA Website Accessibility Lawsuit Recap Report*, USABLENET (December 26, 2018), https://blog.usablenet.com/2018-ada-web-accessibility-lawsuit-recap-report.

[50] *See 60 Minutes: What's a "Drive by Lawsuit"?* (CBS television broadcast, Dec. 4, 2016).

[51] *See* Nathan V. Okelberry, *Monitor ADA Compliance To Prevent 'Surf-By' Lawsuits Against Your Website*, LOS ANGELES BUSINESS JOURNAL (July 19, 2019) https://www.bizjournals.com/losangeles/news/2019/07/29/monitorada-compliance-to-prevent-surf-by-lawsuits.html (using the term "surf-by").

[52] 42 U.S.C. § 12182(a).

[53] 42 U.S.C. § 12182(b)(2)(A)(iii).

to access the services of a place of public accommodation.[54] The DOJ has explained this duty further in its regulations implementing Title III by stating that public accommodations are obligated to "communicate effectively with customers who have disabilities concerning hearing, vision, or speech."[55] Title III further defines "public accommodation" by giving a list of various places such as restaurants, bars, theaters, grocery stores, law offices, and banks, among others, which are public accommodations for ADA purposes.[56] The list essentially covers any *place* a person might go as they carried on their day to day activities.[57]

E. Lack of Clear Standard

In 2010, the DOJ recognized a need for clear guidelines regarding website accessibility and began the rule-making process.[58] The DOJ went as far as releasing a proposed rulemaking notice indicating that the rules it ultimately adopted would be based on the World Wide Web Consortium's (W3C) Web Content Accessibility Guidelines 2.0 Level AA Success Criteria (better known as WCAG 2.0).[59] However, after seven fruitless years, the DOJ withdrew its proposed rulemaking notice altogether, announcing its intent to evaluate whether web accessibility regulations were even necessary.[60]

The immediate result of the DOJ's failure to act was a rash of ADA accessibility suits claiming websites were not accessible to disabled persons.[61] Since its withdrawal of the proposed rulemaking notice, the DOJ has faced repeated calls from members of both the House of

---

[54] Nat'l Fed'n of the Blind v. Target Corp., 452 F. Supp. 2d 946, 955 (N.D. Cal., 2006).
[55] *Id.* (citing 28 C.F.R. § 36.303(b)(2).
[56] 42 U.S.C. 12816(b).
[57] *See id.*
[58] U.S. Department of Justice, 28 C.F.R. parts 35-36; Samuel D. Levy and Martin S. Krezalek, *A Call for Regulation: The DOJ Ignored Website Accessibility Regulation and Enterprising Chaos Ensued,* NEW YORK LAW JOURNAL (2018).
[59] Web Content Accessibility Guidelines 2.0, W3C (Dec. 11, 2008), https://www.w3.org/TR/WCAG20.
[60] U.S. Department of Justice, 28 C.F.R. parts 35-36, https://www.ada.gov/anprm2010/web%20anprm_2010.htm; *see also,* Levy and Krezalek, *supra* note 58.
[61] Levy and Krezalek, *supra* note 58.

Representatives[62] and the Senate[63]to reconsider and get to work delineating website standards which would allow businesses to comply with the ADA.[64] These calls have been echoed by business groups such as the Credit Union National Association,[65] as well as a group consisting of eighteen state attorneys general joined by the Attorney General of Washington, D.C.[66]

In response to the House of Representatives letter, the DOJ responded with a two-page letter of its own in September of 2018.[67] This short letter is rather remarkable in its own right, despite its brevity, for several reasons. First, the DOJ states that the ADA applies to the websites of public accommodations while pointing out that it had made that decision "over 20 years ago."[68] Second, the letter goes on to state that the absence of any specific standard for web site accessibility does not excuse a public accommodation's failure to comply with the ADA.[69] Third, the DOJ dropped a bombshell by stating that compliance with a voluntary technical standard (obviously speaking of WCAG 2.0) "does not necessarily indicate compliance with the ADA."[70] Finally, the letter tosses the ball back to Congress by pointing out the legislative branch's ability to clarify all of the issues surrounding website accessibility simply by passing legislation.[71] Congress accepted the challenge and in 2020, *The Online Accessibility Act* was introduced, , but , did not pass, during the

---

[62] House of Rep. Letter to the Dept. of Justice Regarding Website Access Standards under the ADA, available at: https://www.cuna.org/uploadedFiles/Advocacy/Priorities/Removing_Barriers_Blog/ADA%20Final_06212018.pdf.

[63] Letter from Senators Grassley, Tillis, Cornyn, Rounds, Crapo, Ernst to Attorney General Jeff Sessions, dated September 4, 2018, https://www.judiciary.senate.gov/imo/media/doc/2018-10-04%20Grassley,%20Rounds,%20Tillis,%20Crapo,%20Cornyn,%20Ernst%20to%20Justice%20Dept.%20-%20ADA%20Website%20Accessibility.pdf.

[64] *Id.*

[65] *See* Credit Union Nat. Ass'n. Letter to Attorney General Barr, dated Feb. 19, 2019, https://www.venable.com/-media/cunalettertobarr.pdf?la=en&hash=D7E7CA05C6D74349391BD9CC002A74C4EAECA3D8

[66] *See* Letter from Group of State Attorneys General, dated July 19, 2018, https://www.cuna.org/uploadedFiles/Advocacy/ADAAGLetter71918.pdf.

[67] Assistant Attorney General Stephen E. Boyd's Letter to Congressman Budd, dated September 25, 2018, https://www.adatitleiii.com/wp-content/uploads/sites/121/2018/10/DOJ-letter-to-congress.pdf.

[68] *Id.*

[69] *Id.*

[70] *Id.*

[71] *Id.*

116th session.[72] In the next session, the bill was reintroduced on February 18, 2021 but it has not been passed as of yet.[73]

This lack of a clear standard has predictably resulted in a split among federal courts. The split is primarily over whether a public accommodation's site must have a nexus to a physical location in order to run afoul of Title III.[74] In California, where Mr. Robles filed suit against Dominos, the requirement of a physical nexus between a website and a physical location is firmly entrenched in local Ninth Circuit precedent.[75] In direct contrast, the First and Seventh Circuits have held that the ADA applies to non-physical locations regardless of the existence any connection to a physical location.[76] However, clearly the largest divide among the circuits came on April 7, 2021, created by the Eleventh Circuit's opinion in *Gil v. Winn Dixie*.[77]

In *Gil v. Winn Dixie,* the Eleventh Circuit considered an appeal by Winn Dixie of a trial court's denial of its motion for judgment on the pleadings.[78] A majority of the Court found that *Gil's* complaint about the inaccessibility of Winn Dixie's website for blind people such as himself did not implicate Title III of the ADA because a website is not a place of public accommodation.[79] The majority reached this conclusion by examining the statutory construction of the list of places deemed public accommodations by the Act and noting that all of the places deemed public

---

[72] Bureau of Internet Accessibility, *Congress Did Not Pass ADA Amendment Clarifying Web Accessibility Standards* (January 21, 2021), https://www.boia.org/blog/congress-did-not-pass-ada-amendment-clarifying-web-accessibility-standards.

[73] Press Release, Congressman Ted Budd, *Rep. Ted Budd Introduces Bipartisan Legislation To Stop Frivolous Lawsuits* (February 18, 2021), https://budd.house.gov/news/documentsingle.aspx?DocumentID=1060.

[74] *See e.g.,* National Assn. of the Deaf v. Netflix, 869 F. Supp. 2d 196, 200 (D. Mass., 2012) (not requiring a physical location or nexus between a website and some related physical location); *see also* Cullen v. Netflix, 880 F. Supp. 2d 1017, 1023-24 (N.D. Cal., 2012) (reiterating the Nineth Circuit's precedent requiring a nexus between a website and some physical location related to the public accommodation offered.)

[75] *See* Cullen v. Netflix, 880 F. Supp. 2d 1017, 1023-24 (N.D. Cal., 2012); *see also* Nat'l Fed'n of the Blind v. Target Corp., 452 F. Supp. 2d 946, 952 (N.D. Cal., 2006); *see also* Young v. Facebook, Inc., 790 F. Supp. 2d 1110, 1115 (N.D. Cal., 2010).

[76] *See* Carparts Distrib. Ctr., Inc., v. Auto Wholesaler's Ass'n of New England, 37 F.3d 12, 17 (1st Cir., 1994); *See also,* Doe v. Mutual of Omaha Ins. Co., 179 F.3d 557, 559 (7th Cir., 1999); *See also* Morgan v. Joint Admin. Bd., Ret. Plan of the Pillsbury Co. and Am. Fed'n of Grain Millers, AFL-CIO-CLC, 268 F.3d 456, 459(7th Cir., 2001).

[77] Joshua A. Stein and Shira M. Blank, *The Eleventh Circuit Finally Breaks its Silence on Website Accessibility-But Was Its Decision Worth the Wait?*, THE NATIONAL LAW REVIEW (Apr. 8, 2021), https://www.natlawreview.com /article/eleventh-circuit-finally-breaks-its-silence-website-accessibility-was-its-decision; Gil v. Winn Dixie Stores, Inc., 993 F.3d 1266 (11th Cir., 2021).

[78] Gil v. Winn Dixie Stores, Inc., 993 F.3d 1266 (11th Cir., 2021).

[79] *Id.* at 1277.

accommodation by the text of the ADA are "tangible, physical places" and that there are no examples of "intangible places or spaces, such as websites" listed.[80]   The majority noted that the rules of statutory construction left it no option because the language of the Act is unambiguous and it clearly does not mention or allude to non-physical places.[81]   Dissenting Judge Jill Pryor strenuously objected to the majority's holding in an extensive opinion.[82]   Her position was that the majority's narrow reading of the ADA betrayed the Act's sweeping intent.[83]

However, the precedential value of the Court's decision was extremely short-lived.[84]   In response to Mr. Gil's petition for a panel rehearing the Court agreed with Gill that it should have never decided the case because the issues became moot before the Court got around to deciding it.[85] This decision centered around the injunction granted by the district court giving rise to Winn Dixie's appeal.[86] For whatever reason, the appeal was not decided for several years during which time the interim the injunction expired naturally and, on the proverbially second glance, the Court held that the issue was rendered moot.[87] After finding the issue moot the Court vacated its opinion and judgment, dismissed Winn Dixie's appeal before remanding the case to the district court with instructions to dismiss the case as moot.[88]

II. ROBLES V. DOMINOS

A. Round 1: U.S. District Court

Against this backdrop, on September 1, 2016, Guillermo Robles filed suit against Dominos in the U.S. District Court for the Central District of California, alleging he had made several unsuccessful attempts to place orders via Dominos' website as well as its app.[89] He contends that these attempts were all unsuccessful because neither were accessible to him as

---

[80] *Id.*

[81] *Id.*

[82]*Id.* at 1284-1299.

[83] *Id.* at 1295.

[84] Gill v. Winn Dixie Stores, Inc., 21 F4th. 775, 776 (11th Cir., 2021).

[85] *Id.*

[86] *Id.*

[87] *Id.*

[88] *Id.*

[89] Robles v. Domino's Pizza, LLC, 2017 WL 1330216 (C.D. Cal. Jan. 15, 2019) (not designated for publication) (citing Robles' complaint).

a blind person in violation of Title III's "auxiliary aids and services" provisions.[90]

Robles' complaint alleges Domino's website was inaccessible because it was not compatible with the screen reader he uses for websites.[91] Likewise, he complained Domino's app was inaccessible to him because it was not compatible with the "Voice Over" program on his iPhone he normally uses when using apps.[92] In support of his allegations, Robles pointed out that neither Dominos' website nor app were WCAG 2.0 compliant when he unsuccessfully attempted to use them to order food.[93]

Eventually, Dominos moved for summary judgment asserting several theories, the most notable of which are 1) that its website and app were not public accommodations and 2) that even if its website and app are public accommodations and had fallen short of Title III's requirements, holding the company responsible would violate due process in light of the DOJ's total failure to promulgate the long-awaited accessibility standards.[94]

The Court made short work of Dominos' challenge to the applicability of the ADA to apps and websites by reiterating the jurisdictions' stance that the ADA is concerned with the "services of a place of public accommodation" not services rendered "in a place of public accommodation."[95] Further, the Court pointed to its clear precedent that a website serving to connect consumers to the goods or services of the physical location of a public accommodation are subject to Title III.[96] The Court also noted the incongruity of Dominos' position in the face of the plain language of the ADA.[97] The Court pointed out the company's stance would lead to the conclusion that public accommodations could freely discriminate against the disabled as long as they did not do so on their physical premises.[98] Additionally, the Court pointed out the DOJ's

---

[90] *Id.*

[91] *Id.*

[92] *Id.*

[93] *Id.*

[94] *Id.* (citing Domino's Motion for Summary Judgment/Dismissal/Stay).

[95] *Id.* (quoting Nat'l Fed'n of the Blind v. Target Corp, 452 F. Supp. 2d at 953).

[96] *See* Cullen v. Netflix, 880 F. Supp. 2d 1017, 1023-24 (N.D. Cal., 2012); *see also* Nat'l Fed'n of the Blind, 452 F.Supp.2d at 952; *see also Young v. Facebook, Inc.*, 790 F. Supp. 2d 1110, 1115 (N.D. Cal., 2010).

[97] *Id.* (quoting Nat'l Fed'n of the Blind, 452 F.Supp.2d at 953).

[98] *Id.* (quoting *Nat'l Fed'n of the Blind*, 452 F.Supp.2d at 953).

decades long stance that the websites of public accommodations must be ADA compliant.[99]

Domino's due process claim found considerably more traction with the Court and was ultimately found meritorious.[100] The Court cited the earlier Ninth Circuit opinion from *United States v. AMC Entertainment, Inc.* as support for its decision.[101]

AMC involved a suit brought by the DOJ against the movie theater company over "lines of sight" for customers using wheelchairs.[102] *AMC* successfully pointed out that holding it liable for failing to meet a standard regarding "lines of sight" for patrons in wheelchairs when the DOJ had never actually articulated a standard violated the company's due process rights.[103] The Court quoted a sister court in pointing out "[t]hose regulated by an administrative agency are entitled to know the rules by which the game will be played."[104]

In ruling on Dominos' motion for summary judgment, the trial court interpreted Robles' claims as hinging on his complaint which, in part, sought a ruling stating that all sites and apps belonging to public accommodations must by WCAG 2.0 compliant.[105] The Court found this request flagrantly in violation of due process in light of the Ninth Circuit's precedents from *AMC* and the DOJ's failure to offer "meaningful guidance on this topic."[106] The Court proceeded to dismiss all of Robles' causes of action in the suit.[107] However, in doing so, it utilized the *primary jurisdiction doctrine* which allowed the dismissals to issue without prejudice while awaiting the DOJ to complete its rulemaking process which, at least in theory, would provide the Court the tools necessary to resolve the case in the future.[108] The Court's order granting Dominos' motion for summary judgment concluded with a plea to Congress, the

---

[99] *Id.* (citing *Applicability of the Americans with Disabilities Act to Private Internet Sites: Hearing before the House Subcommittee on the Constitution of the House Committee on the Judiciary,* 106th Cong. 2d Sess. 65-010 (2000); 75 Fed. Reg. 43460-01 (July 6, 2010).

[100] *Id.*

[101] *Id.* (The Court also noted Robles' failure to address Domino's due process claim and the Court's authority to rule in Domino's favor solely due to said failure, however the Court went on to consider the merits of the issue); U.S. v. AMC Entertainment, Inc., 549 F.3d 760, 762-65 (9th Circuit, 2008).

[102] U.S. v. AMC Entertainment, Inc., 549 F.3d 760, 762-65 (9th Circuit, 2008).

[103] *Id.* at 770.

[104] *Id.* at 768 (quoting Alaska Prof'l Hunters Ass'n v. FAA, 177 F.3d 1030, 1035 (D.C. Cir., 1999).

[105] *Id.* (citing Robles' complaint ¶ 36).

[106] *Id.*

[107] *Id.*

[108] *Id.*

DOJ, and Attorney General to finally adopt minimum standards for accessibility for the benefit of all stakeholders.[109]

B. Round 2: Ninth Circuit

Mr. Robles appealed the district court's order granting Dominos' motion for summary judgment to the Ninth Circuit, where the Court subjected it to a full *de novo* review. The court's analysis focused on three questions.[110] The first issue considered by the court was whether the ADA does, in fact, apply to Dominos' website and app.[111] The second question analyzed by the court was assuming the ADA does cover the site and app, would it violate Dominos' right to due process in light of the DOJ's failure to adopt accessibility rules or standards.[112] Finally, the court considered whether a federal court's invocation of the primary jurisdiction doctrine is appropriate under the facts of the case in light of the DOJ's failure to promulgate any guidance on how public accommodations can make their sites and apps ADA compliant.[113]

The Court resolved its first question with relative ease and in doing so echoed the trial court's holding that the ADA applies to websites and apps which facilitate connecting customers with goods and services offered at any public accommodations.[114]

In contrast, the Court answered its second question entirely differently from the lower court, pointedly stating "we hold Domino's has received fair notice that its website and app must comply with the ADA."[115] The Court went on to say that only a statute that is so vague that it fails to give fair notice of what compliance forbids or necessitates violates due process.[116] Further, the Court characterized the ADA as a business or commercial statute subject to a lesser vagueness standard than a standard touching on fundamental rights.[117] As a result, the Court asserted the ADA could only run afoul of due process for vagueness if it wholly failed to articulate a comprehensible standard for those subject to it to follow.[118]

---

[109] *Id.*
[110] Robles v. Domino's Pizza, LLC, 913 F.3d 898, 904 (9th Circuit, 2019).
[111] *Id.*
[112] *Id.*
[113] *Id.*
[114] *Id.* at 906.
[115] *Id.* at 906.
[116] *Id.* at 906 (citing FCC v. Fox Television Stations, Inc. 567 U.S. 239, 253 (2012)).
[117] *Id.* at 906 (citing Botosan v. Paul McNally Realty, 216 F.3d 827, 836 (9th Circuit, 2000).
[118] *Id.*

Having established the standard it would use, the Court determined Title III's "auxiliary aids" section is not vague and, accordingly, Domino's was on notice of its obligation to communicate with their customers effectively.[119] The Court went on to find that the heart of the lower court's logic was flawed. In the Court's view, Domino's due process claim was rooted in its summary judgment argument that "Robles seeks to impose liability based on Domino's failure to comply with WCAG 2.0."[120] The Court found that argument uncompelling. In its view, Robles' causes of action stated a complaint for violating Title III and merely offered an injunction requiring Domino's to require WCAG 2.0 compliance as a potential remedy for the alleged violation(s).[121] Next, the Court distinguished *AMC Theaters*.[122]

The key difference in the Court's view between the facts in *AMC* and the case before it was that AMC Theaters could prove that their theaters had been built years prior to the ADA's passage and the adoption of the rule at issue in the case and would require retrofitting or remodeling its theaters to comply, while Domino's site and app came after both the adoption of the ADA and the DOJ articulating the Act applied to the internet.[123] The Court also noted *AMC* involved a statute ambiguous enough that different circuit courts had examined it and reached different conclusions.[124] In contrast, the court opined, Title III is flexible in the manner an accommodation might comply with it, but it is not ambiguous.[125] The Court concluded its examination of the due process issue by stating:

> [w]hile we understand why Domino's *wants* DOJ to issue specific guidelines for website and app accessibility, the Constitution only requires Domino's receive fair notice of its legal duties, not a blueprint for compliance with its statutory obligations.[126]

The Court also noted its belief that its precedents accurately reflect the law in its jurisdiction that, as a threshold matter, a lack of specific regulations or rules does not relieve a party of their obligations under any statute.[127]

---

[119] *Id.*
[120] *Id.* at 907.
[121] *Id.* at 907-08.
[122] U.S. v. AMC Entertainment, Inc., 549 F.3d 760 (9th Circuit, 2008).
[123] *Id.*
[124] *Id.* at 908 (citing *AMC Theaters,* 549 F.3d at 764-767).
[125] *Id.*
[126] *Id.* at 908.
[127] Fortyune v. City of Lomita, 766 F.3d 1098, 1102 (9th Circuit, 2014).

Finally, the Ninth Circuit ruled that the lower court erred in invoking the primary jurisdiction doctrine. In doing so, the Court pointed out that the controlling factor for consideration before invoking the doctrine is efficiency. The Court further noted that the doctrine does not exist purely to allow a court to receive advice from an agency any time the court is presented with an issue related to an administrative agency's rule making responsibility.[128] In any event, the Court held that efficiency would be in no way served by sending Robles home to wait for the DOJ to issue guidance—which it might very well never do.[129] Further, the Court held that there was no need for guidance from the DOJ in the first place because the trial court is perfectly capable of deciding the merits of the case as "properly framed" by the Court's opinion.[130]

The case was remanded to the trial court to "resolve whether Domino's website and app provide the blind with auxiliary aids and services for effective communication and full and equal enjoyment of its products and services."[131]

C. Round 3: Supreme Court

Domino's filed a Petition for Certiorari with the Supreme Court seeking relief from the Ninth Circuit's opinion.[132] Domino's specific complaint to the Supreme Court was the Ninth Circuit's position that a virtual "place" such as an app or website automatically becomes a public accommodation if it is connected to the goods or services offered by a physical location.[133] Domino's brief goes on to point out an insurmountable contradiction:

> [t]he Ninth Circuit's decision below rests on contradictory logic. Standalone websites cannot qualify as public accommodations, because public accommodations are physical locations. Yet websites maintained by enterprises with brick-and-mortar locations are, in effect, standalone public accommodations. By maintaining a physical presence, companies somehow transform their websites into standalone public accommodations that

---

[128] Robles v. Domino's Pizza, LLC, 913 F.3d 898, 910 (9th Circuit, 2019).
[129] *Id.*
[130] *Id.* at 911.
[131] *Id.*
[132] Domino's Pizza, LLC. v. Robles, Petition for Writ of Certiorari, 2019 WL 2484566 (U.S., 2019).
[133] *Id.*

must meet Title III accessibility requirements. That reasoning cannot be squared with the statutory text and produces illogical results.[134]

Domino's brief received great support from various trade and business groups many of whom filed amicus briefs in support of the Court granting certiorari.[135] However, they would prove to be of no avail.

In October of 2019, three years after Mr. Robles filed suit against Domino's, the Supreme Court declined certiorari.[136] The Court's decision was released unaccompanied by dissent and devoid of comments by the Justices.[137] Accordingly, the case has been returned to district court for trial.[138]

D. Analysis: What Does it Mean for Businesses?

The result of the Supreme Court's refusal to hear Domino's appeal appears to be a mixed bag wholly dependent on one's point of view. On its face, it is merely an exercise of the Court's purely discretionary nature. However, a deeper dive can lead to varying conclusions.

At first glance, people like Guillermo Robles appear to be the clear winners because even if his suit ultimately proves unsuccessful, the Ninth Circuit has made it abundantly clear that any public accommodation with a physical location and any internet-based means of accessing the offering of that location must comply with Title III regarding its web presence. Additionally, with the population of California sitting just south of 40 million people, it would seem to be a market too large to ignore. If the price of doing business in that market is having an accessible website, then logically, it would seem that most businesses would do so.[139] This

---

[134] *Id.*

[135] *E.g.* Brief for Restaurant Law Center as Amicus Curiae in Support of Petitioner, 2019 WL 3216643, *Domino's Pizza, LLC. v.* Robles, 2019 WL 2484566 (U.S., 2019); Brief for Chamber of Commerce of the United States of America and the National Federation of Independent Business as Amici Curiae in Support of Petitioner, 2019 WL 3216645, Domino's Pizza, LLC. v. Robles, 2019 WL 2484566 (U.S., 2019).

[136] Domino's Pizza, LLC. v. Robles, 140 S.Ct. 122 (U.S., 2019) (opinion denying certiorari).

[137] *Id.*; David G. Savage, *Supreme Court Allows Blind People to Sue Retailers if Their Websites Are Not Accessible*, LOS ANGELES TIMES October 7, 2019, https://www.latimes.com/politics/story/2019-10-07/blind-person-dominos-ada-supreme-court-disabled.

[138] *Id.*

[139] World Population Review, available at: https://www.worldpopulationreview.com.

thinking has led disability advocates to regard the Supreme Court's decision as a win for the disabled.[140]

On the other hand, some of the amici who filed briefs in support of Domino's petition to the Supreme Court paint a darker future.[141] In this future, businesses will choose not to create or embrace new technologies which could improve access for the disabled, out of the fear it will only lead to more ADA suits.[142] Others see the Court's declination as a monumental missed opportunity to finally provide a clearly articulated standard businesses could either follow or suffer the consequences.[143]

In this environment, it appears that the only course forward for businesses with any physical footprint in California is to ensure that their websites, apps, and other internet-based activities comply with WACG 2.0 and to hope that compliance is sufficient to shield them from litigation. This uncertainty is destined to continue until either Congress or the DOJ engage in the process and provide the clarity that our legislative and rulemaking processes were intended to provide.

---

[140] *See* Cortnay Cymrot, *Inaccessible Pizza Delivery and the Future of the ADA,* COLUMBIA JOURNAL OF LAW OF SOCIAL PROBLEMS (February 13, 2020) (citing Tucker Higgins, *Supreme Court Hands Victory to Blind Man Who Sued Domino's Over Site Accessibility,* CNBC (October 7, 2019), https://www.cnbc.com/2019/10/07/dominos-supreme-court.html; Stephen Melendez, *Domino's Pizza was Just Dealt a Supreme Court Blow that Could Reshape the ADA in the Digital Era,* FAST COMPANY (October 7, 2019), https://www.fastcompany.com/90414147/dominos-pizza-dealt-scotus-blow-that-could-affect-ada.
[141] Brief for Restaurant Law Center as Amicus Curiae in Support of Petitioner, 2019 WL 3216643, *Domino's Pizza, LLC. v.* Robles, 2019 WL 2484566 (U.S., 2019).
[142] *Id.*
[143] Scott J. Topolski, *The Short-Term And Long-Term Consequences Of The United States Supreme Court's Decision Not To Review Robles v. Domino's Pizza,* CS EMPLOYMENT BLOG (November 18, 2019), https://www.csemploymentblog.com/2019/11/articles/americans-with-disabilities-act/the-short-term-and-long-term-consequences-of-the-united-states-surpreme-courts-decision-not-to-review-robles-v-dominos-pizza/.

BEARING THE COSTS ASSOCIATED WITH SEX TRAFFICKING

CHRISTINA A. CULVER[*]
BENJAMIN RITZ[**]
DIANA BROWN[***]

I. INTRODUCTION

There has been increasing focus on human trafficking issues, and specifically sex trafficking, over the last few decades. That focus led Congress and the states to create statutory liability, not just for the primary actors in trafficking, such as pimps or recruiters, but also for owners of commercial premises or others who know or should know that they benefit from trafficking. When such claims are made against owners of commercial premises, the defendants often seek coverage under their commercial liability policies. This article outlines the potential trafficking liability faced by these secondary actors and issues relating to insurance coverage for such liability.

II. The COMMUNICATION DECENCY ACT

Sex trafficking victims have sued technology companies based upon the use of their internet platforms to contribute to the advertising and exploitation of victims for sex trafficking. The companies are shielded from civil prosecution due to section 230 of the Communication Decency Act ("CDA").[1] Section 230 provides broad civil immunity for computer service providers who publish information posted by others. Courts have interpreted section 230 to allow immunity for technology companies which post third-party content, for criminal activity that is facilitated through their website.[2] A quarter century ago, the Fourth Circuit, in the seminal *Zeran* case, held that Section 230 bars lawsuits which seek to hold a service provider liable for its exercise of a publisher's "traditional editorial functions — such as deciding whether to publish, withdraw, postpone or alter content."[3] However, this may soon change.

---

[*] J.D., Partner, Insurance Coverage Vice Chair, Thompson Coe Cousins & Irons LLP
[**] J.D., Senior Attorney, Thompson Coe Cousins & Irons LLP
[***] J.D., Associate Professor, Sam Houston State University
[1] 47 U.S.C. § 230 (2012).
[2] *See, e.g.*, Zeran v Am. Online, Inc., 129 F.3d 327 (4th Cir. 1997).
[3] Zeran, 129 F. 3d at 331.

A. Justice Thomas Takes Aim At
The Communications Decency Act

The CDA was signed into law in 1996 by President Bill Clinton, as the first attempt to regulate obscene material on the internet.[4] Subsection 230(c) is titled "Protection For 'Good Samaritan' Blocking And Screening of Offensive Material," and states that "[n]o provider or user of an interactive computer service shall be treated as a publisher or speaker of any information provided by another information content provider." Under the statute, technology companies are shielded from liability for "any action voluntarily taken in good faith to restrict access to or availability of material that the provider or user considers to be obscene, lewd, lascivious, filthy, excessively violent, harassing, or otherwise objectionable, whether or not such material is constitutionally protected."[5] Technology companies are also immune from "any action taken to enable or make available to information content providers or others the technical means to restrict access to material described in paragraph (1)."[6] The statute effectively preempts state law by providing that "[n]o cause of action may be brought and no liability may be imposed under any State or local law that is inconsistent with this section."[7]

United States Supreme Court Justice Clarence Thomas issued a statement on October 13, 2020, in the case styled *Malwarebytes, Inc. v. Enigma Software Grp. USA, LLC*, concerning the application of section 230 of the CDA.[8] Noting that when Congress enacted the CDA, the majority of internet platforms that we use today did not exist, Justice Thomas opined that the Supreme Court should consider whether the text of section 230 aligns with the current state of immunity enjoyed by internet platforms.[9] Justice Thomas summarized the purpose of section 230 as protecting companies from publisher liability for unknowingly leaving up illegal third-party content as well as taking down legal third-party content in good faith.[10] Justice Thomas emphasized that this understanding is far

---

[4] See Pub. L. No. 104-104, § 509, 110 Stat. 56.

[5] 47 U.S.C. § 230(c)(2)(A).

[6] 47 U.S.C. § 230(c)(2)(B). Paragraph (1) refers to "information provided by another information content provider."

[7] *Id.*

[8] Malwarebytes, Inc. v. Enigma Software Group USA, LLC, 592 U. S. ——, ——, 141 S.Ct. 13, 13, 208 L.Ed.2d 197 (2020) (statement of Thomas, J., respecting denial of certiorari).

[9] *Id.* at 14.

[10] *Id,* citing § 230(c)(1) and (c)(2)(A).

from what has prevailed because courts often read broader immunity into statutes where, in his opinion, it is not warranted.[11]

Justice Thomas' enumerated concerns with the current interpretation of section 230 include sex trafficking and terrorism, among other modern constructs.[12] One case referenced by Justice Thomas involved an online platform that allegedly facilitated sex trafficking by allowing users to post classified ads for "escorts" and allegedly deliberately structured its website to facilitate illegal human trafficking.[13] The plaintiffs alleged that the company encouraged the illegal activity by accepting anonymous payments, failing to verify e-mails, and stripping metadata from photographs, which made crimes harder to track.[14] The company escaped liability due to due to the prevailing expansive interpretation of section 230.[15]

Justice Thomas stated that a common thread through these cases is that the plaintiffs were not necessarily attempting to hold the defendants liable as a publisher or speaker of third-party content, or for removing content in good faith.[16] Instead, their claims were for the defendants' own misconduct arising from alleged product design flaws, rather than for the content of the published information.[17] According to Justice Thomas, paring back the "sweeping immunity" of section 230 would not render defendants liable for online misconduct, but rather would give the plaintiffs an opportunity to pursue, and potentially prove, their claims.[18]

B. The Texas Supreme Court Speaks

The Texas Supreme Court has recently ruled in the case of *In Re Facebook, Inc. and Facebook, Inc. D/B/A Instagram*.[19] In this case, Facebook sought dismissal of three cases brought by alleged minor trafficking victims who sought to sue Facebook, alleging that Facebook's

---

[11] *Id.* at 15.
[12] *Id.* at 17 (discussing Jane Doe No. 1 v. Backpage.com, LLC, 817 F.3d 12, 16 (1st Cir. 2016)).
[13] *Id.*
[14] *Id.*
[15] *Id.*
[16] *Id.* at 18.
[17] *Id.*
[18] *Id.*
[19] In re Facebook, 625 S.W.3d 80 (Tex. 2021) (orig. proceeding).

failure to warn of, or take adequate measures to prevent, sex trafficking on its internet platforms allowed exploiters to recruit them.[20]

Facebook moved to dismiss the claims against it as barred by section 230 of the CDA.[21] The Texas Supreme Court granted the relief sought by Facebook in part, and denied in part.[22] The Court noted that the CDA has been uniformly interpreted by federal courts to require dismissal of claims alleging that interactive websites like Facebook should do more to protect their users from the malicious or objectionable activity of other users.[23] Accordingly, the Court ordered dismissal of plaintiffs' common-law claims for negligence, negligent undertaking, gross negligence, and products liability under this reasoning.[24] The Court, however, allowed the human-trafficking claims under section 98.002 of the Texas Civil Practice and Remedies Code to proceed.[25]

C. The Supreme Court Agrees to Hear a CDA Case in 2023

The scope of "traditional editorial functions" is at the heart of a case currently on the docket at the Supreme Court.[26] On October 3, 2022, the Supreme Court granted certiorari in an appeal that is challenging whether a social media platform's targeted algorithmic recommendations fall under the umbrella of "traditional editorial functions" protected by the CDA or whether such recommendations are not the actions of a "publisher" and thus fall outside of CDA immunity.[27]

In *Gonzalez*, the Ninth Circuit affirmed the district court's dismissal of claims against Google under the Anti-Terrorism Act[28] for allegedly providing "material support" to ISIS by allowing terrorists to use YouTube (which is owned by Google) as a marketing and recruitment tool to facilitate terrorism.[29] The court found that Google was entitled to CDA immunity for most claims, concluding that "a website's use of content-

---

[20] *Id.* at 83.

[21] *Id.*

[22] *Id.*

[23] *Id.*

[24] *Id.*

[25] *Id.* TRCP section 98.002 provides that a "defendant who engages in the trafficking of persons or who intentionally or knowingly benefits from participating in a venture that traffics another person is liable to the person trafficked ... for damages arising from the trafficking of that person by the defendant or venture."

[26] Gonzalez v. Google LLC, No. 21-1333, 2022 WL 4651229 (U.S. Oct. 3, 2022).

[27] *Id.* The court also granted cert on a related case *Twitter v. Taamneh* which includes similar allegations of social media companies providing material support to ISIS.

[28] 18 U.S.C. § 2333

[29] Gonzalez v. Google LLC, 2 F.4th 871, 883 (9th Cir. 2021).

neutral algorithms, without more, does not expose it to liability for content posted by a third-party."[30]

The question presented in the Gonzalez's petition is: "Does section 230(c)(1) immunize interactive computer services when they make targeted recommendations of information provided by another information content provider, or only limit the liability of interactive computer services when they engage in traditional editorial functions (such as deciding whether to display or withdraw) with regard to such information?"

Given Justice Thomas' pronouncement concerning the CDA, the ruling may be far-reaching. The issues of whether CDA immunity covers algorithm-generated recommendations is one of first impression for the Supreme Court. Additionally, lawmakers from both parties have voiced skepticism with regard to the broad immunity conferred by Section 230, which was drafted when internet bulletin boards were in their infancy. Congress has introduced more than 20 bills that propose to amend or repeal the CDA.[31] Many of these, including the See Something, Say Something Online Act of 2021 and the Protecting Americans from Dangerous Algorithms Act.[32]

III. LEGAL LIABILITY OF COMMERCIAL ENTITIES FOR TRAFFICKING

In order to understand issues what arise with respect to insurance coverage for trafficking liability, it is important to understand the scope of such underlying liability for commercial organizations.

A. Statutory Liability – The Trafficking Victims Protection Act

The primary statute imposing such liability is the Trafficking Victims Protection Act ("TVPA"). Congress initially passed the TVPA in 2000, at which time the statute only created criminal offenses for sex trafficking.[33] However, in 2003, Congress amended the TVPA to create a civil right of action for victims of trafficking against their traffickers: A "victim of a violation of section 1589, 1590, or 1591 . . . may bring a civil

---

[30] *Id.* at 896.

[31] Etta Lanum, *Supreme Court Grants Certiorari in Gonzalez v. Google and Twitter v. Taamneh: An Overview*, (Nov. 8, 2022, 8:31 AM),
https://www.lawfareblog.com/supreme-court-grants-certiorari-gonzalez-v-google-and-twitter-v-taamneh-overview.

[32] *Id. See, e.g.,* S.27 — 117th Congress (2021-2022); H.R.2154 — 117th Congress (2021-2022).

[33] Victims of Trafficking and Violence Protection Act of 2000, PL 106–386 (Division A), Oct. 28, 2000, 114 Stat 1464.

action against the perpetrator . . . [to] recover damages and reasonable attorney[']s fees."[34]

The TVPA defines sex trafficking as the "recruitment, harboring, transportation, provision, obtaining, patronizing, or soliciting of a person for the purposes of a commercial sex act and in which the commercial sex act is induced by force, fraud or coercion."[35] Section 1591 of the Act imposes criminal liability for sex trafficking of children, or of any person by force, fraud, or coercion, to engage in a commercial sex act. Section 1591(a) provides: "Whoever knowingly . . . (1) recruits, entices, harbors, transports, provides, obtains, advertises, maintains, patronizes, or solicits by any means a person; or (2) benefits . . . from participation in a venture which has engaged in an act" with knowledge or reckless disregard . . . shall be punished."[36]

Congress went further in 2008, expanding the victim's right of action in section 1595 to include liability against those who benefited from the trafficking venture, specifically "whoever knowingly benefits, financially or by receiving anything of value from participation in a venture which that person knew or should have known has engaged in an act in violation of this chapter."[37] Several states have also enacted similar criminal and/or civil liability statutes.[38]

As a result, trafficking victims have filed cases around the country, usually against hotels, rest stops or similar entities, for their alleged facilitation and participation in trafficking ventures. The victims typically allege that the brand, owners, and employees all knew that victims were being trafficked, did nothing to prevent the trafficking at their establishments, and financially benefitted from the trafficking operations.

For example, in July 2015, a motel owner, Kanubhai Patel, plead guilty to financially benefitting from a sex trafficking scheme operating out of the Riviera Motel in New Orleans, Louisiana, in which multiple adult women were compelled to engage in prostitution. Evidence presented at court revealed that Mr. Patel acknowledged that, in his role as former owner of the Riviera Motel, he regularly rented rooms to individuals who were charged with sex trafficking as co-conspirators, knowing that they were pimps who forced and coerced women to engage in prostitution. Mr. Patel admitted that, although he never personally

---

[34] Trafficking Victims Protection Reauthorization Act of 2003, PL 108–193, Dec. 19, 2003, 117 Stat 2875.

[35] 22 U.S.C. § 7102.

[36] 18 U.S.C. § 1591(a).

[37] William Wilberforce Trafficking Victims Protection Reauthorization Act of 2008, PL 110–457, Dec. 23, 2008, 122 Stat 5044; 18 U.S.C. § 1595.

[38] *2013 Analysis of State Human Trafficking Laws,* POLARIS PROJECT (Aug. 2013), https://polarisproject.org/wp-content/uploads/2019/09/2013-State-Ratings-Analysis.pdf.

recruited, groomed or coerced any of the victims, he had benefited financially from the sex trafficking operations.[39]

1. *Scienter* Requirements for TVPA Liability

While an organization may be held liable under section 1595 of the TVPA for knowingly benefitting in a venture it should have known engaged in trafficking, there is disagreement among the courts as to whether such liability is predicated on criminal liability.[40] From a recent survey of twenty-one cases submitted to the Judicial Panel for Multidistrict Litigation,[41] the United States District Courts for the Southern District of Ohio and the Western District of Washington took the view that civil liability under section 1595 is distinct from criminal liability under section 1591.[42] The United States District Courts for the Northern District of Georgia and the Southern District of New York, however, require a criminal violation under 1591 before section 1595's civil liability is triggered.[43] In many of the cases, the defendants filed motions to dismiss

---

[39] Press Release Number 5-834, *Louisiana Motel Owner Pleads Guilty in Sex Trafficking Case*, UNITED STATES DEPARTMENT OF JUSTICE (July 1, 2015), https://www.justice.gov/opa/pr/louisiana-motel-owner-pleads-guilty-sex-trafficking-case. "Evidence presented at the plea hearing and court documents establish that Patel would charge the pimps and sex trafficking co-conspirators higher rates than other motel guests, and would open the motel's gate to allow the women to bring customers back to the hotel. Patel learned that members of the sex trafficking conspiracy physically assaulted women they prostituted, including one instance in which a co-conspirator brutally beat one woman with a large piece of wood while she screamed for help, leaving her with multiple lacerations and what appeared to be a broken arm. Patel also saw the damage that a co-conspirator caused to a motel room during a beating, including a broken toilet, a damaged sink and blood on the walls. Patel agreed not to call the police after the co-conspirator paid him for the damage to the room. Patel also knew that, in furtherance of the sex trafficking scheme, members of the sex trafficking conspiracy would take the women's identification cards from them. Patel saw the sex trafficking co-conspirators possessing the women's identification cards and using them to rent hotels. Patel did not report them to police as long as they paid their rent."
[40] *See* A.B. v. Marriott Int'l, Inc., CV 19-5770, 2020 WL 1939678, at *1, 8–14 (E.D. Pa. Apr. 22, 2020) (collecting and discussing trends in sex trafficking cases).
[41] In re Hotel Indus. Sex Trafficking Litig., MDL 2928, 2020 WL 581882, at *3 (U.S. Jud. Pan. Mult. Lit. Feb. 5, 2020) (collecting cases from Georgia, Massachusetts, Michigan, Hampshire, New York, Ohio, Oregon, Pennsylvania, Texas, Virginia, and Washington); *But see also* Florida Abolitionist v. Backpage.com LLC, 617CV218ORL28TBS, 2018 WL 1587477, at *1 (M.D. Fla. Mar. 31, 2018) (involving sex trafficking conducted through the website Backpage.com).
[42] A.B., 2020 WL 1939678, at *8-9.
[43] *Id.*

with mixed results.[44] Either way, courts view claims under the statute in the light of the entire body of allegations.[45] A discussion of one such case from each analysis follows.

a. *M.A. v. Wyndham*

In *M.A. v. Wyndham Hotels & Resorts, Inc.*, the plaintiff M.A. alleged that sex trafficking occurred at Days Inn by Wyndham, Comfort Inn, and Crowne Plaza locations in Columbus, Ohio.[46] M.A. alleged signs of trafficking, including that her trafficker paid in cash for rooms near exits for long stays; the rooms contained used condoms and other paraphernalia; M.A. had bruising and would not make eye contact; her cries for help were ignored by hotel staff; and one online review indicated that the guest was solicited for drugs and prostitutes.[47]

To allege liability under TVPA section 1591, M.A. alleged that Wyndham (1) received a knowing benefit; (2) knew or should have known of a trafficking venture; and (3) participated in a trafficking venture.[48] Wyndham filed a motion to dismiss.

The District Court for the Southern District of Ohio held that as to a "knowing benefit," renting rooms is a sufficient financial benefit.[49] As to the "knew or should have known" element, the court held that M.A's allegations were sufficient for "should have known negligence," but not

---

[44] *Id.*; H.M. v. Red Lion Hotels Corp., No. 19-4859 (N.D. Ga.) (Plaintiff filed a Notice of Voluntary Dismissal without Prejudice of all defendants without ruling on pending motion to dismiss; case closed); H.G. v. Marriott International, Inc., No. 19-13622 (E.D. Mich.) (motions granted); K.B. v. Inter-Continental Hotels Corp., No. 19-1213 (D.N.H.) (granted in part and denied in part); S.J. Choice Hotels Corp., No. 19-6071 (E.D.N.Y) (motions granted in part and denied in part); A.C. v. Red Roof Inns, Inc., No. 19-4965 (S.D. Ohio) (motions denied); C.T. v. Red Roof Inns, Inc., No. 19-5384 (S.D. Ohio) (denied as moot); A B. v. Hilton Worldwide Holdings, Inc., No. 19-1992 (D. Ore.) (granted in part and denied in part); A.D. v. Wyndham Hotels and Resorts, Inc., No. 19-120 (E.D. Va.) (motion denied). Motion to dismiss denied without opinion with plaintiff voluntarily dismissing hotel: L.W. v. Hilton Worldwide Holdings, Inc., No. 19-4171 (S.D. Tex.). Answer, no motion to dismiss: Doe C.D. v. R-Roof Asset, LLC, No. 19-11192 (D. Mass.); V.G. v. G6 Hospitality, LLC, No. 19-6071 (N.D.N.Y.)).

[45] *See* Ricchio v. McLean, 853 F.3d 553, 557 (1st Cir. 2017) (Souter, J. sitting by designation) (reversing the district court's grant of summary judgment to the defendant hotel owner where the kidnapper and hotel manager's high-fives while speaking about "getting this thing going again" was not ambiguous "in light of the allegations of the [hotel manager's] complaisance in response to the several alleged exhibitions of [the kidnapper's] coercive and brutal behavior to a physically deteriorating Ricchio, who pleaded for help.")

[46] M.A. v. Wyndham Hotels & Resorts, Inc., 425 F. Supp. 3d 959, 962 (S.D. Ohio 2019).

[47] *Id.*

[48] *Id.* at 964, 967.

[49] *Id.* at 965.

sufficient to show actual knowledge.[50] To arrive at the decision on the "knew or should have known element," the court provided two examples. On one side is *Ricchio v. McLean*, where the victim alleged the hotel owner witnessed the victim's abuse by the sex trafficker, and the hotel owner and trafficker "high-fived" each other. At the other end of the spectrum is *Lawson v. Rubin*, where the victim alleged only one visit by the police and one by an ambulance to a condominium unit over more than six years.[51] The court held that M.A.'s allegations were sufficient to put the hotel on notice to train their staff to prevent sex trafficking, as well as "signs that should have alerted the staff."[52]

For the third element ("participation in a venture"), the court held that M.A.'s allegations established a "pattern of conduct" indicating that the trafficker and hotel had a "tacit agreement."[53]   To arrive at the definition of "participating in a venture," the court distinguished between the criminal section (§ 1591) and the civil section (§ 1595). While section 1591(e)(4) did define the phrase "participating in a venture" as "knowingly assisting, supporting, or facilitating a violation of subsection (a)(1)," that definition was explicitly limited to section 1591.[54] Section 1595 does not define "participation in a venture."[55] Using common practices of statutory construction to give meaning to every statutory word, the court concluded that applying the criminal definition to section 1595 would void the "should have known" language, rendering it meaningless.[56] Applying the "should have known" language, the court held that M.A. alleged a sufficient continuous relationship and denied the defendants' motion to dismiss in light of M.A.'s pleadings of an agency relationship sufficient to hold the hotels liable.[57]

b. *Red Roof Inn* Cases

The District Court for the Northern District of Georgia took the opposite view of the "participation in a venture" element and granted several defendants' motions to dismiss claims under section 1595. In a series of *Does 1–4 v. Red Roof Inns, Inc.* cases, the court defined

---

[50] *Id.* at 968.
[51] Id. at 966 (citing Ricchio v. McLean, 853 F.3d 553 (1st Cir. 2017) and Hillary Lawson v. Howard Rubin, No. 1:17-cv-6404 (BMC), 2018 WL 2012869 (E.D.N.Y. Apr. 29, 2018)).
[52] *Id.* at 968.
[53] *Id.* at 970.
[54] *Id.* at 969.
[55] *Id.* at 970.
[56] *Id.*
[57] *Id.* at 971.

knowledge for that element as "knowledge as to 'assisting, supporting or facilitating' trafficking."[58] The court imposed the definition of "participation in a venture" in section 1591(e)(4) to section 1595.[59] In making this determination, the court relied on a similar definition established in *Nobel v. Weinstein* from the Southern District of New York.[60] Both the Georgia and New York courts found that association alone could not establish liability, but rather required some level of knowledge and participation in the sex trafficking act.[61] Accordingly, the Georgia District Court dismissed the victims' claims for failure to plead a sufficient knowledge element.[62] The plaintiffs appealed the court's decision.

B. Common Law and Civil Law Liability

In addition to statutory liability, premises owners such as hotels face potential common law liability for injuries on their premises, such as those that can occur in connection with trafficking. The scope of such liability under Texas common law and Louisiana civil law is summarized here for context.

1. Texas Law

"In a [Texas] premises liability case, the plaintiff must establish a duty owed to the plaintiff, a breach of the duty, and damages proximately caused by the breach."[63] Generally, there is no duty to protect another person from the criminal acts of a third party.[64] A property owner or controller of a premises, however, "does have a duty to use ordinary care to protect invitees from criminal acts of third parties if the owner knows or has reason to know of an unreasonable and foreseeable risk of harm to the invitee."[65] Texas uses two tests to determine the presence of a duty: (1)

---

[58] *See* Doe 1 v. Red Roof Inns, Inc., No. 19-3840, 2020 WL 1872335 (N.D. Ga. Apr. 13, 2020); Doe 2 v. Red Roof Inns, Inc., No. 19-3841, 2020 WL 1872337 (N.D. Ga. Apr. 13, 2020); Doe 3 v. Red Roof Inns, Inc., No. 19-3843, 2020 WL 1872333 (N.D. Ga. Apr. 13, 2020); and Doe 4 v. Red Roof Inns, Inc., No. 19-3845, 2020 WL 1872336 (N.D. Ga. Apr. 13, 2020).

[59] *Doe 1*, 2020 WL 1872335, at *3 (citing 18 U.S.C. §§ 1595(a), 1591(a)(2), 1591(e)(4)).

[60] *Id.* (citing Noble v. Weinstein, 335 F.Supp.3d 504, 524 (S.D.N.Y. 2018)).

[61] *Id.*

[62] *Id.*

[63] Del Lago Partners, Inc. v. Smith, 307 S.W.3d 762, 767 (Tex. 2010).

[64] *See* UDR Tex. Props., L.P. v. Petrie, 517 S.W.3d 98, 100 (Tex. 2017).

[65] *Id.*

the foreseeability of similar incidents and the (2) foreseeability of immediately preceding conduct.[66]

To determine the foreseeability of similar incidents, "Texas courts first narrow the relevant criminal history to be included in the foreseeability analysis,"[67] by evidence "of specific previous crimes on or near the premises."[68] "The courts then compare that narrowed criminal history with the crime in question based on the five factors: proximity, publicity, recency, frequency, and similarity."[69] Or, in other words, the court considers: whether any criminal conduct occurred at or near the property;[70] how recently the criminal conduct occurred; how often crime has occurred; how similar the previous crime was to the alleged crime; and what publicity was given to the instances to indicate what the landlord should have known about them.[71] The property owners, however, bear no duty to regularly inspect criminal records to determine the risk of crime in the area.[72] The general idea is that past criminal history will put the hotel on notice.

In *Timberwalk Apartments*, a tenant sued an apartment owner for negligently failing to prevent a sexual assault.[73] The evidence established that there had been no violent crimes in the complex for the preceding ten years (similarity, recency, and frequency), only one sexual assault occurred within one-mile radius in the previous year (similarity, proximity, and frequency), and the remaining six assault-type crimes in neighboring complexes were not publicized or brought to the landlord's

---

[66] Del Lago Partners, Inc., 307 S.W.3d at 768–69 (immediately preceding conduct); Timberwalk Apts., Partners, Inc. v. Cain, 972 S.W.2d 749, 759 (Tex. 1998) (foreseeability of similar incidents).

[67] Jenkins v. C.R.E.S. Mgmt., L.L.C., 811 F.3d 753, 756 (5th Cir. 2016).

[68] Trammel Crow Cent. Tex., Ltd. v. Gutierrez, 267 S.W.3d 9, 12 (Tex. 2008) (quoting Timberwalk Apts, 972 S.W.2d at 756).

[69] *Id.* (citing Timberwalk Apts., 972 S.W.2d at 759). These factors have come to be known as the "*Timberwalk* factors."

[70] After *Trammel*, courts have limited the proximity to the complex in question and its immediate environs. Flanagan v. RBD San Antonio L.P., 04-16-00761-CV, 2017 WL 5615567, at *4 (Tex. App. Nov. 22, 2017) (collecting cases). Previously, some cases looked as far as 3.5 miles. *Id.* Control may still be a key element in determining whether nearby areas like the parking lot are part of that proximity. LaFleur v. Astrodome-Astrohall Stadium Corp., 751 S.W.2d 563, 565–66 (Tex. App.1988) (holding Astrodome operators were not liable for injuries photographer sustained across the street from the Astrodome because the operators had neither control nor the right to control the premises).

[71] Timberwalk Apts., 972 S.W.2d at 759.

[72] *Id.*

[73] *Id.*

attention (similarity and publicity).[74] The Supreme Court of Texas therefore held that the sexual assault was not foreseeable.[75]

In *Trammel Crow Central Texas, Ltd. v. Gutierrez*, the Supreme Court of Texas analyzed the similarity factor in more detail by comparing a murder with armed robberies, while also narrowing the proximity factor to the immediate premises.[76] *Trammel* involved the murder of Luis Gutierrez at the Quarry Market, a shopping mall.[77] In narrowing the relevant criminal history to be included in its foreseeability analysis, the court noted that only violent crimes would signal a future murder:

> In the two years prior to Luis's death, 227 crimes were reported at the Quarry Market. Of these reported crimes, 203 were property and property-related crimes—mostly thefts, but also a handful of burglaries, auto thefts, and incidents of vandalism. Fourteen "other crimes" occurred—thirteen simple assaults and one incident of weapon possession. The remaining ten crimes, all robberies, were classified as violent crimes—a category that also includes murder, manslaughter, rape, and aggravated assault.
>
> Although criminal conduct is difficult to compartmentalize, some lines can be drawn. For instance, we have held that reports of vandalism, theft, and neighborhood disturbances are not enough to make a stabbing death foreseeable. Similarly, although the repeated occurrences of theft, vandalism, and simple assaults at the Quarry Market signal that future property crimes are possible, they do not suggest the likelihood of murder. Accordingly, like the court of appeals, we limit our review to the ten instances of violent crime that took place at the Quarry Market during the two years prior to Luis's death.[78]

The court then applied the five *Timberwalk* factors. As to proximity and publicity, ten other violent crimes all occurred at the market and the property manager knew about the crimes at the time of Luis's

---

[74] *Id.*
[75] *Id.*
[76] Trammel Crow Cent. Tex., Ltd. v. Gutierrez, 267 S.W.3d 9 (Tex. 2008)
[77] *Id.* at 11–12.
[78] *Id.* at 13.

death.[79] As to recency and frequency, the court noted that the market had a relatively low rate of violent crime. The chances of a San Antonio resident suffering a violent crime in general was 44,760-to-1, and the market's expert calculated the odds at the market during the two years prior to Luis's death were 1,637,630 to 1.[80] As to similarity, the robberies were distinct from the murder because the robbers demanded property, rarely with a weapon, and if an attack happened, it occurred after the robbery.[81] In the attack on Luis, the assailant missed one shot before firing four shots at Luis's back, all from a long distance, before taking his wallet.[82] The Court held that this attack was more like murder than an armed robbery.[83] Thus, the court held that the prior robberies would not have put the property manager on notice that it had a duty to prevent the attack.[84]

In *Jai Jalaram Lodging Group, L.L.C. d/b/a Comfort Inn v. Leribeus*, a guest sued a motel for injuries sustained in an armed robbery, kidnapping, and aggravated assault originating from the Comfort Inn's parking lot.[85] In the prior year, the following incidents occurred at the Comfort Inn: "(1) someone jumping on the hood of a car"; (2) "theft of property from the motel rooms"; and (3) "theft of money from the register."[86] The parties debated whether the proximity should extend to a one-mile radius, but even then, none of the violent crimes were of the same variety.[87] Applying the *Timberwalk* proximity and recency factors, evidence showed that no violent crimes occurred at the Comfort Inn and none had been reported at the neighboring motels for two years.[88] Further, applying similarity and frequency factors, the property crimes were not of the kind to facilitate violent crimes nor frequent enough.[89] Also, as to publicity, there was no evidence that criminal activity within a one-mile radius, per police reports, was widely publicized.[90] The El Paso appellate court found that the armed robbery, kidnapping, and aggravated assault was not foreseeable because of insufficient evidence of similar crimes in

---

[79] *Id.* at 15.
[80] *Id.*
[81] *Id.* at 16–17.
[82] *Id.* at 17.
[83] *Id.*
[84] *Id.*
[85] Jai Jalaram Lodging Group, L.L.C. v. Leribeus, 225 S.W.3d 238 (Tex. App.—El Paso 2006, pet. denied).
[86] *Id.* at 244.
[87] *Id.* at 244–45.
[88] *Id.* at 245.
[89] *Id.*
[90] *Id.* at 245–46.

the area.[91] Accordingly, the court reversed the trial court's judgment and rendered a take nothing judgment in favor of the motel.[92]

Texas courts have also considered, after applying the *Timberwalk* factors, if it was reasonably foreseeable that the injured party would be the victim of the crime alleged.[93] In *Mellon Mortgage Co. v. Angela N. Holder*, an off-duty police officer stopped a woman before sexually assaulting her in a nearby parking garage.[94] Applying the *Timberwalk* factors, one would find that a sexual assault might occur.[95] The Supreme Court of Texas found that roughly one violent crime, including rape and murder, occurred every four days at the garage. The court held, however, that the parking garage owner could not anticipate that a policeman would lead a woman from several blocks away to sexually assault her in the garage at three in the morning.[96] The court therefore held that the garage owner owed no duty to Holder.[97]

As an alternative to the *Timberwalk* factors, the Supreme Court of Texas set out an even more straightforward test—the foreseeability of immediately preceding conduct test. In *Del Lago Partners, Inc. v. Bradley Smith*, a bar patron sued the bar owner for injuries from a bar brawl.[98] The Court found that the "nature and character of the premises" (a bar) can make criminal activity (a drunken bar fight) foreseeable.[99] Alternatively, the Court found that the conduct immediately preceding the crime (repeated and aggressive confrontations between patrons about ninety minutes before a bar fight) would allow the owner to anticipate criminal conduct.[100]

Other cases applying the *Timberwalk* factors include: *Flanagan v. RBD San Antonio L.P.*, 04-16-00761-CV, 2017 WL 5615567, at *1 (Tex. App.—San Antonio Nov. 22, 2017, pet. denied) (affirming the hotel's summary judgment where one vehicular burglary in two years was insufficient to satisfy the recency and frequency factors, and "Salmon driving his truck into Flanagan is not similar to a sexual assault inside a hotel"); *Armstrong v. La Quinta Inns, Inc.*, CIV 99-531 BB/LFG, 2000 WL 36739803, at *1–2 (D.N.M. June 13, 2000) (granting judgment as a

---

[91] *Id.* at 246.
[92] *Id.*
[93] Madison v. Williamson, 241 S.W.3d 145, 153 (Tex. App.—Houston [1st Dist.] 2007, pet. denied) (citing Mellon Mortg. Co. v. Holder, 5 S.W.3d 654, 657 (Tex. 1999)).
[94] Mellon Mortg. *Co.*, 5 S.W.3d at 657.
[95] *Id.*
[96] *Id.*
[97] *Id.* at 658.
[98] Del Lago Partners, Inc. v. Smith, 307 S.W.3d 762, 776 (Tex. 2010).
[99] *Id.* at 768.
[100] *Id.* at 769.

matter of law where woman sexually assaulted at a La Quinta did not put on sufficient evidence when the only evidence was the theft of three to four televisions and personal belongings), *aff'd*, 12 Fed. Appx. 879 (10th Cir. 2001); *Fitzgerald v. Patel*, 03-99-00755-CV, 2000 WL 547017, at *1–2 (Tex. App.—Austin May 4, 2000, no pet.) (affirming summary judgment that the hotel had no duty to a woman who was accidently shot in the head by a guest where the evidence showed only property crimes, like robbery, at a rate of one every 2.2 years and one stabbing that did not result in death).

In summary, Texas considers the foreseeability of prior criminal instances (proximity, publicity, recency, frequency, and similarity); whether the victim is a foreseeable victim of such crimes; and whether the hotel had immediate notice that an incident was going to break out like angry drunks starting a bar fight.

2. Louisiana Law

In Louisiana, a negligence action is analyzed under a duty-risk analysis.[101] While a commercial premises owner does not insure its guests against injury or risk from third-party crimes, they have a duty to take a reasonable degree of care against crime.[102] To determine the existence and extent of this duty, a court must weigh the "[t]he foreseeability of the crime risk on the defendant's property and the gravity of the risk."[103] Key considerations consist of (1) the prior occurrence of similar crimes; (2) the location, nature, and condition of the property; and (3) whether management or employees knew that the criminals were about to commit the crime.[104]

For example, in *Dearmon v. St. Ann Lodging, L.L.C.*, Bourbon Orleans Hotel guests were beaten and robbed when they opened the door to criminals posing as police officers. The plaintiffs sued the hotel alleging that it was "negligent in failing to provide the plaintiffs with adequate security." The trial court granted the hotel's motion for summary judgment, holding the victims had presented no admissible evidence to establish that the hotel breached a duty of care owed to them or that the incident was reasonably foreseeable. Plaintiffs appealed.[105] The Louisiana

---

[101] Dearmon v. St. Ann Lodging, L.L.C., 2018-0994 (La.App. 4 Cir. 3/27/19, 2–3); 267 So.3d 639, 642.
[102] *Id.*
[103] *Id.* (quoting Posecai v. Wal-Mart Stores, Inc., 99-1222 (La. 11/30/99, 9); 752 So.2d 762, 768).
[104] *Id.*
[105] *Id.* at 641.

Fourth Circuit Court of Appeals eventually reversed and remanded because the plaintiffs established a genuine issue of material fact as to the extent of the duty owed.[106]

The record contained issues of material fact with regard to (1) prior incidents, (2) the hotel location, and (3) management's knowledge. The hotel offered the affidavit of its general manager attesting to no knowledge of criminal activity in or around the hotel, with the first incident being this incident.[107] In opposition and in support of considerations (1) and (3), the plaintiffs provided an affidavit from a security expert who highlighted one report where an employee stated that "shady" guys had passed the front desk to the elevators, but eventually disappeared.[108] Then security received a noise complaint from the fifth floor where security heard a "commotion and someone shouting 'get on the floor! Put your head down #$&*%!."[109] Security then called the police.[110] As to the location factor (2), the security expert also suggested that Bourbon Orleans Hotel's central French-Quarter location increased the risk of crime.[111] The appellate court held that the trial court erred in granting summary judgment due to the genuine issue of material fact.[112]

This duty will likely not be foreseeable if no criminal activity has been reported. In *Miller v. Threshold BM, L.P. and Westdale Asset Management, Ltd.*, the United States District Court for the Western District of Louisiana granted summary judgment for the apartment owner.[113] Miller was sexually assaulted upon leaving the apartment complex, but presented no reports of sexual or criminal offenses occurring at the apartment complex.[114] The apartment complex therefore had no duty of care, and the court granted summary judgement for the owner.[115] Other cases have found insufficient evidence of criminal activity although there were 25 disturbances of the peace, one armed robbery, and other unreported crimes that were not "real serious offenses."[116]

---

[106] *Id.* at 643.

[107] *Id.*

[108] *Id.* at 643.

[109] *Id.*

[110] *Id.*

[111] *Id.*

[112] *Id.*

[113] Miller v. Threshold Bm, L.P., CV 15-1795, 2016 WL 3440618, at *4 (W.D. La. June 20, 2016).

[114] *Id.*

[115] *Id.*

[116] Young v. Fitzpatrick, 2003-1038 (La.App. 3 Cir. 2/4/04, 9–10); 865 So.2d 969, 976. Arguably, the court also considered the repeated attempts of the night clerk to check on the room alarm in the hotel's favor. *Id.* at 976–79.

This duty may, however, extend to locations adjacent to the property, like a public sidewalk at a mall or a parking lot. In *Banks v. Hyatt Corporation*, the Court of Appeals for the Fifth Circuit held, under Louisiana law, that a Hyatt hotel operator was liable when a guest was shot by an armed robber four feet from the doors of the hotel underneath an overhang that was the second floor of the hotel complex.[117] As to prior incidents supporting the jury verdict, the court considered that Dr. Banks was the second person to be shot at that entrance and the fifth victim of armed robbery at that entrance, along with eleven armed robberies and five simple robberies immediately nearby and during the prior three-month period.[118] Next, the court considered that the hotel was connected to a mall.[119] The management also knew of these problems both through incident reports, security logs, and the off-duty armed police officers Hyatt paid to patrol the outside of the mall.[120] Hyatt foresaw this danger.[121] The court then chose to extend Hyatt's duty to the area around the hotel because the perimeter patrol demonstrated that Hyatt had the power "to take preventative action in the immediate surrounding area."[122] Accordingly, the court affirmed the district court's jury verdict because it "refuse[d] to transform [the entrance] doors into an impregnable legal wall of immunity."[123] Courts have also extended this perimeter duty to parking lots.[124]

But if the property is over 150 yards away without a similar security patrol, the hotel has been found not to be liable. In *Hollander v. Days Inn Motel*, Hollander went jogging in a neighborhood near the Days Inn.[125] He was attacked and beaten 150 yards away.[126] The trial court granted the hotel's motion for summary judgment that they owed no duty

---

[117] Banks v. Hyatt Corp., 722 F.2d 214, 227 (5th Cir. 1984).
[118] *Id.* at 218–19.
[119] *Id.* at 217–18.
[120] *Id.* at 219.
[121] *Id.* at 226.
[122] *Id.* at 227–28.
[123] *Id.*; *see also* Zerangue v. Delta Towers, Ltd., 820 F.2d 130, 132–33 (5th Cir. 1987) (affirming jury's negligence and finding of foreseeability against hotel where guest was raped when hotel lobby door failed to allow her reentry at 3 a.m. and hotel security knew that going outside "would be a dangerous thing to do.")
[124] *See, e.g.*, Landry v. St. Charles Inn, Inc., 446 So.2d 1246, 1249–50 (La. Ct. App.1984) (affirming jury's verdict against hotel operator liable for damages suffered by guest who was robbed in hotel parking lot because hotel failed to provide adequate security. No less than seven robberies or assaults had occurred in the immediate area in the prior year. Also, St. Charles Inn conceded that it had "no security precautions of any kind whatsoever.").
[125] Hollander v. Days Inn Motel, 97-805 (La.App. 3 Cir. 12/10/97, 5); 705 So.2d 1126, 1128, writ denied, 98-0746 (La. 5/1/98); 718 So.2d 417
[126] *Id.*

to warn Hollander, and he appealed.[127] The Louisiana Third Circuit Court of Appeal distinguished *Banks* because this hotel had no security detail exercising control on this more distant public property.[128] The appellate court affirmed the summary judgment in favor of the hotel.[129]

Other incidents of "lack of security" that Louisiana courts found significant include: *Kraaz v. La Quinta Motor Inns, Inc.*, where the Supreme Court of Louisiana affirmed judgment holding an innkeeper liable for damages suffered by guests who were robbed and assaulted inside their hotel rooms when the desk clerk gave the robber the master key;[130] and *Margreiter v. New Hotel Monteleone, Inc. and Liberty Mutual Insurance Company*, where the Fifth Circuit affirmed judgment holding a hotel liable when the hotel had no cameras, heat sensors, adequate alarms or guards to prevent the use of an elevator to a room and an unguarded exit into an alleyway.[131]

IV. INSURANCE COVERAGE FOR TRAFFICKING LIABILITY

Trafficking cases present various coverage issues under different types of liability policies, most commonly general liability policies, but also specialized liability policies such as professional liability and director's and officer's liability policies. These cases also present procedural issues with respect to obtaining a declaration or otherwise resolving such issues. However, there are few published opinions on coverage for trafficking liability cases.

A. Procedural Issues

1. Justiciable Controversy

Like with other disputes, a justiciable controversy is required for a court to decide coverage issues. Where the defendants in a trafficking case did not seek coverage from the insurers, there was no such dispute in the case of *Canopius Capital Two Ltd. v. Jeanne Estates Apartments, Inc.*[132] That case concerned the property and business of Tony Alamo Christian Ministries, which forced minors to become "spiritual wives"

---

[127] *Id.* at 1127.

[128] *Id.* at 1128.

[129] *Id.*

[130] Kraaz v. La Quinta Motor Inns, Inc., 410 So. 2d 1048, 1049, 1053 (La. 1982).

[131] Margreiter v. New Hotel Monteleone, Inc., 640 F.2d 508, 509 (5th Cir.1981).

[132] Canopius U.S. Ins., Inc. v. Johnson, 4:13-CV-4079, 2016 WL 1178793, at *4 (W.D. Ark. Mar. 23, 2016).

before subjecting them to frequent sexual, physical, and psychological abuse.[133] At least one of the underlying complaints alleged trafficking liability under 18 U.S.C. § 1595.[134] In *Canopius Capital*, the United States District Court for the Western District of Arkansas denied the insurer's summary judgment for lack of any remaining justiciable controversy.[135] First, none of the defendant insureds made a direct request to the insurer for defense and/or indemnification.[136] Second, in one of the underlying suits, the plaintiff settled or nonsuited any remaining claims, removing any justiciable controversy for the court to decide.[137] Third, some of the defendant insureds from another underlying suit opposed the summary judgment by citing a duty to defend and indemnify against the judgment.[138] The defendant claimants, however, stipulated that they had not and did not seek insurance proceeds in the collection of these adverse judgments.[139]

2. Intervention

In *M.A. v. Wyndham Hotels & Resorts, Inc.*, the United States District Court for the Southern District of Ohio denied the insurer's late motions to intervene because the insurer had no more than a contingent interest in the underlying action.[140] Erie Insurance Exchange sought to intervene under Federal Rule of Civil Procedure 24 to protect its rights in two sex trafficking cases against hotels insured by Erie.[141] Rule 24(a) requires intervention as a matter of right pursuant to a timely filed motion with a substantial legal interest involved that will be impaired without intervention, and inadequacy of the present parties.[142] Erie argued that it

---

[133] *Id.* at *1.

[134] *Id.*

[135] *Id.* at *6.

[136] *Id.* at *4-5.

[137] *Id.* at *4. Notably, the underlying case did involve a dispute over apartment complex insurance with Truck Insurance Exchange and Farmers Insurance Exchange. *Kolbek v. Truck Ins. Exch.*, 431 S.W.3d 900, 903 (2014). The insurance policy applied to bodily injury, property damage, etc. arising out of the ownership, maintenance, or use of premises. *Id.* at 908. In that case, the Supreme Court of Arkansas ultimately upheld a lower court's findings of fact and conclusions of law finding that none of the Kolbek's allegations were connected to the ownership, maintenance, or use of the apartment premises. *Id.*

[138] *Id.* at *5.

[139] *Id.* (While the court granted summary judgment as to the underlying suit, it did so because the occurrence occurred outside the policy inception.)

[140] M.A. v. Wyndham Hotels & Resorts, Inc., 2:19-CV-755, 2020 WL 1853216, at *1 (S.D. Ohio Apr. 13, 2020).

[141] *Id.*

[142] *Id.* (citing FED. R. CIV. P. 24(a)(2) and Michigan State AFL–CIO v. Miller, 103 F.3d 1240, 1245 (6th Cir. 1997)).

should be permitted to intervene because the defendants sought both defense and indemnity under the policy and potential coverage for some of plaintiffs' claims.[143] The court denied Erie's intervention as a right because Erie's coverage interest was contingent on the underlying action; Erie's right to bring a future declaratory judgment would not be impaired if it did not intervene; and the existing parties were sufficient to decide the underlying case.[144]

In the same case, the court also considered Erie's permissive intervention under Rule 24(b). Under Rule 24(b), Erie argued that its timely motion shared a common question of law or fact with the main action and, as such, intervention would not cause undue delay or prejudice.[145] Erie asserted that its legal obligations rested on the same factual record of the parties.[146] But, as the court explained, this contingent interest focuses on the policy language, which is "wholly separate from the TVPRA [sex trafficking] claims in the main action."[147] The court also found prejudice because it would force the Plaintiff to fight a coverage dispute in which it did not yet have an interest.[148] And the court found Erie's motions untimely because they were filed several months after an earlier insurer's intervention attempts without explanation.[149] The court denied permissive intervention.[150]

In *Lisa Ricchio v. Bijal, Inc. d/b/a Shangri-La Motel*, the United States District Court for the District of Massachusetts eventually permitted intervention by the insurer.[151] Two months after the underlying complaint was filed, Peerless Indemnity Insurance attempted to intervene but was denied.[152] Peerless then filed a separate declaratory judgment, asserting jurisdiction under 28 U.S.C. § 1367, which was stayed.[153] However, after the court lifted the stay, the court then granted Peerless' motion to intervene because it was concerned that § 1367 could not sustain jurisdiction in the independent case.[154]

---

[143] *Id.* at *2.
[144] *Id.* at *2–3 (collecting cases Travelers Indem. Co. v. Dingwell, 884 F.2d 629, 638 (1st Cir. 1989); Nautilus Ins. Co. ex rel. Ecklebarger v. C.C. Rider, Inc., 2002 WL 32073073 (N.D. Ind. Nov. 25, 2002); Nieto v. Kapoor, 61 F. Supp. 2d 1177 (D.N.M. August 4, 1999); Sachs v. Reef Aquaria Design, Inc., 2007 WL 2973841 (N.D. Ill. Oct. 5, 2007)).
[145] *Id.* at *3 (citing FED. R. CIV. P. 42(b)).
[146] *Id.*
[147] *Id.*
[148] *Id.*
[149] *Id.*
[150] *Id.* at *4.
[151] Ricchio v. Bijal, Inc., 424 F. Supp. 3d 182, 185–86 (D. Mass. 2019).
[152] *Id.* at 185.
[153] *Id.* at 186.
[154] *Id.*

Declaratory Judgment Actions

Declaratory judgment actions provide the insurer with a coverage determination sooner rather than later, which the courts, and the parties, prefer. For example, Atain Specialty Insurance Company ("Atain") recently filed a declaratory judgment action against Varahi Hotel, LLC ("Varahi") and Jane Doe 1 concerning the *Red Roof Inn* cases.[155] Atain seeks a declaration that it has no duty to defend or indemnify Varahi for Jane Doe 1's claims and alleged damages based upon several policy terms and conditions, including a physical abuse exclusion. While some declaratory judgment actions seeking to determine coverage will be protracted depending upon the current state of the underlying lawsuit, at least as to the final outcome, the actions offer a vehicle with which the insurer can determine the coverage facts early, and perhaps frame the issues, through discovery taken in the declaratory judgment action.

B. Coverage Issues Under Commercial General Liability Policies

Commercial General Liability ("CGL") insurance policies generally provide the primary liability insurance coverage for most companies. CGL policies typically include two major coverage sections. One section, "Coverage A" includes coverage for "bodily injury" and "property damage." These provide coverage to the insured against claims made for injury to persons, including death, and physical damage to, or loss of use of, tangible property. "Coverage B" includes coverage for "personal and "advertising injury." Personal and advertising injury generally covers claims for torts such as invasion of privacy, slander and libel, as well as false arrest, detention and imprisonment.

1. Personal and Advertising Injury Exclusions

The distinction between Coverage A and Coverage B can raise issues for coverage of trafficking claims under CGL policies because, although trafficking claims often result in bodily injury, such claims may not be covered under Coverage A where they allege liability that would fall within Coverage B but is excluded from Coverage A.

In the *Ricchio* hotel case, Ricchio alleged that she was kidnapped and taken to the Massachusetts hotel, where she was held captive, raped,

---

[155] Atain Specialty Insurance Company v. Varahi Hotel, LLC and Jane Doe 1; Civil Action No. 1:20-cv-01582-WMR; in the United States District Court for the Northern District of Georgia, Atlanta Division.

and abused.[156] Ricchio asserted that the insured hotel knew of the abuse and intentionally assisted with the sex trafficking to profit from it.[157] In turn, Peerless sought summary judgment declaring that it had no duty to defend the insured hotel under either CGL Coverages A and B.[158]

The court found that there was no coverage for the human trafficking under Coverage A because that Coverage was subject to exclusion (o) for "Personal and Advertising Injury," which excluded coverage for "bodily injury arising out of personal injury."[159] The policy defined "personal injury" to include, among other things, "injury, including consequential 'bodily injury' arising out of . . . false imprisonment."[160] Ricchio argued for a narrow interpretation of "arising out of" that mirrored "but for" causation, because a separate asbestos exclusion in the policy used broader language.[161] Rejecting Ricchio's argument, the court held that the exclusions dealt with different topics.[162] The court further explained that Ricchio did not explain how injuries could arise only out of her trafficking without her imprisonment.[163] Accordingly, the court held that because Ricchio's injuries arose out of her false imprisonment, her injuries were excluded coverage under Coverage A of the CGL policy.[164]

However, the court found that the insurer did have a duty to defend the hotel company under Coverage B of the insured's policy, which covered "personal and advertising injury" caused by an offense arising out of the insured's business.[165] The court had already found that the plaintiff's claims arose out of her false imprisonment, which was covered under Coverage B, and rejected the insurer's argument that her injury arose out of the statutory violation alone.[166] The court also rejected the insurer's argument that the plaintiff's injury did not arise out of the hotel company's business because the company is not "in the business of human trafficking" on the grounds that the renting of the room was part of the insured's business.[167]

---

[156] *Id.* at 185.
[157] *Id.* at 185, 194.
[158] *Id.* at 185.
[159] *Id.* at 189.
[160] *Id.*
[161] *Id.* at 191.
[162] *Id.*
[163] *Id.* at 190.
[164] *Id.* at 192.
[165] Id. at 188, 195.
[166] *Id.* at 192.
[167] *Id.*

2. Criminal Acts Exclusions

The *Ricchio* case also raised another common coverage issue for trafficking cases under CGL policies – criminal acts exclusions. Coverage B in the CGL policy at issue had a "Criminal Acts" exclusion which precluded coverage for personal injuries "arising out of a criminal act committed by or at the direction of the insured."[168] Peerless contended that the hotel criminally violated the TVPA to cause Ricchio's injuries, which in turn triggered the exclusion.[169]

The court ruled, however, that the plaintiff's complaint was reasonably susceptible to an interpretation that there was coverage under Coverage B of the insured's policy.[170] The court interpreted the TVPA to permit civil recovery even absent proof of intentional criminal conduct.[171] While Ricchio's claims were focused on intentional conduct, the broad requirements of a duty to defend allowed the complaint to be "reasonably susceptible" to an interpretation of only civil negligence.[172] Thus, the Criminal Acts exclusion did not apply and Peerless had a duty to defend under the policy.[173]

Bodily injury coverage under CGL policies is also typically subject to an exclusion for intended injury, such as: "This insurance does not apply to: . . . 'Bodily injury' or 'property damage' expected or intended from the standpoint of the insured." Depending on the allegations in a trafficking complaint, insurers may also argue that this exclusion applies on the basis that injury from trafficking is expected. Given the availability of "should have known" *scienter* requirements in the TVPA, however, the analysis of the *Ricchio* court may apply to this exclusion as well.

3. Assault & Battery Exclusions

In *Nautilus Insurance Company v. Motel Management Services*, the United States District Court for the Eastern District of Pennsylvania held that the insurer had no duty to defend or indemnify the insured because the alleged sex trafficking claims were barred by an assault or battery exclusion to the CGL policy.[174] Nautilus Insurance Company sought a declaration on its duty to defend and indemnify its insured, Motel

---

[168] *Id.*
[169] *Id.*
[170] *Id.* at 195.
[171] *Id.* at 193–94.
[172] *Id.* at 195.
[173] *Id.*
[174] Nautilus Ins. Co. v. Motel Mgmt. Servs., 320 F. Supp. 3d 636, 643 (E.D. Pa. 2018), *aff'd*, 781 Fed. Appx. 57 (3d Cir. 2019).

Management Services, Inc., a motel in Pennsylvania.[175] At the motel, a minor female allegedly was "held at gunpoint and threatened to engage in sex acts" in violation of several Pennsylvania state kidnapping and rape statutes.[176]

The minor brought claims alleging that the motel knowingly permitted the traffickers' activities, failed to intervene or report the activities, and profited from the rented rooms where the sex acts occurred.[177] She brought her claims under negligence and intentional infliction of emotional distress theories, including a state trafficking law similar to the TVPA.[178] The motel sought coverage under its CGL policy.[179]

The court held that the minor's claims were excluded under the policy's "All Assault or Battery" exclusion which excluded coverage for bodily injury that resulted from any "[a]ctual or alleged assault or battery," regardless of the "culpability or intent of any person."[180] The exclusion also expressly included any act or omission relating to the assault, battery, or prevention of same, including "adequate security," and "emotional distress" arising out of the assault or battery.[181] Thus, the court reasoned that the definitions of assault and battery were broad enough to encompass a negligent insured who did not prevent the assault and battery.[182]

On appeal, the Court of Appeals for the Third Circuit affirmed the District Court, agreeing that coverage was barred by the All Assault or Battery exclusion because the policy excluded claims "arising out of" an assault or battery.[183] Because the assault and battery were the "but for" causes of the minor's injuries—she was ordered at gunpoint to have sex—

---

[175] *Id.* at 637.

[176] *Id.* at 638, 642–43.

[177] *Id.* at 639.

[178] *Id.*

[179] *Id.* at 639, 641.

[180] *Id.* at 641.

[181] *Id.* at 643.

[182] *Id.* The District Court substantiated its conclusion by stating that requiring an insurer to cover claims for intentional torts or criminal acts ran afoul with public policy. *Id.* The District Court stated that "financially benefitting from human sex trafficking is criminalized under the Pennsylvania Human Trafficking Law." *Id.* Thus, Pennsylvania public policy precluded coverage. *Id.* Note that public policy depends on the particular state. For example, there is authority in Texas that public policy prohibits allowing a person from insuring against his intentional misconduct. However, this is subject to exceptions, including that it does not apply to negligent supervision claims. Roman Catholic Diocese of Dallas v. Interstate Fire & Cas. Co., 133 S.W.3d 887, 896 (Tex. App.—Dallas 2004, pet. denied).

[183] Nautilus Ins. Co. v. Motel Mgmt. Services, Inc., 781 Fed. Appx. 57, 60 (3d Cir. 2019).

they arose out the assault and battery.[184] Other cases have upheld similar exclusions.[185]

4. Abuse & Molestation Exclusions

Some CGL policies may include provisions that specifically relate to sexual abuse or molestation, which can impact coverage for trafficking claims. For example, in *Millers Capital Insurance Co. v. Anil Vasant*, the United States District Court for the District of Maryland held that the insurer had a duty to defend the insured because the alleged sex trafficking claims were not barred by an abuse and molestation exception to the CGL policy.[186] In the underlying suit, Jane Doe plaintiffs had been held at an America's Best Value Inn before the traffickers transported them to the insured's Econo Lodge.[187] There they were forced to take provocative pictures that were posted on a website as advertisements and to perform sex acts.[188] The Jane Doe plaintiffs alleged claims of negligence (premises liability), negligent training, retention and supervision, and *respondeat superior*.[189]

An Abuse or Molestation exclusion modified the usual CGL policy at issue by adding an exclusion to the "bodily injury and property damage" and "personal and advertising injury" coverage provisions.[190] Specifically, it excluded those injuries that arise from "the actual or threatened abuse or molestation *by anyone* of any person while *in the care,*

---

[184] *Id.* at 60. The Third Circuit did not address whether public policy would also preclude coverage for the criminal conduct and intentional torts alleged because the policy excluded coverage. *Id.* at 61 n.5.

[185] In *Piligra v. America's Best Value Inn*, the court found that a rape's necessary use of force or violence precluded recovery for plaintiff under the assault and battery exclusion. 2010-254 (La.App. 3 Cir. 10/6/10, 6); 49 So.3d 479, 484. *See also* Espinosa v. Accor N. Am., Inc., 2014-0001 (La.App. 4 Cir. 9/24/14, 13–18); 148 So.3d 244, 253–56 (where a CGL's assault and battery exclusion combined with a reinstating endorsement allowed a limited recovery when insured hotel failed to provide adequate security to guest who was robbed and shot in parking lot), *writ denied*, 2014-2446 (La. 2/13/15); 159 So.3d 466, *and writ denied*, 2014-2453 (La. 2/13/15); 159 So.3d 467; and Ledbetter v. Concord Gen. Corp., 95-0809 (La. 1/6/96, 5–8); 665 So.2d 1166, 1169–71, *amended*, 95-0809 (La. 4/18/96); 671 So.2d 915 (holding that rape was clearly excluded by the assault and battery exclusion, but kidnapping was not because kidnapping did not necessarily involve force or violence upon another person).

[186] Millers Capital Ins. Co. v. Vasant, CV RDB-18-0553, 2018 WL 5295899, at *1 (D. Md. Oct. 25, 2018).

[187] *Id.* at *2.

[188] *Id.*

[189] *Id.* at *3.

[190] *Id.* at *1–2.

custody or control of any insured."[191]   While the court interpreted the language "by anyone" broadly, it interpreted "care custody, and control" as a function of "watching, guarding, or overseeing."[192]   In other words, for a hotel to keep its guests safe, the hotel must be on notice that the invitee is on the premises.[193]   The court explained that a hotel cannot care for or guard a guest whom the hotel has no knowledge or indication is on its premises.[194]

Examining the record, the court held that there was no evidence that the hotel was ever aware that the victims were on its premises.[195] The record showed that no Econo Lodge staff saw the Jane Does, nor did housekeeping come to the rooms; the clients came in at night; the Jane Does did not go to the hotel common areas or office; and "Jane Does #1 and #3 testified that they were not abused or molested while at the Econo Lodge, but were falsely imprisoned at the hotel."[196] Being unaware of the victims, the hotel did not have the victims under its care, custody, or control.[197]   Accordingly, the court granted summary judgment for the insureds, requiring Millers Capital to defend and reimburse defense costs already expended.[198]

Similarly, in *Millers Capital Ins. Co. v. Vasant,* an insurer sought a declaration that it had no duty to defend or indemnify its insured under a general liability policy for allegations in an underlying suit for sex trafficking and prostitution.[199] The insured owned and operated several hotels where the plaintiffs were victims of trafficking and a prostitution ring.[200] The insurer alleged that an "Abuse and Molestation Endorsement" precluded coverage.[201] The court held that since the hotel did not have the victims under its "care, custody or control" the exclusion did not apply, and the insurer had a duty to defend its insured.[202]

In the absence of similar "care, custody, and control" language, however, an abuse or molestation exclusion may apply to preclude coverage. For example, in *Piligra v. America's Best Value Inn*, a Louisiana appellate court affirmed a trial court's holding that the CGL policy's

---

[191] *Id.* at *2 (emphasis added).
[192] *Id.* at *4–5.
[193] *Id.* at *6.
[194] *Id.* at *6.
[195] *Id.* at *7.
[196] *Id.* at *6–7.
[197] *Id.* at *7.
[198] *Id.*
[199] No. CV RDB-18-0553, 2018 WL 5295899, at *7 (D. Md. Oct. 25, 2018)
[200] *Id.*
[201] *Id.*
[202] *Id.*

sexual abuse and/or molestation exclusion applied.[203] Piligra had lost consciousness by consuming alcohol at a nightclub within the hotel.[204] An employee escorted her to a room, leaving her with an unknown male who allegedly raped her.[205] Piligra alleged negligence of an innkeeper's standard of care.[206]

The *Piligra* hotel's sexual abuse and/or molestation exclusion excluded bodily injury for "the actual or threatened abuse or molestation . . . culminating in any sexual act."[207] It also excluded negligent hiring or supervision of an employee.[208] The court explained that molestation implied "a degree of unwanted touching."[209] Piligra's allegations of rape, *i.e.* nonconsensual sex, supported the trial court's finding that the sexual molestation exclusion applied.[210] In this case, the absence of control language preserved the exclusion.

An Abuse & Molestation Exclusion was also interpreted in *OTRA, LLC v. Am. Safety Indem. Co.,* a coverage dispute as to whether the insurer should defend an insured against claims that it negligently allowed sex trafficking to occur in a strip club. [211] The court held that the Expected Or Intended Injury Exclusion did not apply because the alleged conduct was "negligent" rather than "intentional."[212] The court further found that a "Abuse, Molestation, Sexual Assault" exclusion did not apply because there were at least some allegations within coverage that were sufficient to invoke the duty to defend, specifically that the insured failed to discover that customers touched the plaintiff in non-sexual ways on the club's premises and failed to prevent them from doing so.[213]

Still other policies may include express coverage for abuse or molestation claims. For example, the Fifth Circuit has interpreted a policy with an endorsement providing: "[I]t is hereby understood and agreed that Bodily Injury and Property Damage includes any act, which may be considered sexual in nature and could be classified as an Abuse, Harassment, Molestation, Corporal Punishment or an Invasion of an

---

[203] Piligra, 49 So.3d at 488.

[204] *Id.* at 482.

[205] *Id.*

[206] *Id.*

[207] Piligra, 49 So.3d at 484.

[208] *Id.* at 485.

[209] *Id.*

[210] *Id.* The policy also included a "Restaurant, Bar, Tavern, Night Clubs, Fraternal and Social Clubs Endorsement," which also excluded coverage. *Id.*

[211] Case No. 3:20-CV-01063-SB, 2020 WL 6828738, at *1 (D. Or. Nov. 20, 2020).

[212] *Id.*

[213] *Id.*

individual's right of Privacy or control over their physical and/or mental properties by or at the direction of an Insured . . . ."[214]

C. Other Potentially Applicable Policies

Depending on the claims alleged there may be coverage under other liability policies for trafficking-related claims. Issues under such policies include the following:

Professional Liability Policies: Professional liability policies typically cover claims against the insured for alleged conduct in providing professional services. The professional services covered vary considerably policy. If a claimant alleges that the insured's conduct in participating in a trafficking venture involves the insured's professional services, then such allegations could trigger coverage under professional liability policies.

Directors and Officers ("D&O") Liability Policies: D&O policy terms also vary, but they usually cover a company's directors and officers for claims against them for "wrongful acts," which is typically broadly defined, performed in their capacity as directors and officers of the company. Private company D&O policies also cover the company itself broadly for "wrongful acts." Public company D&O policies, on the other hand, typically only cover claims against the company by shareholders or alleging violation of securities regulations or laws. Accordingly, if shareholders were to assert claims against a public company or its directors or officers alleging that trafficking liability resulted in a stock drop or other damage to the shareholders, such claims could be covered under a D&O liability policy. D&O policies typically do not have specific exclusions for sexual conduct; however, they typically exclude bodily injury, so they are less likely to apply to direct trafficking claims.

---

[214] Western Heritage Ins. Co. v. Magic Years Learning Centers and Child Care, Inc., 45 F.3d 85, 88 (5th Cir. 1995); see also, e.g., McCain v. Promise House, Inc., 2018 WL 2042009, at *1 (Tex. App.—Dallas May 2, 2018, no pet. h.) (enforcing settlement of negligence claims against employer relating to sexual abuse where the policy explicitly covered bodily injury "arising out of 'sexual or physical abuse'").

V. CONCLUSION

The International Labor Organization estimates that sex trafficking generates $99 billion globally.[215] As the trafficking problem has grown in magnitude, the federal government and the states have enacted legislation in an attempt to combat the problem. These statutes include both criminal and civil liability. Businesses facing civil liability often seek indemnity for such civil losses from their insurers. Common policy provisions may preclude coverage for liability arising from sexual trafficking, however, as with all other coverage issues, the language of the applicable policy is paramount.

---

[215] *Profits and Poverty: The Economics of Forced Labour,* INTERNATIONAL LABOUR ORGANIZATION (2014), https://www.ilo.org/global/topics/forced-labour/publications/profits-of-forced-labour-2014/lang--en/index.htm

HAUNTINGLY FUN LEGAL ENVIRONMENT OF BUSINESS TOPICS FOR A HALLOWEEN-THEMED CLASS

MICHAEL CONKLIN[*]

I. INTRODUCTION

This Teaching Note provides potential topics for an engaging and informative Halloween-themed Legal Environment of Business class activity. Each topic is in some way related to Halloween and can be used to illustrate a variety of legal principles. Instructors are encouraged to really lean into the theme by dressing up, playing haunted house background music,[1] and dimming the lights. A Halloween-themed class also serves as a welcome break from the traditional lecture for both instructor and students. There are enough potential topics listed in this Teaching Note to cover an entire week of lectures; a single class; or even just a 15-minute, interactive, themed quiz using Kahoot!, Quizlet, or Poll Everywhere. Note that this activity does not have to be limited to legal topics covered up to this point in the semester. This lighthearted, relaxed environment in which a variety of topics are casually discussed is an excellent method to get the class excited about—and considering the implications of—topics to come later in the semester.

From personal experience, I can attest that this class activity is not only the highlight of the semester for myself and the students as far as entertainment value but is also a powerful catalyst for sparking deeper interest in the subject. Weeks after the activity, students will poignantly refer back to principles initially discussed in the Halloween activity. And students frequently mention in their end-of-semester evaluations how much they enjoyed the activity. Teaching pedagogy research confirms these anecdotal findings as to how effective themed class periods that utilize pop culture are at engaging learners.[2] Note that this Teaching Note

---

[*] Assistant Professor, Powell Endowed Professor of Business Law, Angelo State University.

[1] This is available on YouTube by searching for "haunted house sounds."

[2] Ana M. H. Kehrberg, *Halloween as an Opportunity for Teaching Biological Psychology*, in 15 ESSAYS FROM E-XCELLENCE IN TEACHING: REDUCING UNDERGRADUATE WRITING APPREHENSION WITH THE BASIC PSYCHOLOGICAL NEEDS 23, (William S. Altman, Lyra Stein & Jonathan E. Westal eds., 2016), https://www.researchgate.net/profile/Jacqueline-Espinoza/publication/327190241_E-xcellence_in_writing_Reducing_undergraduate_writing_apprehension_with_the_basic_p sychological_needs/links/5b7f18fca6fdcc5f8b6370c5/E-xcellence-in-writing-Reducing-undergraduate-writing-apprehension-with-the-basic-psychological-needs.pdf; Victoria

is a resource for instructors and not a handout to students. Therefore, a moderate knowledge base of the law is assumed. Furthermore, it is intentionally not a step-by-step guide; rather, it is a list of topics with brief descriptions that can then be customized by the instructor to match his or her teaching style, along with time, modality, and class size constraints.

II. HAUNTING RAMIFICATIONS OF REAL ESTATE CONTRACTS

A homeowner in Nyack, New York, lived in a three story, fifteen-room Victorian house that he claimed was haunted by poltergeists.[3] The homeowner recounted stories of the allegedly paranormal activity in local news accounts and in an article published in *Reader's Digest*.[4] The homeowner then sold the house to a buyer from New York City.[5] The homeowner was never asked, and never mentioned, the allegedly haunted nature of the house.[6] Before moving in, the buyer heard about the house's reputation of being haunted and sued to rescind the contract and recover the down payment.[7]

A New York court cheekily held that normally the plaintiff wouldn't have a "ghost of a chance" because there is generally no duty to warn a home buyer of alleged hauntings.[8] However, the court was nevertheless "moved by the spirit of equity" to rule in favor of the plaintiff.[9] In considering whether to apply the strict rule of caveat emptor to a potentially haunted house, the court asked, "Who you gonna' call?"[10] This is not just a clever reference to the movie *Ghostbusters* but a valid point. Was the buyer expected to bring a "psychic or medium [to accompany] the structural engineer and Terminix man on an inspection of

---

Bryant, *Harry Potter and the Osteopathic Medical School: Creating a Harry Potter-Themed Day as a High-Yield Review for Final Exams*, 31 MED. SCI. EDUCATOR 819 (2021); Jeffrey M. Craig, Renee Dow & Mary Anne Aitken, *Harry Potter and the Recessive Allele*, 436 NATURE 776 (2005); Susan Hatters Friedman & Ryan C. W. Hall, *Teaching Psychopathology in a Galaxy Far, Far Away: The Light Side of the Force*, 39 ACAD. PSYCHIATRY 719 (2015); Lisa Tessier & Jack Tessier, *Theme-Based Courses Foster Student Learning and Promote Comfort with Learning New Material*, 11 J. FOR LEARNING THROUGH ARTS 1 (2015); Renee Sorrentino et al., *Sex on the Silver Screen: Using Film to Teach About Paraphilias*, 42 ACAD. PSYCHIATRY 237 (2018).
[3] Christina Poletto, *'Legally' Haunted New York Manor Is for Sale Again*, N.Y. POST (Sept. 19, 2019, 12:17 AM), https://nypost.com/2019/09/19/legally-haunted-new-york-manor-is-for-sale-again/.
[4] Stambovsky v. Ackley, 572 N.Y.S.2d 672,   674 (1991).
[5] *Id.*
[6] *Id.*
[7] Id.
[8] *Id.* at 675.
[9] *Id.*
[10] *Id.*

every home subject to a contract of sale?"[11] "[T]he notion that a haunting is a condition which can and should be ascertained upon reasonable inspection of the premises is a hobgoblin which should be exorcised from the body of legal precedent and laid quietly to rest."[12] The general rule that non-disclosure does not constitute misrepresentation is only applicable when the undisclosed fact is patent or when the plaintiff has equal opportunities to obtain the information.[13] The court ruled in favor of the buyer, and he was able to rescind the contract and recover his down payment.[14]

Some media accounts of this case claimed that "New York's Supreme Court ruled that the home was officially haunted."[15] This is somewhat misleading. The court did not hear evidence for and against the existence of a poltergeist in the house. Rather, the court created a legal fiction that the house was haunted by estopping the seller from denying the existence of a poltergeist because the seller made previous claims of its existence.[16]

It is interesting to note that the once notorious reputation of the house may now serve as a selling feature. Haunted tourism is a $300 million-a-year industry in America.[17] Former owners of the Nyack, New York, house now include film director Adam Brooks, singer-songwriter Ingrid Michaelson, and Orthodox Jewish rapper Matisyahu, although none of these owners have reported anything supernatural.[18]

Pictures of the beautiful Victorian house are easily found by searching "Nyack haunted house" on the internet and can be shown to the class for context. This case allows for numerous hypotheticals to pose to the class. For example, if a seller did not believe the house was haunted and never claimed it was haunted, but the buyer came to believe it was haunted after signing the contract, could the buyer void the contract? In

---

[11] *Id.*

[12] *Id.*

[13] *Id.*

[14] *Id.*

[15] Poletto, *supra* note 3. Note that New York is one of the few states where the trial-level courts are referred to as Supreme Court and the highest court is referred to as the Court of Appeals.

[16] *Stambovsky*, 572 N.Y.S.2d at 674 ("Whether the source of the spectral apparitions seen by defendant seller are parapsychic or psychogenic, having reported their presence in both a national publication (Readers' Digest) and the local press (in 1977 and 1982, respectively), defendant is estopped to deny their existence and, as a matter of law, the house is haunted.").

[17] Elizabeth Yuko, *The Terrifying Rise of Haunted Tourism*, BLOOMBERG (Oct. 28, 2021, 6:00 AM), https://www.bloomberg.com/news/features/2021-10-28/when-ghost-hunters-become-historic-preservationists.

[18] Poletto, *supra* note 3.

this instance, the answer is probably not. The buyer of the Nyack house was only allowed to void the contract because the seller had made numerous claims that the house was haunted. The best argument available to the buyer in this hypothetical is likely that modern law imposes an implied warranty of habitability, ensuring that a home will not have defects that substantially impair the enjoyment of the residence.[19] A hyperactive poltergeist would certainly be a breach of this implied warranty, but the buyer would have the onerous burden of proving not only that such a poltergeist exists but also that it existed at the time the house was purchased—as opposed to moving in with the buyer.

III. A DEVILISH DEFENDANT

If there is anyone who deserves to be held liable for bad acts, surely it is Satan. In 1971, a man attempted to hold him liable by filing a civil rights action against Satan for allegedly placing deliberate obstacles in his way that caused his downfall.[20] The court rejected the claim for not providing a cause of action upon which relief can be granted.[21] Furthermore, the court explained that it lacked personal jurisdiction over the defendant, Satan, as "[t]he complaint contains no allegation of residence in this district."[22] Finally, the court noted that the plaintiff failed to file the required form for the U.S. Marshal to serve process on the defendant.[23]

IV. ETHICAL CANNIBALISM?

The classic law school case of *R v. Dudley & Stephens* is an unsettling tale involving cannibalism.[24] The eerie tale begins with a capsized ship 700 miles away from land.[25] All four crewmembers escaped on a lifeboat, where they faced shark attacks, starvation, and dehydration.[26] One of the crewmembers, a teenaged cabin boy with no family, fell ill from drinking sea water, which he was advised against

---

[19] Melvin A. Eisenberg, *Disclosure in Contract Law*, 91 CAL. L. REV. 1645, 1679–80 n.79 (2003).
[20] *United States ex rel. Gerald Mayo v. Satan and His Staff*, 54 F.R.D. 282, 282–83 (W.D. Pa. 1971).
[21] *Id.* at 283.
[22] *Id.*
[23] *Id.*
[24] R v. Dudley & Stephens, [1884] 14 Q.B.D. 273.
[25] Elizabeth Gam, *The Queen vs. Dudley Stephens*, HARV. L. (June 25, 2018), https://h2o.law.harvard.edu/text_blocks/30824.
[26] *Id.*

drinking.[27] On the twentieth day, the other three crewmembers agreed to kill and eat the cabin boy, which they did.[28] They were rescued three days later.[29] They were then tried for murder, during which two of them, Dudley and Stephens, were initially sentenced to death but later had their sentences commuted to six months in prison.[30]

This gruesome tale elicits discussion about a number of legal and ethical issues, including:

- What is the purpose of criminal sanctions (retributive, restorative, or preventative)?
- The "necessity" defense.
- Is the value of human life relative to factors such as age, career position, and reliance from family members?
- Utilitarian versus deontological ethics.
- The crew members debated using a lottery to decide who to kill and eat.[31] Is that any better?
- Would it have been wrong to eat the cabin boy after he died from dehydration?

For more information, Michael Sandel has an excellent class discussion about this case available on YouTube.[32]

V. INTELLECTUAL PROPERTY RIGHTS, IT'S ALIVE, IT'S ALIVE!

The creation of Frankenstein's monster implicates numerous legal issues regarding intellectual property (and ethics!). In the 1957 movie version of the story, Dr. Frankenstein worked with his partner Paul Krempe. United States patent law allows for the issuance of a patent to co-inventors even if they did not contribute equally to the invention.[33] So Dr. Frankenstein might have to share the fruits of such a patent with Krempe—that is, assuming the patent is not denied on the ground of being for an illegal purpose. Perhaps the scariest aspect of Dr. Frankenstein patenting

---

[27] *Id.*
[28] *Id.*
[29] *Id.*
[30] *Id.*
[31] *Id.*
[32] Harvard University, *Justice: What's the Right Thing to Do? Episode 01 "The Moral Side of Murder,"* at 29:30 (Sept. 4, 2009), https://youtu.be/kBdfcR-8hEY.
[33] Brian Weissenberg, *U.S. Patent No. '666 to V. Frankenstein and P. Krempe?*, LEGAL GEEKS (October 27, 2020), https://thelegalgeeks.com/2020/10/27/u-s-patent-no-666-to-v-frankenstein-and-p-krempe/.

the process of how to reanimate dead tissue is that it would then be made public information!

VI. ESTABLISHMENT CLAUSE

The Halloween season brings about a variety of issues regarding the Establishment Clause. For example, in 2007 a government employee sued the federal government, alleging that Halloween decorations that included depictions of witches violated the Establishment Clause of the First Amendment.[34] The court ruled against the plaintiff, explaining that generic Halloween decorations are secular in nature and do not promote witchcraft.[35]

Another Halloween-themed Establishment Clause issue is found in the peculiar standoff between Christian groups who promote the placement of the Ten Commandment monuments on state grounds and Satanist organizations who counter by proposing the placement of an over seven-foot-tall statue of Baphomet, a winged, half-goat-half-man pagan deity adorned with Satanist symbols.[36] This provides a real-life example of First Amendment protections. Students often initially express the opinion that, since promoting the Ten Commandments is "good" and promoting Baphomet is "bad," allowing the placement of the former and not the latter on state grounds is acceptable. But of course, the personal preference of a judge—or even society at large—for one message over another is not justification for selective censorship. The First Amendment is needed to protect unpopular opinions, not popular ones.

VII. FRANKENSTEIN FOODS

"Frankenstein Foods" is a derogatory term used to refer to food produced from genetically modified plants and animals.[37] This is an engaging topic to discuss because opinions on the subject are so disparate. Depending on who you ask, they are either one of the greatest inventions

---

[34] Ruiz v. Gonzalez-Galoffin, No. 06-1093CCC, 2007 U.S. Dist. LEXIS 69905 (D.P.R. Sept. 20, 2007).

[35] *Id.*

[36] Vanessa Romo, *Satanic Temple Protests Ten Commandments Monument with Goat-Headed Statue*, NPR (Aug. 17, 2018, 7:27 PM), https://www.npr.org/2018/08/17/639726472/satanic-temple-protests-ten-commandments-monument-with-goat-headed-statue.

[37] *Frankenstein Food*, DICTIONARY.COM, https://www.dictionary.com/browse/frankenstein-food (last visited Nov. 10, 2021).

that have saved over a billion people from starvation[38] or an unethical tactic by greedy corporations that could lead to disastrous results.[39] This topic also opens a variety of legal topics to discuss. Was the Supreme Court's 1980 ruling that genetically modified food can be patented consistent with the purpose of patent law?[40] Should genetically modified foods be required to expressly state their nature on the packaging?[41] If only a few states required special labels that identify the food as genetically modified, would that violate the Dormant Commerce Clause?[42] What are the implications of allowing patents on genetic material? Human genes are unpatentable due to being a product of nature, so why are genetically modified foods treated differently?[43]

VIII. POP ROCKS AND COKE, A DEADLY COMBINATION?

An urban legend that started in the 1970s claimed that drinking Coke with the volatile candy Pop Rocks in your mouth could lead to death.[44] This false rumor resulted in plummeting sales of Pop Rocks, nonstop inquiries from concerned venders and parents, and a $500,000 advertising campaign to counter the rumor.[45] Unfortunately, the advertising campaign failed, and Pop Rocks were discontinued in 1982, although they have been brought back since.[46] If the person who started the rumor that led to so much harm was identified, could he or she be successfully sued for defamation? Could others who repeated the claim

---

[38] Salil Singh, *Norman Borlaug: A Billion Lives Saved*, AGBIOWORLD, http://www.agbioworld.org/biotech-info/topics/borlaug/special.html (last visited Nov. 6, 2021).

[39] Joanna Blythman, *'Frankenstein Food' a Good Thing? It's All Great GM Lies*, DAILY MAIL (Dec. 18, 2012, 3:19 AM), https://www.dailymail.co.uk/news/article-2249687/Frankenstein-foods-good-thing-Its-great-GM-lies.html.

[40] Diamond v. Chakrabarty, 447 U.S. 303 (1980).

[41] Brad Plumer, *What's the Debate Over Labeling GM Foods?*, VOX (July 22, 2015, 12:24 PM), https://www.vox.com/2014/11/3/18092756/whats-the-debate-over-labeling-gm-foods.

[42] Almost certainly not. *See, e.g.*, George A. Kimbrell & Aurora L. Paulsen, *The Constitutionality of State-Mandated Labeling for Genetically Engineered Foods: A Definitive Defense*, 39 VT. L. REV. 341, 388–99 (2014).

[43] Ass'n for Molecular Pathology v. Myriad Genetics Inc., 569 U.S. 576 (2013).

[44] Natalie O'Neil, *How the Explosive 'Pop Rocks and Coke' Legend Destroyed an Iconic Candy Brand*, THRILLIST (Oct. 5, 2017, 4:00 AM), https://www.thrillist.com/eat/nation/pop-rocks-urban-legend-mikey-death.

[45] *Id.*

[46] *Id.*

not knowing that it was false be liable for defamation?[47] If it were true that consuming Pop Rocks with Coke could lead to death, would Pop Rocks have a duty to warn? Would it have to stop selling the product? Even though Coke was in existence first, would it have a duty to warn or a duty to cease all sales?

IX. REAL-LIFE CONSEQUENCES OF A FICTIONAL MONSTER

In 2009, a member of an internet forum community created the legend of the Slender Man.[48] The legend varies, but the Slender Man is generally depicted as over seven feet tall; impossibly skinny; wearing a black suit; and possessing an amorphous, blank, white face.[49] Unfortunately, two twelve-year-old girls read about the Slender Man, lured a classmate to a park, and then stabbed her nineteen times, allegedly believing that this would please the Slender Man.[50] One of the girls was sentenced to twenty-five years in a mental institution, but after serving less than six years, she was released.[51] This incident sparks discussion about potential liability for the creator, the limits of but-for causation, the purpose of criminal sanctions (retributive, restorative, or preventative), and *mens rea*.

X. CEMETERIES BURIED IN DEBT

Many cemeteries are structured as nonprofits, but like any business they need their income to cover their expenses in order to stay in operation. However, the business model of a cemetery is somewhat antithetical to accomplishing this. Cemeteries are generally paid upfront but then obligated indefinitely to expend money on upkeep.[52] Some cemeteries are able to delay the inevitable by expanding in order to sell

---

[47] Generally, repeating defamation is still defamation. However, the company that makes Pop Rocks may be classified as a public figure, which would require the additional element of malice to be proven.
[48] Caitlin Dewey, *The Complete History of 'Slender Man,' the Meme That Compelled Two Girls to Stab a Friend*, WASH. POST (July 27, 2016), https://www.washingtonpost.com/news/the-intersect/wp/2014/06/03/the-complete-terrifying-history-of-slender-man-the-internet-meme-that-compelled-two-12-year-olds-to-stab-their-friend/.
[49] *Id.*
[50] Isabella Grullon Paz, *Teen Participant in 'Slender Man' Stabbing to Be Released from Mental Hospital*, N.Y. TIMES (Sept. 11, 2021), https://www.nytimes.com/2021/09/11/us/slender-man-anissa-weier-release.html.
[51] *Id.*
[52] Sarah Stone, *What Happens if a Cemetery Goes Under?*, TODAY I FOUND OUT (April 14, 2015), http://www.todayifoundout.com/index.php/2015/04/happens-cemeteries-go/.

more plots.[53] And some cemeteries even implement a "dig and deepen" strategy in which existing bodies are exhumed and reburied deeper so that new bodies can be buried in the same plot.[54] In the instance of a bankruptcy or foreclosure of a cemetery, a local municipality may offer to take over the maintenance duties.[55] But it is possible for a cemetery to go bankrupt, be foreclosed on, and later repurposed for commercial or residential use.[56] But anyone who has ever watched scary movies knows you should never build on a former cemetery!

XI. THE OUIJA BOARD THAT RENDERED A GUILTY VERDICT

In 1994, English jurors in a murder trial tried to use a Ouija board to help inform their verdict.[57] Believing they had contacted the spirit of the murder victim, they asked if the defendant on trial was the murderer.[58] The Ouija board allegedly indicated a positive response to this question and then spelled out "vote guilty tomorrow."[59] The jurors then rendered a guilty verdict.[60] A UK Court of Appeals quashed the murder conviction from this jury and ordered a new trial, which also returned a guilty verdict.[61] Perhaps the Ouija board was right! This fascinating case brings up numerous topics about what jurors are allowed to hear, juror misconduct, the inability of jurors to ignore evidence and testimony when instructed to do so, the requirement that criminal verdicts be unanimous, the importance of jury selection, and the standards for overturning a jury verdict.

XII. EXORCISING LEGAL LIABILITY

The 2005 move *The Exorcism of Emily Rose* is a scary movie that revolves around the wrongful death trial of a priest who performed an

---

[53] *Id.*
[54] *Id.*
[55] *Id.*
[56] *Id.*
[57] Michael Dulaney & Damien Carrick, *'Who Killed You?' The Jurors Who Used a Ouija Board to Find a Murderer Guilty*, ABC NEWS (May 7, 2018, 5:00 PM), https://www.abc.net.au/news/2018-05-08/ouija-board-juror-misbehaviour-murder-trials/9734868.
[58] *Id.*
[59] *Id.*
[60] *Id.*
[61] *Id.*

exorcism on Emily Rose that resulted in her death.[62] The movie is loosely based on the real-life 1970s West Germany case in which Anneliese Michel displayed disturbing and erratic behavior due to schizophrenia and epilepsy.[63] Anneliese and her mother solicited a priest to perform an exorcism.[64] After being rejected by numerous priests who urged her to seek medical help instead, two priests were located and performed 67 exorcisms on Anneliese, which resulted in her death from dehydration and malnourishment.[65] The two priests were sentenced to six months in prison as a result.[66] This case brings up issues of consent, contributory negligence (if it were a civil case), an unwritten preference of courts to not pry into the legitimacy of religious beliefs, and the purpose of criminal sanctions (retributive, restorative, or preventative).

XIII. THE HAUNTED HOUSE OF 1,000 TORTS

By their very nature, haunted house attractions are overflowing with potential tort liability. They are dark, frequently utilize strobe lights, and are designed to scare people. Because customers entering a haunted house are aware that the purpose is to scare them, the operators generally do not have a duty to warn against injuries that occur from frightened customers. For example, a haunted house in Louisiana was not held liable when a scared customer ran into a brick wall.[67] Likewise, a haunted corn maze was not held liable when a customer tripped and injured himself after being chased by an actor with a chainsaw.[68]

Assumption of risk is a strong defense available to haunted house attractions whose customers willingly and knowingly partake in the experience. But one does not assume the risk of injury from being scared simply by going out in public during the Halloween season. Consider the lawsuit involving a fifteen-year-old student who tripped and fractured his knee after his teacher tricked him into answering a door from which burst

---

[62] *The Exorcism of Emily Rose*, IMDB, https://www.imdb.com/title/tt0404032/plotsummary (last visited Nov. 1, 2021).
[63] Brynne Ramella, *The Exorcism of Emily Rose True Story Explained*, SCREEN RANT (July 9, 2020), https://screenrant.com/exorcism-emily-rose-true-story-explained/.
[64] Gabe Paoletti, *Anneliese Michel and the Shocking Images from the Exorcism of the Real Emily Rose*, ALL THINGS INTERESTING (Aug. 20, 2021), https://allthatsinteresting.com/anneliese-michel-exorcism.
[65] *Id.*
[66] *Id.*
[67] Mays v. Gretna, 668 So. 2d 1207 (La. Ct. App. 1996).
[68] Durmon v. Billings, 873 So. 2d 872 (La. Ct. App. 2004).

a masked man carrying a running chainsaw.[69] This student did not assume the risk of injury from being scared merely by attending class during the Halloween season. This case brings up issues of the varying duties owed to invitees, licensees, and trespassers.

XIV. IIED, THE PATRON TORT OF HALLOWEEN

If there is any tort that should be closely associated with Halloween, it is intentional infliction of emotional distress ("IIED"). And if there is anything that illustrates potential IIED liability, it is the prank show *Scare Tactics*. The show puts unsuspecting people in elaborately fabricated scenarios during which they are led to believe that they are seconds away from being murdered or severely injured.[70] This is clearly extreme and outrageous conduct and could easily result in severe emotional harm, the two elements of IIED. Another entertaining example of IIED is explicitly found in the parody business advice television show *Nathan For You*. In season 1 episode 5, Nathan advises the owner of a struggling haunted house attraction to do something so over-the-top that he gets sued for IIED and therefore receives free publicity as the scariest haunted house.[71] To accomplish this, Nathan devises a scheme in which two patrons are tricked into thinking they contracted a deadly disease while in the haunted house. They are transported in an ambulance by actors to a supposed hospital, where they are greeted by actors in hazmat suits claiming to be doctors. When they exit the ambulance, they see a sign that reads "Haunted House Exit" and are greeted by a real-life attorney asking them if they are interested in suing the haunted house for IIED.

Another potential example of IIED is found in the classic horror film *The Shining*, in which lead actress Shelley Duvall did an exceptional job portraying a scared woman tormented by a husband who is losing his sanity. Unfortunately for Duvall, this exceptional performance was due to director Stanley Kubrick's abusive treatment of her on set.[72] Kubrick insisted that the rest of the cast ignore her in an effort to evoke genuine

---

[69] *Taunton Family Filing Lawsuit After Halloween Prank Mishap at School*, CBS BOSTON (Sept. 14, 2011, 6:19 PM), https://boston.cbslocal.com/2011/09/14/taunton-family-filing-lawsuit-after-halloween-prank-mishap-at-school/.

[70] For short clips of the show, view their page on YouTube at https://www.youtube.com/c/ScareTactics/videos.

[71] *Nathan for You: Haunted House/The Hunk*, IMDB, https://www.imdb.com/title/tt2780864/ (last visited Nov. 10, 2021).

[72] Emmeline Saunders, *Shining Star Shelley Duvall Destroyed by Stanley Kubrick Abuse—Hair Loss, Bleeding Wounds & Crying Fits*, MIRROR (Mar. 7, 2020, 8:56 AM), https://www.mirror.co.uk/3am/celebrity-news/how-shining-star-shelley-duvall-21615871.

fear and terror in Duvall.[73] And he infamously demanded 127 takes of the intense baseball bat scene, which left Duvall exhausted, hoarse, and dehydrated from crying.[74] This treatment led to illness, bleeding wounds, and hair loss in Duvall.[75] It is debatable if the context of a famous actress on the scene of a big-budget horror movie would result in this behavior not being considered extreme and outrageous conduct. Additionally, one could argue against IIED by pointing out that Duvall was technically free to leave at any time—although doing so would incur an extreme harm to her reputation as an actress, and might have had contractual implications for her as well.

XV. THE INNOCUOUS COSTUME THAT CAUSED GREAT HARM

When thinking about potentially dangerous Halloween costumes, Mary and her little lamb is likely not the first to come to mind. Unfortunately for husband and wife Susan and Frank Ferlito, this costume proved highly dangerous. The husband's lamb costume was constructed by gluing cotton batting manufactured by Johnson & Johnson to long underwear.[76] While at a Halloween party, the husband tried to light his cigarette with a butane lighter, which accidentally made contact with his costume, igniting the cotton balls and severely burning him.[77] The Ferlitos sued Johnson & Johnson in a products liability action, alleging that Johnson & Johnson failed to warn them of this danger.[78] The trial court awarded them $625,000 in damages.[79]

Johnson & Johnson filed a motion for judgment notwithstanding the verdict.[80] The appeals court explained that "[a] manufacturer has a duty 'to warn the purchasers or users of its product about dangers associated with intended use.'"[81] Conversely, manufacturers have no duty to warn about dangers that may arise from unforeseeable misuse of its product.[82] The appeals court ruled that

---

[73] Id.

[74] Id.

[75] Id.

[76] Ferlito v. Johnson & Johnson Prods., Inc., 771 F. Supp. 196, 198 (E.D. Mich. 1991).

[77] Id.

[78] Id. at 199.

[79] Id. at 198.

[80] Id.

[81] Id. at 200 (quoting Rusin v. Glendale Optical Co., Inc., 805 F.2d 650, 653 (6th Cir. 1986)).

[82] Id.

no reasonable jury could find that [Johnson & Johnson's] failure to warn of the flammability of cotton batting was a proximate cause of plaintiff's injuries because plaintiffs failed to offer any evidence to establish that a flammability warning on the cotton batting would have dissuaded them from using the product in the manner that they did.[83]

Furthermore, the Ferlitos admitted at trial that they were aware that cotton batting was flammable.[84]

This combustible case ignites discussion on the applicable standard of review for a motion for judgment notwithstanding the verdict, pragmatic implications of allowing appeals court judges who were not present at trial to overturn the jury's verdict, and various issues regarding products liability and the duty to warn.

XVI. DEATH PENALTY

While the death penalty is traditionally not covered in a Legal Environment of Business course, it is an intriguing topic with which to illustrate numerous legal principles. It demonstrates how the law is often not as objective as people think. For example, students will have wildly different opinions on what constitutes cruel and unusual punishment. It is interesting to note that even death by firing squad currently does not violate constitutional protections against cruel and unusual punishments, and some activists are even calling for the firing squad to replace lethal injection to better protect death row inmates from the latter, more painful method of death.[85]

Death penalty jurisprudence also demonstrates how legal standards evolve over time. What is considered a cruel and unusual punishment today may not have been 100 years ago. Likewise, what is an acceptable punishment today may be held to be cruel and unusual in the future. This topic also brings up comparisons that many find highly inconsistent. For example, it is currently not cruel and unusual to execute someone, while it is cruel and unusual—and therefore unconstitutional—

---

[83] *Id.*
[84] *Id.*
[85] Michael Conklin, *No, the Firing Squad Is Not Better than Lethal Injection: A Response to Stephanie Moran's A Modest Proposal*, 44 SEATTLE U. L. REV. 357 (2021).

to punish a U.S. citizen with deportation.[86] This strikes many as inconsistent, as being deported is far more preferable than being executed. Finally, the death penalty naturally elicits questions regarding the purpose of criminal sanctions (retributive, restorative, or preventative).

XVII. Pet Cemetery Switcheroo

Pet aftercare is big business. There are over 700 pet funeral homes in America.[87] Businesses that offer pet cremation often sell either a group cremation service or a more expensive individual service.[88] In the group option, the remains of the pet are cremated along with other pets, and the owner receives a portion of the remains, which would include ashes of his or her pet along with others.[89] In the more expensive individual cremation, only the owner's pet's remains are cremated, and the owner receives the ashes of only his or her pet.[90] At least, that is what is supposed to happen. An investigation using fake dead cats (rabbit fur stuffed with hamburger meat) discovered that many crematories were charging for the individual service but only providing the group service.[91]

Any civil trial arising out of such a practice would have the peculiar task of establishing a dollar value for damages. There is, of course, no inherent harm that comes from learning that the ashes one possesses include ashes of other pets in addition to the owner's pet, as opposed to only that of his or her pet. Regardless, one could imagine how such a revelation could cause mental pain and suffering to a plaintiff. Although amorphous and difficult to quantify, pain and suffering damages are nonetheless compensatory (they compensate the plaintiff for actual harm) and a legally recognized damage that can be sought. To make such a case even more peculiar, one could argue that the proximate cause of the damages was not the crematory's fraudulent practice but, rather, the person who informed the owner of the deceased pet of the fraud. After all, the former pet owner could have gone the rest of his or her life incurring no damages but for this person revealing the fraud. An energetic

---

[86] *Grounds for Deportation from the United States*, Shouse Cal. L. Grp., https://www.shouselaw.com/ca/immigration/deportation-defense/grounds-for-deportation/ (last visited Nov. 6, 2021). However, there is an exception that a U.S. citizen can be deported if he or she committed fraud to obtain citizenship. *Id.*

[87] Stephen J. Dubner, *The Troubled Cremation of Stevie the Cat*, Freakonomics (Oct. 14, 2013, 9:20 AM), https://freakonomics.com/podcast/the-troubled-cremation-of-stevie-the-cat-a-new-freakonomics-radio-podcast/.

[88] *Id.*

[89] *Id.*

[90] *Id.*

[91] *Id.*

discussion can be had by simply asking the class if they would prefer to be informed of the truth of the ashes of their deceased pets and incur the harm associated with the information or continue in blissful ignorance.

Despite these potential issues, a study involving a mock trial of this practice resulted in damages against the defendant crematory for intentional infliction of emotional distress and negligence and an additional $3 million in punitive damages. The mock trial even awarded the plaintiff compensation from the veterinary clinic that outsourced its cremation services to the crematory, reasoning that the clinic should have done more to confirm that the crematory it used was not engaging in this fraudulent practice.[92]

Would the answer to these questions be different if the cremation involved human remains? In 2002, a man operating a crematorium was convicted of improperly disposing more than 300 human bodies and served twelve years in jail for the crime (a class action civil suit was settled out of court).[93] The man was charging people for a cremation, discarding the bodies in the woods behind his business, and then delivering concrete dust to the consumers.[94]

XVIII. LIL NAS X "SATAN SHOES"

In 2021, rapper Lil Nas X launched "Satan Shoes."[95] They were made by taking Nike Air Max 97s, adding a bronze pentagram, an inverted cross, and a drop of real human blood.[96] The limited run of exactly 666 sold out in less than one minute.[97] Nike had no part in designing the shoes and did not endorse them.[98] After a lawsuit by Nike, Lil Nas X agreed to voluntarily recall the shoes as part of a settlement agreement.[99]

Nike alleged that the shoe misled consumers into believing that Nike was involved and that it was an unauthorized use of the Nike Swoosh

---

[92] *Id.*

[93] *Brent Marsh Released from Prison After Serving 12-Year Sentence*, WTVC (June 29, 2016), https://newschannel9.com/news/local/brent-marsh-released-from-prison-after-serving-12-year-sentence.

[94] *Id.*

[95] Oscar Holland & Jacqui Palumbo, *Lil Nas X's Unofficial 'Satan' Nikes Containing Human Blood Sell Out in Under a Minute*, CNN (Mar. 29, 2021), https://www.cnn.com/style/article/lil-nas-x-mschf-satan-nike-shoes/index.html.

[96] *Id.*

[97] *Id.*

[98] *Id.*

[99] *Nike Ends Lawsuit over Lil Nas X 'Satan Shoes,' Which Will Be Recalled*, CNBC (Apr. 8, 2021, 6:26 PM), https://www.cnbc.com/2021/04/08/nike-settles-lawsuit-against-maker-of-lil-nas-x-satan-shoes-.html.

trademark.[100] Nike further alleged that the alterations to the shoe may pose a safety hazard.[101] Nike suffered harm in that people called for a boycott of Nike products after seeing the Satan Shoes and incorrectly believing Nike was responsible.[102] Nike settled the lawsuit with MSCHF, the manufacturer of the Satan Shoes.[103]

This illustrates the interesting tradeoff between intellectual property rights and free speech rights, as the modified shoes are clearly an artistic expression that garners free speech protections. The creators explain that they were "intended to comment on the absurdity of the collaboration culture practiced by some brands, and about the perniciousness of intolerance."[104]

XIX. VIRTUAL PITCHFORKS

In 2015, Yale's Intercultural Affairs Committee sent out an email urging students not to wear Halloween costumes that might be viewed by some as offensive.[105] Erika Christakis, a Yale lecturer in early childhood development and a *New York Times* bestselling author, sent an email to the students in her residential college that applauded the goal of the Intercultural Affairs Committee email, while questioning if perhaps censorship has gone too far.[106] Christakis's email posited that if one sees a Halloween costume he or she personally does not like, tolerating the free speech expression of the individual may be a better response.[107] Over 700 Yale students signed a petition stating that Christakis's email was "jarring" and "invit[es] ridicule and violence."[108] After forceful calls by students

---

[100] Complaint, Nike, Inc. v. MSCHF Prod. Studio, Inc., No. 21-cv-1679 (E.D.N.Y. Mar. 29, 2021).

[101] *Id.*

[102] Allana Akhtar, *Nike Is Suing the Maker of Lil Nas X's Blood Shoe, Alleging It Has 'Suffered Significant Harm' — Including Complaints from Customers Who 'Believe That Nike Is Endorsing Satanism,'* BUS. INSIDER (Mar. 29, 2021, 6:18 PM), https://www.businessinsider.com/nike-lil-nas-x-satan-blood-shoe-mschf-lawsuit-2021-3.

[103] Adi Robertson, *Nike and MSCHF Settle Satan Shoe Lawsuit, Say Any 'Confused' Buyers Can Get a Refund*, THE VERGE (Apr. 8, 2021, 6:22 PM), https://www.theverge.com/2021/4/8/22374480/nike-mschf-lil-nas-x-unauthorized-satan-shoes-lawsuit-settled.

[104] *Nike Ends Lawsuit*, *supra* note 99.

[105] Libby Nelson, *Yale's Big Fight over Sensitivity and Free Speech, Explained*, VOX (Nov. 7, 2015, 5:50 PM), https://www.vox.com/2015/11/7/9689330/yale-halloween-email.

[106] *Id.*

[107] *Id.*

[108] Letter from Concerned Yale Students, Alumni, Family, Faculty, and Staff to Erika Christakis, Assoc. Master, Yale, Univ.,

that Erika Christakis and her husband—also a Yale instructor—resign, they did.[109]

This episode elicits numerous legal and ethical issues for class discussion. While Yale is a private school—and the initial email only advocated for self-censorship—the issue of public university censorship is timely and engaging. While a public university could ban inherently dangerous costumes, banning costumes simply because others may find them offensive clearly violates free speech protections. This illustrates the expansive nature of what is considered "speech" under the First Amendment.

Finally, this topic provides a great opportunity to discuss that while one may be legally allowed to do something, that does not mean that he or she should. And while one has free speech rights, he or she does not have consequence-free speech rights. The First Amendment offers no protections from the consequences of wearing an offensive costume. These consequences may include being fired by a private employer, losing friends, the withdrawal of financial support from parents, and being dumped by a significant other. For example, in 2013, twenty-two-year-old Alicia Lynch dressed up as a Boston Marathon bombing survivor for Halloween, and tweeted a photo of her costume.[110] The public found out where she was employed and made numerous calls to her employer demanding she be fired.[111] Ultimately, she was terminated..[112]

XX. A Gruesome—Yet Protected—Message

In 2017, Kathy Griffin posted a picture of herself stoically holding a severed replica head of then President Donald Trump.[113] The image was widely criticized by both conservatives and liberals, and Griffin issued an

---

https://docs.google.com/forms/d/e/1FAIpQLSexdyJZ2UBCB9Isl7vP2rTfLXuO2F22yn5 Sj9ZRizsxxKisJw/viewform (last visited Nov. 1, 2021).

[109] Conor Friedersdorf, *The Perils of Writing a Provocative Email at Yale*, ATLANTIC (May 26, 2016), https://www.theatlantic.com/politics/archive/2016/05/the-peril-of-writing-a-provocative-email-at-yale/484418/.

[110] Rachel Zarrell, *What Happens When You Dress as A Boston Marathon Victim and Post It on Twitter*, BUZZFEED NEWS (Nov. 2, 2013, 2:24 PM), https://www.buzzfeednews.com/article/rachelzarrell/what-happens-when-you-dress-as-a-boston-marathon-victim.

[111] *Id.*

[112] *Id.*

[113] Christopher Rosen, *Donald Trump Blasts Kathy Griffin for Beheading Photo*, ENT. WKLY. (May 31, 2017, 7:46 AM), https://ew.com/news/2017/05/31/donald-trump-blasts-kathy-griffin/.

apology.[114]   This gruesome image illustrates some often-misunderstood aspects of the First Amendment. While the image insinuated the violent murder of a sitting president, it fell far short of what is required to constitute the incitement to riot exception to free speech. Under the *Brandenburg* test, speech must be directed to inciting or producing imminent lawless action and be likely to incite or produce such action.[115] Donald Trump alleges that his then eleven-year-old son Barron saw the image on television, believed his father had literally been decapitated, and screamed for his mother.[116]   One might be tempted to point out that this arguably meets the requirements of IIED in that it was extreme and outrageous conduct and resulted in severe emotional harm. However, the limited case law on this issue supports the notion that Griffin's free speech rights would take precedence over the IIED claim.[117]

This incident also illustrates the often-misunderstood distinction between public and private censorship. Griffin maintained First Amendment protections for her speech, but that only protected her from government censorship and punishment. The First Amendment did not protect her from the consequences from private parties. For example, Griffin was fired from CNN, many of her tour dates were cancelled, and she lost a spokeswoman job as a result of her decision to take part in this photoshoot.[118]

XXI. A HALLOWEEN PARADE WITH A FRIGHTENING ENDING

In 2003, the city of York, Pennsylvania, held a Halloween parade.[119]   An anti-abortion group was issued a permit to enter a float in the parade.[120]   The float was entitled "Dr. Butcher's Chop Shop of Choice

---

[114] *Id.*

[115] Brandenburg v. Ohio, 395 U.S. 444 (1969).

[116] Martha Ross, *Did Barron Trump Really Fear That Kathy Griffin's Beheading Image Showed His Father?*, MERCURY NEWS (June 1, 2017, 7:26 AM), https://www.mercurynews.com/2017/05/31/barron-trump-really-feared-kathy-griffins-beheading-image-showed-his-father-report-says/.

[117] Heath Hooper, *Sticks and Stones: IIED and Speech After* Snyder v. Phelps, 76 MO. L. REV. 1, 2 (2011) (considering the two cases of *Hustler Magazine, Inc. v. Falwell*, 485 U.S. 46 (1988) and *Snyder v. Phelps*).

[118] Scott D. Pierce, *Kathy Griffin's Punishment Didn't Fit Her 'Crime' — and CNN Should Have Rehired Her for New Year's Eve Show*, SALT LAKE TRIB. (Dec. 28, 2017, 3:05 PM), https://www.sltrib.com/artsliving/tv/2017/12/28/kathy-griffins-punishment-didnt-fit-her-crime-and-cnn-should-have-rehired-her-for-new-years-eve-show/.

[119] Grove v. City of York, 342 F. Supp. 2d 291, 298 (M.D. Pa. 2004).

[120] *Id.*

Cuts" and featured large signs depicting mutilated fetuses.[121] Due to strong public outcry and the city fearing violence, the group was informed on the day of the parade that its float would be last in line and that, while it could hand out material, it could not display large images of mutilated fetuses as planned.[122] The city argued that this was a reasonable time, place, and manner restriction, a recognized exception under the First Amendment.[123] The court rejected the city's claim and held that the censorship was not content neutral, nor was it narrowly tailored to their public safety concerns.[124] While the actual case involved additional, complex issues regarding the group walking up and down the path of the parade passing out flyers, the basic elements mentioned in this paragraph illustrate the expansive nature of free speech protections and the invalid nature of the heckler's veto as a defense.

XXII. Urban Legends

Urban legends provide a variety of topics with which to pose hypothetical fact patterns in class. The following are examples of urban legends that are ripe for such treatment:

- The often-warned-about but rarely true stories of razor blades in Halloween candy can be used to discuss assault and battery, IIED, issues of evidence gathering, and products liability (perhaps candy wrappers were not designed to sufficiently reduce the risk of tampering).
- The fanciful story of a helicopter scooping up water to put out a fire, unknowingly scooping up a scuba diver, and dropping him on the fire can be used to discuss negligence, assumption of risk, and foreseeability.
- Stories of a possessed video that—if watched—will lead to the death of the viewer unless he or she shows the video to someone else, thus transferring the curse to the next viewer can be used to discuss the mental states necessary for homicide offenses, a creative self-defense argument, and transferred intent.

---

[121] *Anti-Abortion Float Prompts Organizers to Pull Out of York Parade*, WGAL 8 (July 28, 2005, 10:36 AM), https://www.wgal.com/article/anti-abortion-float-prompts-organizers-to-pull-out-of-york-parade/6193876.
[122] *Grove*, 342 F. Supp. 2d 291 at 299.
[123] *Id.* at 300.
[124] *Id.* at 302.

- The famous curse of the Bambino can be used to discuss, interference with a contractual relationship, damages, and what could be presented as evidence at trial to prove the curse is what caused the damages.
- Triskaidekaphobia is the fear of the number thirteen. Some hotels label their thirteenth floor as fourteen because customers do not want to stay on an unlucky floor. There is an urban legend that someone attempting to bungee jump from a high floor in a hotel building died because the person did not account for the omission of the thirteenth floor and therefore let out too much bungee cord. If this were to happen in real life, would the decedent's estate have any valid grounds to sue the hotel? Perhaps if the hotel had reason to believe that this was going to happen?

XXIII. VOIDING A DEAL WITH THE DEVIL

Depictions of a desperate person selling his or her soul to the Devil in exchange for some earthly reward are present in numerous movies and television shows. Applying real-life contract jurisprudence to such a transaction is an engaging illustration of the nuanced aspects of contract formation. Such an agreement might be held voidable for a lack of definiteness—what exactly is a "soul," and what are the consequences of losing it? As mentioned in the Suing Satan section, there are inherent jurisdiction and service of complaint issues with litigation against the Devil.

Generally, courts will not consider the adequacy of consideration in a bargained-for exchange; people are free to enter into, and courts will enforce, contracts in which one side is clearly receiving the better deal.[125] So the fact that an eternity in Hell is wildly disparate from some earthly temporary gain does not per se invalidate the contract. However, such an extreme difference in consideration is perhaps so disparate as to be unenforceable due to unconscionability. Contracts of adhesion are ones in which there is unequal bargaining power among the parties, there is very little opportunity for the weaker party to negotiate the terms, and it is a take-it-or-leave-it offer.[126] Those three elements appear to be met in these contracts with the Devil. However, contracts of adhesion—such as iTunes user agreements, waivers signed at a hospital, and cell phone contracts, are

---

[125] 17 C.J.S. *Contracts* § 175 (2021) ("In the absence of fraud, the law generally will not weigh the adequacy of the consideration for a contract; so long as it is something of real value, it is sufficient.").

[126] Donald P. Harris, *Trips and Treaties of Adhesion Part II: Back to the Past or a Small Step Forward?*, 2007 MICH. ST. L. REV. 185, 191 (2007).

not per se unenforceable. It is only when they rise to the level of unconscionability that they are voidable. However, one could argue under a theory of promissory estoppel that it would be unjust to allow a person to receive the benefit of the agreement and then be absolved of fulfilling his end of the bargain.

In most jurisdictions, the statute of frauds requires that contracts that cannot be performed in less than one year must be in writing to be enforceable.[127] Students often misinterpret this to mean that contracts that will normally take more than a year must be in writing. A hypothetical contract for a soul helps illustrate why this is wrong. Assuming the Devil takes possession of the contracting party's soul at the time of his death, such an agreement *could* be completed in less than a year, since it is not guaranteed that one will not die within a year.

XXIV. MISCELLANEOUS

Potential topics fit for discussion in a Halloween-themed class are too numerous to enumerate in this Teaching Note. The following are some miscellaneous topics for consideration:

- Whether the actions of the Ghostbusters satisfy the requirements of false imprisonment[128]
- State statutes that criminalize the practice of wearing masks or disguises[129]
- Whether property owners could seek compensation for destruction to property caused by Godzilla[130]
- Potential liability for the decision to keep the beach open in the movie *Jaws*[131]
- The distinction between public domain monsters, such as zombies, Dracula, werewolves, and Frankenstein's monster, versus protected monsters, such as Godzilla, Thanos, Michael Meyers, and Freddy Kreuger

---

[127] 9 WILLISTON ON CONTRACTS § 24:1 (4th ed. May 2021 update).

[128] Josh Gilliland, *Ghostbusters & False Imprisonment*, THE LEGAL GEEKS (Oct. 29, 2012), http://thelegalgeeks.com/2012/10/29/ghostbusters-false-imprisonment/.

[129] Christine Sellers, *Double, Double Toil and Trouble, Fire Burn and Caldron Bubble*, LIBR. OF CONG. (Oct. 31, 2011), https://blogs.loc.gov/law/2011/10/double-double-toil-and-trouble/.

[130] Josh Gilliland, *Who Pays the Clean-Up Costs for Acts of Godzilla*, THE LEGAL GEEKS (May 21, 2014), https://thelegalgeeks.com/2014/05/21/who-pays-the-clean-up-costs-for-acts-of-godzilla/.

[131] The Legal Geeks Law and Pop Culture Podcast, *Jaws & Liability for the Island of Amity* (Sept. 1, 2012) (downloaded using iTunes).

- Liability of the high school in *Buffy the Vampire Slayer*[132]
- Criminal liability for killing someone who had been bitten by a zombie but not yet turned into a zombie
- Criminal liability for the Jigsaw Killer from the *Saw* movies, who technically never kills anyone but puts them in diabolical scenarios that frequently lead to death
- "Zombie Laws," which are undead laws because they are no longer enforced but remain on the books
- Legal considerations of organ donation and the ability to contract for your organs
- Suing from beyond the grave (right of third parties to sue on behalf of the deceased)
- Could the Ghostbusters be liable if they do not answer your call for assistance?[133]
- Efforts to ban or otherwise censor scary movies and violent video games
- Could the ghosts in *Beetlejuice* retain ownership of the house under a theory of adverse possession?[134]
- In 1989, members of a vampire cult murdered someone and then drank the victim's blood.[135] This case illustrates the standard for the often-misunderstood insanity defense, which was ultimately unsuccessful.
- Legality of COVID-19 trick-or-treat bans
- Could a haunted house be considered an "attractive nuisance," therefore creating an exception to the general rule that landowners owe only the duty of willful and wanton harm to trespassers?
- Is Jack Skellington from *The Nightmare Before Christmas* guilty of false impersonation?[136]

---

[132] The Legal Geeks Law and Pop Culture Podcast, *School Liability & Buffy the Vampire Slayer* (Sept. 1, 2012) (downloaded using iTunes).

[133] Steve Chu, *Can the Ghostbusters Be Sued for Not Coming to Your Assistance?*, THE LEGAL GEEKS (Oct. 24, 2018), https://thelegalgeeks.com/2018/10/24/can-the-ghostbusters-be-sued-for-not-coming-to-your-assistance/.

[134] Gaby Schneider, *Betelgeuse Said "Ghost Rights!": The Property Law of Haunted Houses*, THE LEGAL GEEKS (Oct. 30, 2019), https://thelegalgeeks.com/2019/10/30/betelgeuse-said-ghost-rights-the-property-law-of-haunted-houses/.

[135] State v. Erickson, 449 N.W.2d 707 (Minn. 1989).

[136] Josh Gilliland, *What's This? What's This? Jack Skellington and False Impersonation*, THE LEGAL GEEKS (Oct. 31, 2012), https://thelegalgeeks.com/2012/10/31/whats-this-whats-this-jack-skellington-false-impersonation/.

- A property rights battle between residents who argued that a local pumpkin patch violated environmental protection laws[137]
- Using the Salem Witch trials as an issue-spotting exercise to list the legal protections under current criminal law that the accused were denied. This includes right to counsel, right to confront one's accuser, protections against cruel and unusual punishment, a jury of one's peers, protection from unconstitutionally vague laws, admissibility of evidence, due process, and cruel and unusual punishment.
- Justice Gorsuch's colorful opinion regarding a haunted house attraction and an insurance dispute[138]
- Is it error for a judge to tell potential jurors during voir dire about a legend that the ghost of a Confederate soldier haunted the courthouse?[139]
- Look for urban legends and ghost stories for your college campus and town that can be used to illustrate legal principles

XXV. CONCLUSION

Themed classes such as this Halloween-themed one provide numerous positive benefits. They are a welcome break from traditional lectures for both instructor and students. The format of jumping from topic to topic and provocative subject matter keeps the class engaged. It reignites interest in previously covered topics and sparks curiosity for topics to come later in the semester. And in a traditional, fifteen- or sixteen-week fall semester, this activity can fit conveniently after the midterm in mid-October.

As mentioned in the introduction, this Teaching Note is intentionally not a step-by-step guide for conducting the activity. Instead, instructors are encouraged to pick and choose which topics fit best for their class and to experiment with creative methods for implementation. Above

---

[137] Friends of Temescal Canyon, Inc. v. City of Los Angeles, No. B178063, 2005 WL 1524201 (Cal. Ct. App. June 29, 2005).
[138] W. World Ins. Co. v. Markel Am. Ins. Co., 677 F.3d 1266, 1267 (10th Cir. 2012) ("Haunted houses may be full of ghosts, goblins, and guillotines, but it's their more prosaic features that pose the real danger. Tyler Hodges found that out when an evening shift working the ticket booth ended with him plummeting down an elevator shaft. But as these things go, this case no longer involves Mr. Hodges. Years ago he recovered from his injuries, received a settlement, and moved on. This lingering specter of a lawsuit concerns only two insurance companies and who must foot the bill. And at the end of it all, we find, there is no escape for either of them.").
[139] United States v. Shuff, 470 Fed. Appx. 158 (4th Cir. 2012).

all else, instructors are encouraged to have a frighteningly good time with it, Mwahahaha!

EXPLORING THE ETHICAL AND INSTRUCTIONAL POSSIBILITIES OF GROUPME IN BUSINESS LAW AND BUSINESS COMMUNICATION COURSES

LINDSAY CLARK[*]
ASHTON MOUTON[**]
TRACI AUSTIN[***]

I. INTRODUCTION

At many universities, students communicate with each other about their classes using different types of technological tools, including email, learning management systems, and mobile instant messaging (MIM) apps. One such MIM is GroupMe, a free, mobile- and web-based app created in 2010 and now owned by Microsoft.[1] Users can create an unlimited number of groups–social, family, work-based, or educational–through which they can share text, photos, and videos using a variety of devices.[2] At the authors' university, the use of the application GroupMe is a common communication tool for students to share information, ask questions, and coordinate interactions (like team projects) for specific courses. As many faculty are aware, however, GroupMe is not always used for honorable purposes, for students also use the app to cheat on tests, quizzes, and other assignments–an activity that is not specifically prohibited by Microsoft's Service Agreement.[3]

While the academic literature on GroupMe is sparse, the literature that does exist reflects both the positive and negative possibilities of GroupMe for students and instructors. On the positive side, Gronseth and Hebert argue for the usefulness of GroupMe in facilitating communication

---

[*] Ph.D., Assistant Professor of Business Administration, Sam Houston State University
[**] Ph.D., Assistant Professor of Business Administration, Sam Houston State University
[***] Ph.D., Associate Professor of Business Administration, Sam Houston State University
[1] GROUPME, https://groupme.com/en-US/ (last visited Jun. 16, 2022).
[2] GROUPME, About, https://groupme.com/en-US/about
[3] MICROSOFT. (2021, April 1). The Microsoft Services Agreement Code of Conduct prohibits anything illegal, exploitative or harmful to children, spam or phishing, inappropriate content (including pornography, graphic violence or criminal activity, among others), fraudulent, false or misleading statements, harmful conduct (stalking, hate speech, advocating violence, among other things), infringing on others' rights (sharing copyrighted materials), invading the privacy of others, as well as helping others break the rules. https://www.microsoft.com/en-us/servicesagreement/default.aspx (subpart 3.a.i.-x.)

in both face-to-face and online courses.[4] Analyzing over 900 posts from students in educational technology courses, they found that GroupMe allowed for focused and productive course discussions and encouraged interaction and engagement between students. Students use the GroupMe chats to ask questions and continue discussions about course related content without having to wait until the next class period; in large courses, it provides an avenue for more students to participate in the discussion rather than only those who participate in the classroom setting.[5] Similarly, Ly's analysis of GroupMe posts and follow-up interviews from her composition students demonstrated rhetorical decision-making, arguing that "computer-mediated communication is a valuable space...that is rich with rhetorical activities, critical thinking, and identity/voice negotiations."[6] Carpenter and Green also reported that students learn about social media literacy and appropriateness through GroupMe chats. Moreover, with instructor-created GroupMe chats, professors can extend the possibilities of discussion with the professor outside the classroom through engaging course discussions, alternate avenues of answering questions, announcements and reminders, and even community building with the class as a whole.[7] As such, GroupMe provides the possibility for students to build key skills related to communication, critical-thinking, and decision-making regarding course-specific content.

However, on the negative side, there have been several accounts of GroupMe being used as a channel for cheating and other violations of universities' codes of conduct in recent years. In *Peden v. W. Ky. Univ.*, the appellate court upheld Michael Peden's expulsion from both Western Kentucky University and Gatton Academy for using the GroupMe chat to secure answers on an exam for his astronomy course.[8] Under both academic honesty policies, his actions qualified as cheating on an exam, even without mention of MIMs in the policy.[9] Over the last two years of online and hybrid courses in response to the COVID-19 pandemic, many

---

[4] Susie Gronseth & Waneta Hebert, *GroupMe: Investigating Use of Mobile Instant Messaging in Higher Education Courses*, 63 TECHTRENDS 15, 22 (2019). See also Jeff Carpenter & Tim Green, *Connecting and Engaging with Students Through GroupMe*, 61 TECHTRENDS 1 (2017).

[5] Carpenter & Green, *supra* note 7.

[6] Quang C. Ly, *The Case for GroupMe: Rhetorical Thinking Thrives Among Students Using App*, 21 JOUR. LIT. TECH. 110, 149 (2020).

[7] Carpenter & Green, *supra* note 7; *see also,* Joy L. Daggs, Creating and Extending Classroom Community with GroupMe (Mar. 2018). NATIONAL COMMUNICATION ASSOCIATION, https://www.natcom.org/sites/default/files/pages/eTools_GroupMe_March_2018.pdf

[8] No. 2021-CA-0106-MR, 2022 WL 815458 (Ky. Ct. App. Mar. 18, 2022) (not designated for publication).

[9] *Id.*

universities have reported a surge in code-of-conduct violations via GroupMe, prompting several universities to adopt explicit statements about MIM apps into their academic integrity policies.[10]

The Ohio State University penalized 83 students for "unauthorized collaboration" (explicitly prohibited in the university's honor code) on a GroupMe chat in a business course, raising some questions about whether or not innocent students were implicated in the penalty.[11] Similarly, after two University of Texas students sent information about an upcoming exam over the app, the university threatened failing grades or expulsion of all 70 students on the chat.[12] At Georgia State University, cheating specifically related to GroupMe increased when courses moved online in the spring of 2020 and have stayed elevated ever since.[13] At Georgia State, revisions to the academic honesty policy specify that all students in a GroupMe chat are implicated in cheating even if they did not participate and were unaware that cheating occurred.[14] While students do not want to be implicated when others cheat, there are strong deterrents that prevent them from reporting ethics violations, including perceived avenues of retribution from peers, being labeled a *tattle-tale* or *rat*.[15] The goal here is to incentivize students to gather evidence, report it to the Dean of Students office, and to leave these GroupMe chats.[16]

Yet students typically will not report cheating or tattle on their peers in a GroupMe for fear of being labeled a *tattle-tale*; instead, students just leave the GroupMe chat.[17] Louisiana State University contacted GroupMe directly, requesting information related to suspected cheating, and although GroupMe admits that academic cheating is not a violation of

---

[10] Jada Jones, Georgia State Students Warn about Cheating through GroupMe, THE GEORGIA STATE SIGNAL (Nov. 17, 2020), https://georgiastatesignal.com/georgia-state-students-warn-about-cheating-through-groupme/

[11] Nick Roll, Cheating without Intent? INSIDE HIGHERED (2017, Nov. 14, 2017), https://www.insidehighered.com/news/2017/11/14/could-groupme-lead-cheating-guilt-association

[12] Autumn Rendall, UT GroupMe Cheating Scandal Causes Students to Resent App. THE DAILY COUGAR (Oct. 23, 2019), http://thedailycougar.com/2019/10/23/ut-groupme-cheating-scandal/; *see also,* Libby Cohen, Is It Cheating to Use GroupMe for College Classes?, DAILY DOT (2019, November 26), https://www.dailydot.com/irl/groupme-cheating-college/

[13] Jones, *supra* note 13.

[14] *Id.*

[15] Donald McCabe, Kenneth D. Butterfield, & Linda Klebe Trevino, *Academic Dishonesty in Graduate Business Programs: Prevalence, Causes, and Proposed Action,* 5 ACAD. OF MGMT. LEARN. & ED. 294 (2006) https://www.jstor.org/stable/40214383

[16] Jones, *supra* note 13.

[17] *Id.*

their Terms of Service, they forward all of those requests to Microsoft, who will release them to universities under the right circumstances: "According to Microsoft's privacy statement, private information, including content like emails or messages, may be shared if it is requested through valid legal processes."[18] GroupMe does not employ end-to-end encryption, and the company's privacy policy falls under Microsoft's general Privacy Policy, which allows them to collect and store your data; under the right circumstances, they can and will share GroupMe chat data with third parties.[19] This back-door access to GroupMe chats provides universities with more information about who is using the app for academic dishonesty and more evidence to enforce their academic honesty policies.

The issue of academic dishonesty is of particular interest to business communication and business law because of higher-than-average rates of cheating among students in those disciplines. McCabe and Trevino focused on students in business, law, and medicine at 31 of the United States' most competitive colleges, and their results demonstrated that students in all disciplines cheat.[20] Of their respondents, 67% admitted cheating once while completing their undergraduate degree, 38% reported cheating at least three times, and 15% reported cheating only on tests/exams.[21] More importantly for this data-set, business students were among the most likely to cheat and engage in unethical academic behaviors; second to business students were law students.[22] Pfeffer and Fong argue that the problems with cheating and ethics, specifically for business schools, stem from the lack of ethics in business, and encourage business schools to develop better ethics policies, specifically related to

---

[18] Luke Jeanfreau, LSU Students Using GroupMe for Class Could be in Violation of Code of Student Conduct, LSU REVEILLE (Mar. 21, 2018), https://www.lsureveille.com/daily/lsu-students-using-groupme-for-class-could-be-in-violation-of-code-of-student-conduct/article_a53985bc-2c73-11e8-b1fb-a71c5c3a66ae.htm; see MICROSOFT, Privacy Statement, https://privacy.microsoft.com/en-us/privacystatement (last updated Apr. 2022): "How we use personal data…We also use the data to operate our business, which includes analyzing our performance, *meeting our legal obligations*, developing our workforce, and doing research." (emphasis added).
[19] Lora Ivanova, *GroupMe Review: A Team Chat Made for Friends*, BROSIX BLOG (Feb. 10, 2021), https://www.brosix.com/blog/groupme-review/
[20] Donald McCabe & Linda Klebe Trevino, *Cheating Among Business Students: A Challenge for Business Leaders and Educators*, 19 J. of MGMT. EDU. 205, 218 (1995).
[21] *Id.*
[22] *Id.*

cheating.[23] Moreover, McCabe and Trevino encourage professors to visit ethical decision-making in their classrooms.[24]

McCabe, Butterfield, and Trevino confirmed that the trend of business students cheating holds even in graduate school, as business graduate students cheat more than their non-business student peers in law, medicine, and the liberal arts. Their results also indicated specific correlations with business student cheating: (1) perceived certainty that peers also cheat; (2) perceived certainty of being reported for cheating; and (3) the importance of academic integrity policies and/or honor codes as well as the students' acceptance of them, with peer behaviors having the biggest impact.[25] Competitive grading scales might be one method of increasing student reporting of their classmates' cheating. In a meta-analysis of literature on student academic dishonesty McCabe, Trevino, and Butterfield confirmed that student cheating has increased dramatically over the last 30 years. The authors assert that business, law, and medical students cheat more than any other college students, specifically because there is a pressure to do well, placement in advanced degree programs is a challenge, and many want prestigious positions in business/management.[26] Not only does the group chat function in GroupMe provide students with up close and personal evidence that peers are cheating, the use of GroupMe over time demonstrates to students that their peers will not report each other. Without a serious honor code or an academic honesty policy that specifically includes MIMs in combination with incentivized ethical decision-making, there is no incentive not to cheat.

While these studies predate the existence of GroupMe as an educational tool, the results in these studies hold to the present, with even more cheating taking place through online learning and throughout the COVID-19 pandemic.[27] The simplicity of GroupMe as a communication tool, coupled with the prevalence of cheating and COVID-19 factors on student learning, presents a unique opportunity for cheating in today's academic environment. In the business college at the authors' institution, faculty have discussed the benefits and drawbacks of these student-initiated channels of communication; on one hand, the authors recognize the potential of GroupMe for coordinating virtual collaboration and

---

[23] Jeffery Pfeffer & Christina Fong, *The Business School 'Business': Some Lessons from the US Experience*, 41 J. of MGMT. STUD., 1501 (2004), https://onlinelibrary.wiley.com/doi/10.1111/j.1467-6486.2004.00484.x
[24] McCabe & Trevino, *supra* note 23.
[25] McCabe, Butterfield, & Trevino, *supra* note 18.
[26] Donald McCabe, Linda Klebe Trevino, & Kenneth D. Butterfield, *Cheating in Academic Institutions: A Decade of Research*, 11 ETH. & BEH. 219, 232 (2001).
[27] Jones, *supra* note 13.

managing team projects, as well as disseminating course-related announcements and reminders. Conversely, many faculty discussed issues of academic dishonesty (*e.g.*, sharing exam information and homework answers). Finally, other negative activities, such as the dissemination of incorrect information regarding expectations or due dates and even libel about instructors, have prompted discussion of ways to block communication between students in online courses (*e.g.*, disabling email through the Learning Management System ("LMS").

This research investigates students' perceptions of the GroupMe app, specifically focusing on students taking business law and business communication courses. Specifically examined were the students' perceived value of that channel, their various reasons for joining group chats, and the perceived value of having a student-only communication channel. The purpose of this manuscript is to share an appreciation for the possibilities the channel offers to both professors and students, while uncovering ways to mitigate the challenging and potentially unethical aspects, thus leveraging the positive aspects of GroupMe in the classroom. GroupMe and similar mobile instant messaging platforms are here to stay, especially in the post-pandemic academic landscape, which witnessed an explosion of virtual communication in all forms. A greater understanding of GroupMe and its uses opens the door to a productive, rather than adversarial, relationship between instructors and the app.

II. METHOD

To gather data for this project, the authors surveyed students in a college of business at a regional university in the Southwestern United States from spring 2020 through spring 2022. The student participants were enrolled in business law and business communication courses, from the sophomore to the graduate level. The anonymous survey consists of closed, open-ended, multiple-choice, and multiple-selection questions that sought input on the students' experience with the GroupMe app. The questions addressed the following topics:

- The frequency and pervasiveness of class-focused, student-created GroupMe chats
- The students' purpose in joining and using GroupMe
- Instances in which students have felt uncomfortable in or left a GroupMe
- The perceived impact of GroupMe on their success in the course
- The impact of the pandemic-related university shutdown on the frequency and pervasiveness of student-led GroupMe chats

- Students' attitudes toward instructor presence on a class-centered GroupMe

These questions sought to determine if students used GroupMe to communicate about courses as suspected, if their usage changed in response to online/hybrid learning resulting from the COVID-19 pandemic, and if they would be open to instructors using this tool to communicate during the semester. After reaching half of the targeted number of responses, and confirming suspected usage preferences, the focus shifted to understanding the nuances of student usage of this app, including topics discussed, perceptions about the value of this communication tool, and the ethical implications of using this tool in an educational space.

Those closed questions were analyzed for frequency, while open-ended answers were analyzed for recurring themes. The open-ended data was coded using MaxQDA and Nvivo to identify emergent topics, as they are beneficial for managing large quantities of data and ensuring consistency and rigor in qualitative data analysis.[28] The data was then mined for representative quotes that add important contextual information about student preferences and behavior about the GroupMe application. The goal of the data analysis was two-fold: first, to capture students' experience with and attitudes toward GroupMe; second, to provide practical recommendations from the analysis to inform classroom management, exploring ways in which professors can adapt to and perhaps even direct the presence of GroupMe chats associated with their individual courses. At the end, pedagogical innovations that might encourage students to think critically about ethics and communication are provided.

III. FINDINGS AND DISCUSSION

In total, the authors received 410 individual responses to the survey after polling 16 sections (10 business communication courses and 6 business law courses) in person and online. After analyzing both the quantitative and qualitative data, the results indicate two major findings relevant to business law and business communication pedagogy: (1) GroupMe can be used as a communication tool for students and instructors, and (2) there are ethical and legal considerations associated with students' use of GroupMe that can be mitigated by pedagogical interventions.

---

[28] Joy D. Bringer, Lynne Halley Johnston, & Celia H. Brackenridge, *Using Computer-Assisted Qualitative Data Analysis Software to Develop a Grounded Theory Project*, 18 FIELD METH. 245 (2006).

A. A Communication Tool for Students and Instructors

While the student use of GroupMe has been of interest to college faculty since the app was created, the COVID-19 pandemic created a new sense of urgency around, and created opportunities for, this study starting in early 2020. First of all, an increase was suspected in the use of GroupMe chats as students adjusted to online learning in the wake of pandemic-related shifts to virtual teaching; this offered a unique opportunity to study students' attitudes toward and use of the app. Also, many instructors themselves were considering new tools to bolster teaching amid the changes–some temporary, some enduring–caused by the pandemic, and had begun to consider GroupMe as an option for this. Each semester of this project, students were asked if they use GroupMe consistently. In both phases of the project, the majority of respondents continue to report using the GroupMe app to communicate with classmates (81.2%, n=333). In the first research phase, students were asked if they were using the app prior to the COVID-19 pandemic and universities moving to online/hybrid learning in spring 2020. Interestingly, little change to this trend was observed, with students reporting consistent use of the app both prior to and after the beginning of the pandemic.

It is clear, then, that students have recognized the value of GroupMe to their own educational and social goals for many years; many instructors, however, still see student-only GroupMe chats as problematic. Many professors at the authors' institution have mentioned that students sometimes share incorrect due dates or interpretations of course objectives in the GroupMe, resulting in confusion or poor performance on assignments. With this in mind, during the first research phase, students were asked if they would invite their instructor to join the GroupMe chats they create for classes. The authors have all been accidentally invited, as students use the LMS email function to send the chat link out to their classmates, but intentionally chose not to join. Other instructors have opted to join quietly to monitor the chat for cheating, intervening only when information about exams is shared. Initial survey results from 284 respondents suggest that only about half would invite an instructor to their student-created GroupMe chat (52%, n=147). When explaining their choice, this subset of students cited the importance of faster responses to questions, clearer answers about course information and expectations, and the possibility of mitigating academic integrity violations such as cheating and unauthorized collaboration.

Still, almost half of respondents answer "No" or "Maybe" when asked if they would invite an instructor to their student GroupMe. When explaining why, students emphasized the value of having a student-only space. Their responses focused on two recurring themes: fear of getting in trouble if someone were to send answers over the chat and fear of "looking stupid" for asking clarifying questions about activities and assignments with the instructor present. These student-created chats function as a safe space to express confusion and frustration, and many students acknowledge that the nature and frequency of communication may change if they know an instructor is "watching."

While students can email their professors directly through the university LMS, the authors sought to better understand their preferences towards this direct communication channel. Considering the impact an instructor-created GroupMe may have on minimizing misinformation or confusion, students were also asked if they would join a GroupMe created by an instructor: 91.7% (n=257) said they would join to get quicker answers and information "straight from the horse's mouth," as well as to avoid the perceived delay of email responses. Only 4.6% said they would not join an instructor-created GroupMe, saying they might feel intimidated or silenced by the instructor's presence, prefer private communication with the instructor, or feel fear of being "monitored" or "ridiculed" for asking for clarification or help. Overall, students like quick, direct, easy communication with the instructor and each other. Students are open to an instructor-created GroupMe for specific courses, suggesting a preference toward this channel over email.

When asked to indicate what topics are typically discussed in course GroupMe chats, respondents were offered eight possible categories, an option to indicate no participation in GroupMe, and a field to enter other topics not included. Overall, the results proved the list to be comprehensive, highlighting students' preferences for using the app to navigate coursework. As shown in Table 1 below, the two most reported uses for joining a GroupMe chat were "Questions about assignments, homework, tests, or other activities" (342 responses) and "Reminders about due dates or course/assignment requirements" (341 responses). Other frequent course-related uses for GroupMe are detailed in Table 1, including helping each other and coordinating team projects:

Table 1: Frequency of reported uses for GroupMe (n=410)

Reported uses for GroupMe	Totals
Questions about assignments, homework, tests, or other activities	342
Reminders about due dates or course/assignment requirements	341
Helping each other understand coursework, assignments, or topics	318
Organizing course-related events, meetups, or teamwork sessions	226
Frustration about expectations, assignments, or the instructor	212
Coordinating contact with the instructor to address questions or concerns	183
Celebrating individual or class "wins" and achievements	128
Non-school related or social topics	101
I do not use GroupMe.	22
Other	4

Moreover, students indicated that they use GroupMe to coordinate contact with the instructor to address questions or concerns (183 responses). Specifically, students will identify or volunteer someone in the class to contact the instructor on behalf of the class, disseminating that information back out on the GroupMe channel. The motivation behind this coordination is certainly information-seeking; however, students also explain that they try to minimize the amount of messages or avoid sending the same messages to an instructor.

With these insights in mind, last semester, one author created

GroupMe chats for her courses and invited her students to join. Mirroring the findings, almost all students joined the course GroupMe chats (even choosing to contact her through GroupMe over Remind, which does not require an app). This affirms that students are active, consistent users of GroupMe each semester; this direct line to the instructor is perceived as less laborious than email. While she primarily used the course GroupMe chats to send reminders about due dates (one of the primary stated reasons for joining course GroupMe chats), she also received several messages on the group thread as well as direct messages. Whereas more formal messages about grade disputes or class performance typically came through email, these types of messages were sent through GroupMe. Additionally, when questions or confusion was expressed on the group thread, she noticed students liking the comment, as if to emphasize or agree.

Though questions and confusion could be addressed, expectations explained, and information shared quickly, this instructor using a GroupMe chat to communicate with her students also seemed to make issues with the course more visible than before. For example, if a student emails about a broken link for a reading on the LMS, an instructor could correct that, potentially before other students notice. This semester, a student sent a message over the chat indicating that a link to one reading was broken, which prompted the instructor to have to respond to the whole class that it was repaired. Similarly, a student expressed confusion about assignment guidelines for the class to see; rather than responding to this classmate, the students seemed to wait for the instructor to answer. Though this transparency does clarify and potentially mitigate misinformation being shared between students, might it also affect instructor credibility? While this would require additional exploration, the study affirms that students will still interact in student-only GroupMe spaces and interact differently.

Early in the semester, this instructor announced class cancellation via the GroupMe, asking students to also make an announcement on the student GroupMe (unsure if that other chat existed). It was quickly confirmed that student-created chats were running parallel to hers. This was also suggested in the data through comments about the value of a student-only space, as well as the use of these student-only chats for non-class related communication. Therefore, it seems that an instructor-created GroupMe would not prevent the creation of student-only chats and would not forestall the cited negative aspects of GroupMe and similar apps, such as cheating and potentially libelous statements.

B. Ethical and Legal Considerations

Indicated by the survey data and evidenced by university cases and instructor experiences, violations of academic integrity are prolific on GroupMe.[29] These violations include sharing answers to assignments and exams, sending pictures or videos of exams, and coordination of cheating or unauthorized collaboration. Realizing that GroupMe is used for more than just discussions about class, students were asked about the ways they choose *not* to interact on the chat that perhaps others do. Not surprisingly, the vast majority of students report that they do not engage in cheating behaviors. However, recognizing that students may not self-implicate, regardless of the anonymous nature of the survey, it is safe to assume that students are aware that cheating happens on GroupMe or even participate in it. Also, academic dishonesty may actually be hiding in plain sight in the responses students gave to the survey. As seen in Table 1, "Questions about assignments, homework, tests, or other activities" or "Helping each other understand coursework, assignments, or topics" constitute two of the three most common activities on GroupMe. Previous scholarship indicates that students are often confused about what does and does not constitute academic dishonesty or misconduct. This is a particular issue when students are asked by instructors to collaborate on formal or informal group activities in class.[30] Often, the line between "Helping each other understand" assignments and "unauthorized collaboration" is not always explicitly addressed, so it is possible that students cross that line, whether they realize it or not.

Academic dishonesty is not the only negative activity taking place on student-created GroupMe chats. In qualitative explanations of one of the items in Table 1, "Frustration about expectations, assignments, or the instructor," some students pointed out that expressing "frustration" often took the form of "trash-talking" the instructor and, occasionally, other students. While further research is necessary, anecdotal evidence indicates that these situations arise when students feel that the instructor has been unfair, disengaged, or unsympathetic to students. As in other social media platforms, conversations in GroupMe can be subject to "emotional contagion," a phenomenon in which people's emotions tend to echo those of the people they are exposed to in a group.[31] This is especially true if

---

[29] Jones, *supra* note 13.

[30] Charles B. Shrader, Susan P. Ravenscroft, Jeffery B. Kaufmann, & Timothy D. West, *Classroom Cheating and Student Perceptions of Ethical Climate*, 13 TEACH. ETH. 105 (2012).

[31] Steffen Steinert, *Corona and Value Change: The Role of Social Media and Emotional Contagion*, 23(Suppl. 1) ETH. & INFO. TECH. 59 (2021).

the emotions are intense and negative.[32]   Emotional contagion goes beyond feelings, however, as emotions impact how people act, think, speak, and write.[33] Thus, a critical comment about a teacher, classmate, or situation on GroupMe may escalate, fueling additional negative comments in an emotionally-laden spiral that has the potential to culminate in defamatory or threatening language. While there are no obvious instances in the literature of cases of libel originating from class-focused GroupMe chats, other social media platforms have been the origin and focus of defamation cases.[34] Thus, the potential for similar instances on GroupMe is real.

In many cases described in the literature, cheating via GroupMe or other virtual platforms has most commonly been understood as the purview of university academic dishonesty policies or honor codes; recently, however, the issue of "virtual" cheating has begun to be reframed as a violation of civil law and thus subject to the legal system. In 2022, for instance, David Berkovitz, an assistant professor of business at Chapman University, sued students for copyright infringement for sharing answers to his exams with Course Hero.[35] Course Hero calls itself "an online learning platform for course-specific study resources."[36] The majority of Course Hero's "resources" are submitted by students: class notes, assignments, visuals aids, lectures, etc. Posting exam questions and answers technically violates Course Hero's own honor code, but these materials can still be commonly found on the site.[37] Because the submissions can be anonymous depending on the email used and the username students pick, Dr. Berkovitz did not know the identity of the students who shared his materials, and thus the university was unable to address the actions under their honor code policies.[38] Therefore, Berkovitz is suing the students as John Does and plans to subpoena Course Hero to compel the company to release the students' identities.[39]   This case represents a shift from dealing with virtual cheating within the confines of

---

[32] Carolina Herrando & Erthymios Constantinides, *Emotional Contagion: A Brief Overview and Future Directions.* 12 FRONT. PSYCH. (2021).

[33] Steinert, *supra* note 34.

[34] E.S.Yost,. (2020). *Tweet, Post, Share... Get Haled into Court? Calder Minimum Contacts Analysis in Social Media Defamation Cases.* 73 SMU L. Rev. 693 (2020).

[35] *Berkovitz v. Does 1-5*; Cause No. 2:22-CV-01628; in the United States District Court Central District of California.

[36] COURSE HERO, About Us, https://www.coursehero.com/about-us/ (last visited Jun. 16, 2022).

[37] *Id.*

[38] *Berkowitz*, Pet. 2, ECF No. 1

[39] Colleen Flaherty, Suing John Doe Students over Copyright, INSIDE HIGHER ED (Mar. 18, 2022), https://www.insidehighered.com/news/2022/03/18/suing-students-who-shared-exams-online-identify-them

the university to addressing it under the auspices of the legal system. While this case seems to be the first of its kind, other individuals may pursue similar means to address cheating on other social media and digital services, including GroupMe, given that the Microsoft Services Agreement prohibits unauthorized dissemination of copyrighted materials via their platform.[40]

Instructors and administrators may be tempted, then, to implement ethics education initiatives in an attempt to forestall cheating. However, studies show that ethics instruction (*e.g.*, a business ethics unit or course) alone is only minimally effective when it comes to increasing ethical behavior, as it changes attitudes, but not necessarily behavior.[41] As an example, Kean University requires all professors to discuss the academic honesty policy in detail in their classes, and how violations are incurred on their specific assignments in their specific courses. According to the policy, MIMs should be discussed in every single course as they relate to the course and the academic honesty policy. Despite this policy, students are still encouraged by their professors to drop classes when they are caught cheating on GroupMe, suggesting that a discussion of how the policy applies to the course and assignments is still not enough to prevent cheating through GroupMe.[42]

Instead, instructors should engage in a variety of pedagogical practices, such as implementing competitive grading scales, discussing and creating strong, actionable course-specific honor codes, and utilizing cases and/or hidden curriculum – all of which are discussed below – which, in combination, curb unethical behaviors such as unauthorized collaboration or cheating.[43] First, utilizing a competitive grading scale (*e.g.*, a forced bell curve) incentivizes students to report each other for cheating, especially in a GroupMe where evidence is available to each student on the chat, because it ranks students based on their performance.[44] If students know that allowing someone else to cheat might ultimately mean they receive a lower grade, they are less likely to tolerate their peers' cheating. Second, honor codes can be university implemented or course generated, but they are intentional documents specifying ethical and unethical behaviors as well as their consequences that students must sign. Instructors looking to increase ethical decision-making in their classes,

---

[40] Microsoft, *supra* note 21.

[41] Ethan P. Waples, Alison L. Antes,Stephen T. Murphy, Shane Connelly, & Michael D. Mumford, *A Meta-Analytic Investigation of Business Ethics Instruction*, 87 J. OF BUS. ETH. 133 (2009).

[42] Davaughnia Wilson, Students Caught Cheating Using GroupMe, THE TOWER (Mar. 24, 2021), http://kutower.com/2021/03/24/students-caught-cheating-using-groupme-app/

[43] McCabe, Butterfield, & Trevino, *supra* note 18.

[44] McCabe, Trevino, & Butterfield, *supra* note 29.

specifically on campuses that do not have campus-wide honor codes, should "consider establishing a classroom honor code—one that places appropriate responsibilities and obligations on the student, not just the faculty member, to prevent cheating."[45] Although honor codes do not stop cheating completely, they do increase students' belief that they will be penalized for their actions and provide professors with stronger avenues for punishing students who do cheat.

Third, another avenue to discourage cheating via GroupMe is to implement cases about unethical decision-making regarding GroupMe itself. Student involvement in discussions of ethics, with discussion of discrete cases and examples, has been shown to reduce cheating.[46] For example, the *Peden* case can be used to discuss cheating, contracts, and other ethical implications of GroupMe in business law classes.[47] In addition, other universities that have penalized, suspended, and/or expelled students based on cheating through GroupMe could be used as examples to discuss ethics (*e.g.*, The Ohio State University, University of Texas).[48] These recent examples highlight the decisions and consequences of students using GroupMe unethically on college campuses.

Finally, another approach may be the creation of a broader ethical community within courses and programs. In one such approach, McCabe *et al.* propose the creation of a "hidden curriculum" in which ethical issues are raised–implicitly, not explicitly–in the classroom for students to parse and evaluate through discussions with peers and instructors. Using cases drawn from students' lived experiences in the higher education environment or other common contexts, the "hidden curriculum" prompts students to make decisions and plan actions that call upon their ethics and values.[49] For example, a case involving cheating or disparaging language on a GroupMe chat will not necessarily be labeled and presented by the instructor as simply that; instead, the issues of copyright, libel, or the ethics of collaboration will arise organically as the students explore the details of the cases together.

IV. CONCLUSION

It is common for instructors to have a negative attitude toward GroupMe: at best ambivalent, and at worst adversarial. However, the

---

[45] McCabe, Trevino, & Butterfield, *supra* note 29, at 229.
[46] Pfeffer & Fong, *supra* note 26.
[47] No. 2021-CA-0106-MR, 2022 WL 815458 (Ky. Ct. App. Mar. 18, 2022) (not designated for publication).
[48] Roll, *supra* note 14; Rendall, *supra* note 15.
[49] McCabe, Trevino, & Butterfield, *supra* note 29.

survey results show that GroupMe often plays a crucial, practical role in student success in and satisfaction with a course, and, indeed, the platform seems to be offering a place for support, communication, and collegiality that students feel is not available elsewhere. Additionally, the results suggest that students would be open to an instructor-created GroupMe for specific courses, suggesting a preference toward this communication channel over email. By better understanding the reasons why students join course-specific GroupMe chats, instructors can, perhaps, find ways to capitalize on the positive aspects of GroupMe, counteract its negative tendencies, and provide other ways of achieving the collegiality, safety, and practical, real-time communication students seem to be seeking in GroupMe. Moreover, the situations students encounter in these spaces could offer instructors pedagogical opportunities and material to discuss interpersonal communication, collaboration, and ethics, using these real-world examples to explore these issues.

Though the survey was anonymous, it is important to note that student respondents may have responded in ways to not self-implicate when discussing ethical and academic integrity behavior issues that arise on a GroupMe chat. However, the survey provided insight into the prevalence of cheating and other negative interactions that take place in these student-initiated conversations. Anecdotally, students have reported that they will leave the chat if this behavior is observed; however, additional research would be required to better explore students' perceptions of these negative aspects and how they choose to respond to these situations. More broadly, the study of student use of GroupMe can provide valuable insight into how students understand and navigate the boundaries between "cheating" and academic misconduct on the one hand and legitimate collaboration or "helping" fellow students on the other. Generation Z, which was raised in a more collaborative and connected environment than any previous generation, may very well define those boundaries in new and challenging ways. Therefore, it is important for business law and business communication instructors to acknowledge the differences in the ways in which students may view collaborative technologies like GroupMe and the roles these platforms play in students' educational experience. With a deeper understanding of the needs that GroupMe and similar apps fill for students, instructors may be able address those needs in the classroom in more innovative, intentional, and effective ways.

www.ingramcontent.com/pod-product-compliance
Lightning Source LLC
Chambersburg PA
CBHW071200210326
41597CB00016B/1615